Sacramentals

RALPH WEIMANN

Sacramentals
Their Meaning and Spiritual Use

SOPHIA INSTITUTE PRESS
Manchester, New Hampshire

Copyright © 2023 by Ralph Weimann
Printed in the United States of America. All rights reserved.

Cover Designer: Joshua Facemyer, Impressus Art LLC (ImpressusArt.com)

Cover art: *Crucifix ink drawing*

Unless otherwise stated, the Scripture citations used in this work are taken from the *New American Bible, revised edition* © 2010, 1991, 1986, 1970 by the Confraternity of Christian Doctrine. In some places, the author has added italics for emphasis. Excerpts are from the United States Conference of Catholic Bishops website, www.usccb.org.

Excerpts from the English translation of the *Catechism of the Catholic Church* for use in the United States of America copyright © 1994, United States Catholic Conference, Inc. — Libreria Editrice Vaticana. English translation of the *Catechism of the Catholic Church: Modifications from the Editio Typica* copyright © 1997, United States Conference of Catholic Bishops — Libreria Editrice Vaticana.

No part of this book may be reproduced, stored in a retrieval system, or transmitted in any form, or by any means, electronic, mechanical, photocopying, or otherwise, without the prior written permission of the publisher, except by a reviewer, who may quote brief passages in a review.

Sophia Institute Press
Box 5284, Manchester, NH 03108
1-800-888-9344
www.SophiaInstitute.com

Sophia Institute Press is a registered trademark of Sophia Institute.

paperback ISBN 978-1-64413-949-3

ebook ISBN 978-1-64413-950-9

Library of Congress Control Number: 2023938893

First printing

Contents

Foreword ix
Abbreviations xv

FIRST PART
Theological Foundation of the Sacramentals

1. **Historical Background and the Magisterium of the Church** 11
   1.1. Sacramentals and Magisterial Texts. 15
   1.2. The Problem Regarding the Right Hermeneutic. 26
2. **The Theological Notion of Sacramentals** 31
   2.1. Basic Distinctions 32
   2.2. Four Different Categories of Sacramentals within the
        Church 36
       2.2.1. Consecrations/Dedications. 36
       2.2.2. Blessings. 42
       2.2.3. Exorcisms. 43
       2.2.4. Sacred Objects and Places. 43
   2.3. The Theological Nature of Sacramentals. 44
       2.3.1. Original Sin and Its Consequence 44
       2.3.2. The Biblical Foundation of Sacramentals. 48
       2.3.3. The "Incarnational Principle". 51
       2.3.4. Ecclesiological Considerations 55
       2.3.5. Sacramentals as Liturgical Actions. 59
           2.3.5.1. Reference to a Past Reality 62
           2.3.5.2. Reference to the Present Reality. 65
           2.3.5.3. Reference to the Future Reality 66
       2.3.6. Systematic Considerations 67

3. The Use and the Effects of Sacramentals 75
   3.1. *Ex Opere Operantis Ecclesiae* in Contrast to *Ex Opere Operato* 76
   3.2. *Participatio Actuosa*: Devout Participation 81
   3.3. Participated Effects of the Sacramentals 89
   3.4. Importance of the Formula 92
   3.5. Essential Characteristics of the Revised *De Benedictionibus* 101
   3.6. Importance of the Signs 112
   3.7. Conclusion 115

4. The Minister and the Recipient 119
   4.1. Introduction 119
   4.2. Spiritual Fruits Obtained by the Minister and the Recipient 121
   4.3. The Spiritual Effects of Consecrations and Blessings . . 124
   4.4. The Minister of Sacramentals 125
   4.5. The Common or Ministerial Priesthood 131
   4.6. Theological Considerations 138

SECOND PART
Pastoral Considerations of the Sacramentals

5. Invocations of the Name of Jesus Christ 149
   5.1. The Biblical Foundation of Invocations 150
      5.1.1. Salvation 151
      5.1.2. Purification, Sanctification, and Justification . . . 152
      5.1.3. Healing 154
      5.1.4. Protection and Liberation against Demonic Actions 154
      5.1.5. Do Everything in the Name of the Lord Jesus . . . 155
   5.2. Invocations: Practical Application 156
      5.2.1. Imperative Invocations 158

      5.2.2. Deprecative Invocations 161
  5.3. Spiritual Effects Achieved through the Invocation of the
      Name of Jesus Christ 162

6. **The Sign of the Cross** 165
  6.1. The Biblical Foundation. 167
  6.2. Some Theological Considerations 171
  6.3. Some Practical Considerations 175
  6.4. Spiritual Effects and the Sign of the Cross. 178
      6.4.1. Fruits of Purification and Liberation 179
      6.4.2. Fruits of Sanctification 182

7. **Exorcisms and Their Anti-Demonic Character** 185
  7.1. Introduction. 185
  7.2. Some Necessary Premises 189
      7.2.1. Angels — Spiritual Beings 191
      7.2.2. The Fallen Angels 193
      7.2.3. People Looking for an Exorcist. 197
      7.2.4. Priests and Exorcism 198
  7.3. The Work of the Devil 201
      7.3.1. Ordinary Actions of the Devil 202
      7.3.2. Extraordinary Actions of the Devil 204
      7.3.2.1. Infestation *(Infestatio)*. 206
      7.3.2.2. Vexation *(Circumsessio)*. 211
      7.3.2.3. Obsession *(Obsessio)*. 213
      7.3.2.4. Possession *(Possessio)* 217
  7.4. Overcoming Extraordinary Actions of the Devil. 227
      7.4.1. Liberation from Infestations 227
      7.4.1.1. The Minor Exorcism of Pope Leo XIII 234
      7.4.1.2. Commentary on the Prayer. 237
      7.4.2. Liberation from Vexations and Obsessions 243
      7.4.3. The Major Exorcism 248
      7.4.4. Healing and Deliverance. 251

- 7.5. Concluding Remarks 255
8. **Blessings of the Church** 261
    - 8.1. God, the Source of All Blessings 261
    - 8.2. Efficiency and Symbolism 264
    - 8.3. What Can and Cannot Be Blessed 267
    - 8.4. Some Basic Elements Concerning Blessings in Practice 270
        - 8.4.1. Blessing of Persons 273
            - 8.4.1.1. Constitutive Blessings 275
            - 8.4.1.2. Consecration to the Immaculate Heart of Mary 281
            - 8.4.1.3. Invocative Blessings of Persons 284
        - 8.4.2. Blessing of Objects 287
            - 8.4.2.1. Holy Water 291
            - 8.4.2.2. The St. Benedict Medal and the Miraculous Medal 296

Conclusion 305
Glossary 313
Bibliography 319
Appendix 1 341
Appendix 2 347
About the Author 351

Foreword

FR. RALPH WEIMANN'S BOOK, *Sacramentals: Their Meaning and Spiritual Use*, fills a gap in theological research — it is a long-awaited desideratum. When I was the Prefect of the Congregation for Divine Worship and the Discipline of the Sacraments, it became clear to me that sacramentals are often neglected because the theological justification behind them and the explanation for them are lacking or deficient. The *Catechism of the Catholic Church* has explicitly reminded us: "Holy Mother Church has, moreover, instituted sacramentals. These are sacred signs which bear a resemblance to the sacraments. They signify effects, particularly of a spiritual nature, which are obtained through the intercession of the Church. By them men are disposed to receive the chief effect of the sacraments, and various occasions in life are rendered holy."[1] Despite this teaching, it is not uncommon that even priests and religious do not know how to administer the sacramentals.

Fr. Weimann has succeeded in closing this gap with his vital publication. His book offers not only an excellent theological justification from a sacramental-theological perspective, but also practical and pastoral guidance that provides basic orientation for any priest, deacon, or lay person. He proceeds in the following way.

---

[1] *Catechism of the Catholic Church*, 1667.

First, he describes how the sacramentals have developed in the tradition of the Church. Because of their spiritual effects, they have always enjoyed great popularity among the faithful. In modern times, however, there has been a crisis in the use of the sacramentals — a crisis aggravated by rationalism. Underlying is the question of good hermeneutics — namely, about the interpretation and understanding of these sacramentals. Fr. Weimann addresses this difficulty and, at the same time, shows the only viable way out of the crisis through a development of the theological understanding of sacramentals. This must begin from a hermeneutics of reform that proceeds in continuity with the Tradition of the Church. In this way, he avoids the trap of dualism, which drives a wedge between the dimensions of the natural and the supernatural. Rather than falling into this trap, he brings these two dimensions together in the duality of being. Accordingly, he provides answers that meet the demands of both reason and revelation. This necessary, basic presupposition leads to unfolding the theological nature of the sacramentals. Other Catholic authors and teachers should take their cue from him in this regard; it is a path uniquely able to order, fathom, and explain the greatness and beauty of the Faith with regard to the sacramentals.

From this perspective, Fr. Weimann goes on to explain the theological concept of sacramentals, beginning with an important distinction. After explaining the meaning first of sacred signs and then of sacramental actions, he identifies four categories of sacramentals: consecrations, blessings, exorcisms, and sacred objects and places. Although there is no general consensus on these categories, the division that he provides proves to be extremely valuable precisely because it allows a closer theological classification.

The resulting theological differentiation with regard to sacramentals is also helpful because it repeatedly refers back to Sacred Scripture and Tradition, while at the same time giving sufficient space to Original Sin and its consequences for readers to be provided with a realistic look at human life. From this basic understanding of Catholic Faith, one can see better why the sacramentals must necessarily contain apotropaic elements, i.e., actions or prayers designed to ward off the influence of Satan. In his theologically profound commentary, Fr. Weimann starts from the Incarnation as the central moment of Christian faith, but, at the same time, he takes into account the ecclesiological and the liturgical dimension of the sacramentals. They touch the past, present, and future, which is also reflected, even though in a different way, in the trinitarian structure that is fundamental to the sacramentals. In this way, grace perfects creation by elevating it.

This is followed by an explanation of the administration and spiritual effects of the sacramentals. The principle of *ex opere operantis Ecclesiae* (due to the action and prayer of the Church) marks an essential difference from the mode of action of the sacraments, the latter acting *ex opere operato* (by the mere fact that the rite is performed), and, at the same time, serves as a key for the theological understanding. Therefore, conscious, active, and fruitful participation (*participatio actuosa*) is of particular importance insofar as the spiritual effects are achieved through a participation based on a living faith — meaning that the dispositions of both the minister and the recipient are of special significance.

The liturgical formula also has an indwelling efficacy, especially when it is part of the flow of the living tradition. Since, unfortunately, this principle has not always been taken into account in the "renewal" of the sacramentals, the recommendations for a "reform of the reform," as expressed by Joseph Ratzinger/Benedict XVI throughout the course of his life, deserve special attention. Sacred signs and rituals are not invented at a desk, and neither are they the work of academic effort; rather, they are the expression of the living Faith of the Church as it comes to us through Scripture and Tradition. And yet the spiritual fruits of these signs and rituals depend not only on the intercessory power of the Church, but also on the holiness of both the minister and the recipient. The lives of so many saints illustrate this in a striking way.

These theologically profound explanations lead into the second part of the book: "Pastoral Considerations." With this progression, Fr. Weimann clarifies which spiritual effects can be achieved by invoking the name of Jesus Christ; this invocation can be made in an imperative as well as in a deprecative way. This is followed by important explanations of the sacred signs, among which the sign of the cross is of utmost importance. It is the sign of salvation, the sign of triumph over sin and the devil, and it must therefore never be absent from any blessing. This becomes evident in the spiritual effects caused by the proper use of this sacred sign, such as purification, liberation, and sanctification. It is also the special merit of Fr. Weimann to have given the subject of exorcisms a sufficiently large frame in his book. This delicate subject is often neglected; even priests usually do not know what to do when confronted with preternatural things.

Following the International Association of Exorcists and the orientation guide published by these experts, the author also succeeds in filling a gap in this field, providing valuable grounding and insight. In these matters, the devil acts both through ordinary and extraordinary actions. Thus, based on texts of the Church's Magisterium, Fr. Weimann draws distinctions among infestations, vexations, obsessions, and possessions. He does not leave it at mere descriptions of these extremely disturbing phenomena—he also shows how to overcome them. Because Jesus Christ is ontologically present in him, any priest is able to remedy most of these phenomena if he is properly prepared and educated. For this reason, too, this book is especially important and should be given a permanent place in the formation of priests and seminarians. Finally, the ecclesiastical blessings are mentioned, whereby a distinction is made between the blessing and the consecration of persons and objects. In this distinction, the spiritual effect associated with these blessings is illustrated from a sacramental-theological perspective. It becomes clear not only why the blessings are so important, but also how they can become fruitful in the life of the faithful.

Much like the sacraments, sacramentals are entrusted to the Church to help us on our journey to God. Because wonderful graces emanate from them, priests in particular — and laypeople, up to a point, which is also clearly described in the present book — should make generous use of them.

In every day and age, sacramentals have had great importance, but they are especially important in our own day and age. It is the merit of Fr. Ralph Weimann to have opened up their meaning anew in his book, offering to all of us a key to understanding them.

On the feast of the Visitation, May 31, 2023
Robert Card. Sarah
Prefect Emeritus of the Congregation for Divine Worship
and the Discipline of the Sacraments

Abbreviations

AAS	*Acta Apostolicae Sedis*
IAE	International Association of Exorcists, *Guidelines for the Ministry of Exorcism*
ASS	*Acta Sanctae Sedis*
BoB	Book of Blessings
ca.	circa
can.	canon
cann.	canons
CCC	*Catechism of the Catholic Church*
CCEO	*Codex Canonum Ecclesiarum Orientalium*
CDF	Congregation for the Doctrine of the Faith
cf.	confer
chap.	chapter
CIC	*Code of Canon Law*
DH	Denzinger Hünermann
DV	Dogmatic Constitution *Dei Verbum*
DS	Denzinger-Schönmetzer
GS	Pastoral Constitution *Gaudium et Spes*
ed./eds	editor/editors

et al.	et aliae
etc.	et cetera
ibid.	ibidem
JRGS	Joseph Ratzinger *Gesammelte Schriften* (Collected Works)
LF	Encyclical Letter *Lumen Fidei*
LG	Dogmatic Constitution *Lumen Gentium*
LThK	*Lexikon für Theologie und Kirche*
NAB	The New American Bible
NOrd	*Die Neue Ordnung*
RR	*Rituale Romanum*
SC	Constitution *Sacrosanctum Concilium*
✠	Sign of the Cross
SP	Motu Proprio *Summorum Pontificum*
SS	Encyclical Letter *Spe Salvi*
STh	*Summa Theologiae*
TDL	Cyprian Vagaggini, *Theological Dimensions of the Liturgy*
TL	Joseph Ratzinger, *Theology of the Liturgy*
USCCB	United States Conference of Catholic Bishops
trans.	translated
vol.	volume

Sacramentals

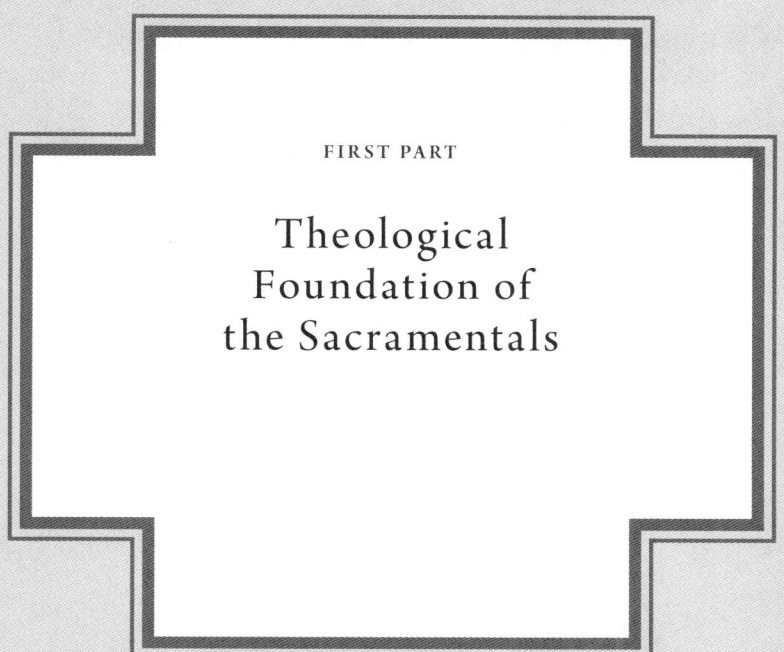

FIRST PART

Theological Foundation of the Sacramentals

✠ ✠ ✠

THERE IS A GROWING confusion about the doctrine of Faith — and there is a corresponding "profound crisis of faith that has affected many people."[2] This confusion is especially notable regarding the administration of the sacramentals, for they are related in a special way to the reality of faith. Without an understanding that their starting point is in our Faith, they become, at the same time, both incomprehensible and powerless.

It is a fact that the crisis of faith is quite advanced. According to a survey from 2019, just one-third of U.S. Catholics believe in transubstantiation — that is, that the bread and wine become truly the Body and Blood of Jesus Christ.[3] Others reject the most central belief in the Resurrection. Cardinal Eijk, quoting Pope John Paul II, speaks even about the great apostasy, which he witnessed in the

---

[2] Benedict XVI, Apostolic Letter *Porta Fidei*, October 11, 2011, 2, in http://www.vatican.va/content/benedict-xvi/en/motu_proprio/documents/hf_ben-xvi_motu-proprio_20111011_porta-fidei.html [10.5.2023]. For a more detailed analysis see Ralph Weimann, "The Crisis of Faith and the Crisis of the Church," in *Nova et Vetera*, vol. 19, no. 2 (2021): 199–216.

[3] Cf. Gregory A. Smith, "Just one-third of U.S. Catholics agree with their church that Eucharist is body, blood of Christ," August 5, 2019, in https://www.pewresearch.org/fact-tank/2019/08/05/transubstantiation-eucharist-u-s-catholics/ [10.5.2023].

Netherlands.[4] If faith in the central supernatural realities is abandoned, one might question how this will affect sacramentals such as exorcism, for example. The former chief exorcist of Rome, Gabriele Amorth (d. 2016), reported that this unbelief takes its toll on the clergy as well as the laity; the faith of even bishops and cardinals, the dispensers of these sacramentals, is not what it should be.[5]

When faith becomes weaker, superstition grows. This is reflected in the increase of esoteric practices such as yoga, reiki, Zen meditation, and others; rather than being given a wide berth, they are tolerated, accepted, and sometimes even promoted by priests and religious. It is noteworthy that, to the degree in which the sacramentals are neglected and rejected, these practices become proportionally more popular. People dedicate much time, effort, and money to these practices that are foreign to our Faith, but they no longer trust in the healing and liberating power of the sacramentals.

This crisis of faith has led to the sad situation in which people, especially priests and religious, are often quite ignorant regarding the sacramentals. It may happen that they hold a doctorate in theology, but they do not know how to impart certain blessings, they do not know what a consecration is and how it works, and only very few are familiar with prayers of liberation. With this, a huge problem regarding the current study of "theology" becomes evident, namely, that it is all too frequently based only upon human reasoning, so-called "scientific" results, and sociological studies — rather than on the reality of supernatural faith.

The biggest problem regarding theology in general, and the sacramentals in particular, becomes evident: a lack of faith. Indeed, the

---

[4] Cf. Willem Jacobus Eijk with Andrea Galli, *Dio vive in Olanda. "Ma il Figlio dell'uomo, quando verrà, troverà la fede sulla terra?" Lc 18,8*, (Milan: Ediziones Ares, 2020), 53.

[5] Cf. Gabriele Amorth with Paolo Rodari, *L'ultimo Esorcista. La mia battaglia contro Satana*, (Milan: Piemme, 2011), 191.

sacramentals cannot be understood without rediscovering that faith is a "supernatural gift"[6] that comes with transforming power.[7] For that reason, our Lord said to the apostles, when they were unable to expel a demon, that their failure was "Because of your little faith. Amen, I say to you, if you have faith the size of a mustard seed, you will say to this mountain, 'Move from here to there,' and it will move. Nothing will be impossible for you" (Matt. 17:20). With this in mind, it is worth noting a certain distinction between sacramentals and the seven sacraments: the effectiveness of each sacramental depends, to a certain degree, on one's faith. Therefore, it is important to recall to mind the words from the Letter to the Hebrews:

> Faith is the realization of what is hoped for and evidence of things not seen. Because of it the ancients were well attested. By faith we understand that the universe was ordered by the word of God, so that what is visible came into being through the invisible. By faith Abel offered to God a sacrifice greater than Cain's. Through this he was attested to be righteous, God bearing witness to his gifts, and through this, though dead, he still speaks. By faith Enoch was taken up so that he should not see death, and "he was found no more because God had taken him." Before he was taken up, he was attested to have pleased God. But without faith it is impossible to please him, for anyone who approaches God must believe that he exists and that he rewards those who seek him. (Heb. 11:1–6)[8]

From the outset, it must be emphasized that sacramentals have nothing to do with superstition, nor with magic. Rather, they are intrinsically related to our belief in Jesus Christ, who is the source of their effectiveness. The encyclical letter *Lumen fidei* offers a precise and profound overview about the relation between the act of faith and its

---

[6] Francis, LF, 4.
[7] Cf. Benedict XVI, Apostolic Letter *Porta Fidei*, 10. See also Benedict XVI, SS, 2.
[8] All Bible quotations according to the NABRE.

spiritual effects. The first three chapters especially provide a solid theological ground, helpful in evaluating the importance and effectiveness of sacramentals.[9]

Another aspect of sacramentals must also be mentioned right from the start, an aspect which serves as a point of reference. When considering the sacramentals — just as with any other subject related to theology — it must be affirmed that *they are related to the Faith as expressed in revelation and through dogma*. There is no contradiction between dogma and its pastoral practice, since any pastoral approach independent of dogma would break off the relationship between the *lex credendi* and — in this case — the *lex celebrandi*.[10] In short, the way the sacramentals are celebrated must correspond to the Faith of the Church. Without this connection, the use of sacramentals would become an empty gesture, producing no spiritual effects. A correct understanding of the sacramentals has to be solidly grounded in revelation. The invisible reality of God was made known through the Incarnation of Jesus Christ and is linked to the authority of the Church. Revelation, because it comes to us through Scripture and Tradition, is accessible to us.[11] Sacramentals have to be considered from a perspective solidly grounded in this "divine wellspring" of revelation, which is the reason for their existence and the source of their effectiveness.

---

[9] Cf. Francis, LF, 1–19.

[10] Cuthbert Johnson emphasizes this aspect when he writes: "The dogmatic character of the Liturgy derives from the fact that in the Liturgy the Church confesses and lives her faith. . . . The Liturgy is the 'authentic expression of the faith' of the Church and is the basis of Pope St. Celestine's axiom 'ut legem credendi lex statuat supplicandi.'" Cuthbert Johnson, *Prosper Gueranger (1805–1875) A Liturgical Theologian. An Introduction to his liturgical writings and works*, Analecta Liturgica 9, (Rome: Edizioni Abbazia S. Paolo, 1984), 283.

[11] DV, 9.

Given the crisis of faith, it is no surprise that, during the past decades, sacramentals have been marginalized, even though they are supposed to be the daily bread of any priest, as well as of the laity. With the collective disintegration of faith, i.e., the breakdown of the *sensus fidei*, foreseen by Cardinal Joseph Ratzinger in the 1980s,[12] many of the "faithful" today are actually incapable of a comprehensive view of the contents of their faith. As said before, this incapacity has had a significant impact concerning the sacramentals in particular; all too often, they have been simply abandoned or neglected.

This has not just happened because of a lack of faith, however. Sometimes it has been a result of a well-meaning but imbalanced overemphasis on the sacraments, which leaves no room for the sacramentals. As a result, because they are not *as* important or powerful as the sacraments, they are considered superfluous. Regardless of the secondary nature of their importance in relation to the seven sacraments, however, they are in fact significant means ordered toward the sacraments that can produce real spiritual effects in the daily life of the faithful.

---

[12] Cf. Joseph Ratzinger with Vittorio Messori, *The Ratzinger Report: An Exclusive Interview of the State of the Church*, trans. Salvator Attanasio and Graham Harrison, (San Francisco: Ignatius Press, 1985), 73.

ONE
✣ ✣ ✣
Historical Background and the Magisterium of the Church

EVEN THOUGH THE SACRAMENTALS were always practiced within the Church, the word *sacramentals* was not used until the twelfth century. Peter Lombard (d. 1160), a Scholastic theologian and a bishop of Paris, wrote a famous textbook of theology called *Libri Quatuor Sententiarum* (Four Books of Sentences). He began to distinguish sacraments from sacramentals, which, up until then, had been referred to as *sacramenta minora* (minor sacraments) or by other similar names.[13] At this time, theologians developed their theology in fidelity to revelation and based upon reason. This led to a golden age of theological precision. Each theologian tried to find the most precise concepts to express the mysteries of faith. In this respect, it is worth mentioning St. Thomas Aquinas (d. 1274), who explained in the *Summa Theologiae* how the study of theology needs to be undertaken. Specifically, Thomas answered whether sacred doctrine is a matter of argument:

> This doctrine is especially based upon arguments from authority, inasmuch as its principles are obtained by revelation: thus, we ought to believe on the authority of those to whom the revelation

[13] Cf. John M. Huels, "A Juridical Notion of Sacramentals," in *Studia canonica*, 38 (2004): 345–368, here 346.

has been made. Nor does this take away from the dignity of this doctrine, for although the argument from authority based on human reason is the weakest, yet the argument from authority based on divine revelation is the strongest. But sacred doctrine makes use even of human reason, not, indeed, to prove faith (for thereby the merit of faith would come to an end), but to make clear other things that are put forward in this doctrine. Since therefore grace does not destroy nature but perfects it, natural reason should minister to faith as the natural bent of the will ministers to charity. Hence the Apostle says: "Bringing into captivity every understanding unto the obedience of Christ." (2 Cor. 10:5)[14]

Theology therefore must be developed based on revelation. The words of the prologue of the Gospel of John indicate the way: "In the beginning was the Word, and the Word was with God, and the Word was God" (John 1:1). The starting point of theology is not an opinion — not a mystical revelation or an affirmation of any ecclesiastical authority — but Divine Revelation. When Peter Lombard considered the *sacramentalia*, he related them immediately to revelation and to its most effective realization: the sacraments. Even though there had been no precise concept or agreement on the notion of sacramentals among Scholastic theologians, this concept began to develop in the twelfth century.

At that time, the term *sacramentals* was considered primarily as meaning the ritual ceremonies within the celebration of the sacraments. As time went on, they came to be considered as distinct from their divinely instituted essence, namely, the sacraments themselves.[15] According to the understanding of these Scholastics, the sacraments were the essential part of the divine action since they were instituted by Christ. In contrast, these other parts that

---

[14] Thomas Aquinas, STh I. q.1; a.8. English Translation available at http://www.newadvent.org/summa/1001.htm [10.5.2023].

[15] Cf. José Bonet Alcón, *Los Sacramentos menores. Estudio histórico sobre la naturaleza de los sacramentales*, (Buenos Aires: ACS Publications, 1993), 33–51.

accompanied the sacraments — e.g., the other rites namely, the sacramentals — were considered as instituted by the Church. This distinction is of great importance, and it would be developed over the next centuries with more precision. For one thing, *sacramentalia* were characterized as instituted by the Church, since it is up to the Church to define them. Consequently, theologians expanded the meaning of sacramentals, which would soon include even acts of piety and other gestures, pious common objects, invocations, and so on. John Huels writes:

> By the thirteenth century, theologians and canonists expanded the meaning to include other rites, objects, pious acts, etc. They offered lists of sacramentals that varied considerably, including the rites other than the sacraments, blessings, symbolic gestures, prayers, blessed objects, the eating of blessed bread, public confession of sins apart from the sacrament of penance, almsgiving and certain other pious works, the sign of the cross, exorcisms, ritual anointings, the invocation of the name of Jesus, and similar sacred signs other than the sacraments. Given such diversity, authors could not agree on a precise notion of sacramentals.[16]

For this reason, the concept of sacramentals was not accepted everywhere. The Council of Trent (1545–1563), while treating the ritual elements of the sacraments, did not actually use the word *sacramentals*; instead, it spoke of the *ceremonies* or *rites* of the sacraments to describe what Peter Lombard had called *sacramentals*. For example, "If anyone says that the received and approved rites of the Catholic Church, accustomed to be used in the administration of the sacraments, may be despised or omitted by the minister without sin and at their pleasure,

---

[16] John M. Huels, "A Juridical Notion," 346. Something similar is affirmed by William J. Barry, *The Sacramentals of the Holy Catholic Church, or Flowers from the Garden of the Liturgy*, (London: FB &c Ltd., 2017), 14–15.

or may be changed by any pastor of the churches to other new ones; let him be anathema."[17]

The Council's use of the words *rite* and *ceremonies* served as a clarification on which it would continue to elaborate, one that would be of great importance, because it led to a clear distinction and a better understanding of what are called sacramentals today. In the period after the Council of Trent, there was a renewal of the Church from within; theologians and clergy related dogma to revelation and applied it to their concrete pastoral situations. This strengthened the Catholic identity and missionary spirit, bringing forward many fruits of holiness. In this period, the sacramental practices of the Church were revised; this is reflected concretely with the 1614 publication of the *Rituale Romanum*.[18] It was an organic development from already existing forms, especially from the *Ceremonial of Bishops*. As a result, the dominant tendency of the scholars was to use the term *ceremonies* for those rites of the sacraments that did not pertain to their substance. The term *sacramentals* was used for things and actions employed outside the sacraments. Even though this caused a certain shift regarding the theological understanding, sacramentals were still considered with a certain similarity and in analogy to the sacraments. Over the centuries, there were continuously new editions of the *Rituale Romanum* published, adding new blessings. For example, Pope Leo XIII approved a typical edition in 1884, published by the German publisher Pustet.[19]

[17] See Session VII, can. 13, in *Canons and Decrees of the Council of Trent*, trans. H.J. Schroeder, (Rockford: TAN Books, 1978), 53.
[18] It was recently reprinted in Germany in a revised version including the modifications realized by Pius XII: *Rituale Romanum, Pauli V Pontificis Maximi iussu editum aliorumque Pontificum cura regognitum atque ad normam codicis iuris canonici accommodatum SSMI D.N. PII Papae XII auctoritate ordinatum et actum*, (Bonn: Nova et Vetera, 2010).
[19] A good overview of the historical development of the different publications is provided by Florian Kluger, *Benediktionen. Studien zu kirchlichen*

By the beginning of the twentieth century, the Belgian-French theologian Henri Leclercq (d. 1945) asserted that "at present *sacramentalia* is exclusively reserved for those rites which are practiced apart from the administration of the seven sacraments, for which the word ceremonies is used."[20] Prior to the *Code of Canon Law* from 1917, there were different definitions and explanations of the term *sacramentals*. *Die Sacramentalien der Katholischen Kirche*,[21] written by the Austrian theologian Franz Schmid (d. 1922), became one such work of reference. He enumerated twelve different definitions of sacramentals, quoting prominent theologians in support of his definitions. The most specific information he could provide was limited to only common theological opinions on the definition of sacramentals; the Magisterium had not, as yet, given any official statement in this regard. But this changed after the publication of the *Code of Canon Law* of 1917. This very fact underlines why the Magisterium of the Church must provide clarity and unambiguous definitions; doing so helps the whole Church by stimulating theological research, from which both the faithful and theologians can benefit.

1.1. Sacramentals and Magisterial Texts

The first definition of sacramentals to be offered by the supreme legislator was that of canon 1144 of the 1917 *Code of Canon Law*:

Segensfeiern, (Regensburg: Verlag Friedrich Pustet, 2011), 6–47. A very detailed overview of the sacramentals in the Middle Ages is offered in the two-volume work by Adolph Frank, *Die Kirchlichen Benediktionen im Mittelalter*, vol. 1–2, (Bonn: Nova et Vetera, 2006).

[20] Henri Leclerq, "Sacramentals," in Charles G. Herbermann et al. (eds.), *The Catholic Encyclopedia*, vol. 13, (New York: Robert Appleton, 1912), 293.

[21] Cf. Franz Schmid, *Die Sacramentalien der Katholischen Kirche: in ihrer Eigenart beleuchtet*, (Brixen: Verlag der Buchhandlung der Kath.-polit. Pressvereins, 1896).

Latin	English
Sacramentalia sunt res aut actiones quibus Ecclesia, in aliquam Sacramentorum imitationem, uti solet ad obtinendos ex sua impetratione effectus praesertim spirituales.	Sacramentals are things or actions that the Church, in a certain imitation of the Sacraments, is wont to use to obtain, by her imprecation, effects that are primarily spiritual.[22]

The location in the text of this discussion of sacramentals is actually key to understanding them; they were cited in the first part of the third book, namely, the book on sacraments. This context underlines the close relationship between sacraments and sacramentals. Although the sacramentals were somehow considered an "imitation" of the sacraments, their effectiveness depends on other criteria. They are "things or actions" of the Church. The theological meaning of this definition will be explained later on; nevertheless, it has to be underlined that the Church approves and — to a certain degree — establishes the sacramentals, which are in close relation to the sacraments themselves, instituted by Christ. The effects of the sacramentals are obtained above all through the intercession of the Church and the fruitful participation of the recipient and minister. Special emphasis is put on the spiritual effects they produce. All this is reflected in the definition of can. 1144, which became the standard description of sacramentals among most authors until Vatican II.

This definition was modified through the publication of the Constitution on the Sacred Liturgy, *Sacrosanctum Concilium*. It presented a revised explanation of sacramentals in No. 60:[23]

---

[22] Edward N. Peters (ed.), *The 1917 or Pio-Benedictine Code of Canon Law*, (San Francisco: Ignatius Press, 2001), 393.
[23] SC, 60.

Latin	English
Sacramentalia praeterea sancta Mater Ecclesia instituit. Quae sacra sunt signa quibus, in aliquam Sacramentorum imitationem, effectus praesertim spirituales significantur et ex Ecclesiae impetratione obtinentur. Per ea homines ad praecipuum Sacramentorum effectum suscipiendum disponuntur et varia vitae adiuncta sanctificantur.	Holy Mother Church has, moreover, instituted sacramentals. These are sacred signs which bear a resemblance to the sacraments: they signify effects, particularly of a spiritual kind, which are obtained through the Church's intercession. By them men are disposed to receive the chief effect of the sacraments, and various occasions in life are rendered holy.

This definition appears in Chapter II of the Constitution, entitled "The Other Sacraments and the Sacramentals." The context is once again the same: the sacramentals are presented in close relationship to the sacraments. Furthermore, the Constitution makes clear that sacramentals are liturgical acts. Number 7 explains what the Council intended when referring to liturgical acts: "Rightly, then, the liturgy is considered as an exercise of the priestly office of Jesus Christ. In the liturgy the sanctification of the man is signified by signs perceptible to the senses, and is effected in a way which corresponds with each of these signs; in the liturgy, the whole public worship is performed by the Mystical Body of Jesus Christ, that is, by the Head and His members."[24] At this point, it becomes clear why the Constitution considered the sacramentals as a liturgical act: they are intrinsically related to the exercise of the priestly office of Jesus Christ, which underlines the strong Christocentric dimension of the sacramentals.[25] Thus, the Second Vatican Council considered sacramentals as "sacred signs"; they bear spiritual effects and are obtained through the Church. Similarly, the 1983 *Code of Canon Law* (CIC) defines them just as SC did:[26]

---

[24] SC, 7.
[25] See chap. 2.3.2.
[26] CIC/1983, can. 1166.

Latin	English
Sacramentalia sunt signa sacra, quibus, ad aliquam sacramentorum imitationem, effectus praesertim spirituales significantur et ex Ecclesiae impetratione obtinentur.	Sacramentals are sacred signs by which effects, especially spiritual effects, are signified in some imitation of the sacraments and are obtained through the intercession of the Church.[27]

In the revised *Code of Canon Law*, the sacramentals are discussed in "Other acts of divine worship [cann. 1166–1204]" which is the second part of the fourth book, "The Sanctifying Office of the Church"; the CIC dedicates various canons to this topic. Again, this placement emphasizes that, like the sacraments, the sacramentals are acts of divine worship — however, they differ from them in origin and nature: "The seven sacraments were instituted by Christ and cannot be substantially changed or abolished. The sacramentals are instituted by the Church; new ones can be created and old ones suppressed."[28] Sacramentals may refer to objects, for example, holy water, blessed candles, and the like, or to actions, such as sprinkling holy water, the sign of the cross, and such.

Since the CIC offers a solid foundation for a correct understanding and application of sacramentals, it is helpful to go through the canons that discuss them. This provides a solid basic orientation for divine worship, offering some principles that indicate how to understand them.

"Canon 1167§1. The Apostolic See alone can establish new sacramentals, authentically interpret those already received, or

---

[27] The English translation — here and throughout — is taken from: John P. Beal et al. (eds), *New Commentary on the Code of Canon Law*, Commissioned by The Canon Law Society of America, (New York: Paulist Press, 2000), 1401.

[28] John M. Huels, "Part II Other Acts of Divine Worship [cann. 1166–1204]," in John P. Beal et al. (eds.), *New Commentary on the Code of Canon Law*, (New York: Paulist Press, 2000), 1400–1423, here 1401.

abolish or change any of them."[29] In other words, it is up to the Holy See to approve or disapprove of individual sacramentals. If it chooses to grant approval for and so maintain any given practice, its approval and oversight guarantees that the faithful are not exposed to irregularities and arbitrariness. Frequently, for example, so-called charismatic groups invent new forms or elements of sacramentals, and some use them even within the Eucharist. However, such practices do not do justice to the sacrament of the Eucharist itself nor to the nature of the sacramentals. Since the effects of the sacramentals are obtained through the Church, it corresponds to the inner logic that their use and practice can only be authorized by the Apostolic See.

For that reason, §2 adds: "In confecting or administering sacramentals, the rites and formulas approved by the authority of the Church are to be observed carefully."[30] In a commentary on this paragraph, John Huels argues that a bishop's conference might compose new blessings. However, the canon must be interpreted "to refer to entirely new classes of sacramentals, not to new sacramentals within the same category."[31]

It also matters who administers or carries out the practice of sacramentals.[32] For this reason, canon 1168 states: "The minister of sacramentals is a cleric who has been provided with the requisite power. According to the norm of the liturgical books and to the judgment of the local ordinary lay persons who possess the appropriate qualities can also administer some sacramentals."[33] Moving on from there, the next canon (can. 1169 §1) provides an overview of the function of clerics and a broad meaning of sacramentals:

[29] can. 1167 §1.
[30] can. 1167 §2.
[31] John M. Huels, "Part II Other Acts of Divine Worship," 1402.
[32] See chap. 4.
[33] can. 1168.

"Those marked with the Episcopal character and presbyters permitted by law or legitimate grant can perform consecrations and dedications validly. §2. Any presbyter can impart blessings except those reserved to the Roman Pontiff or bishops. §3. A deacon can impart only those blessings expressly permitted by law."[34] Sometimes, even priests are not aware that certain blessings — especially consecrations — are reserved for higher clergy; it is beyond their faculty to use them. This is in fact similar to what can be seen within the sacrament of Penance; the absolution of certain sins cannot be granted by just any priest. There are reasons for this that are necessary to explain; details will be provided on the particularities of some of the sacramentals — specifically which can and cannot be administered by a priest or by a lay person — in chapter 4.

Regarding the sacramentals that take the form of blessings, canon 1170 makes it clear that they are never an offense; therefore, they should never be skipped over because of a false or misguided sense of human respect or political correctness: "Blessings, which are to be imparted first of all to Catholics, can also be given to catechumens and even to non-Catholics unless there is a prohibition of the Church to the contrary."[35] The theological understanding of this canon will be explained in chapter 2. For now, it suffices to emphasize that canon law says that blessings "are to be imparted." This matters to an imperative degree because it is intrinsic to the nature of the priestly existence to administer divine grace to everyone who does not openly contradict the belief and practice of the Church. Priests are to serve and bring grace to everyone whom they encounter, not just to professed Catholics.

Canon 1171 discusses sacred objects, emphasizing that they are essential parts of the sacramentals: "Sacred objects, which are designated for divine worship by dedication or blessing, are to be treated reverently and are not to be employed for profane or inappropriate use

[34] can. 1169 §1–3.
[35] can. 1170.

even if they are owned by private persons."[36] Dealing correctly with sacred objects is important and therefore, the "diocesan bishop has the right of visitation of places where blessed objects are kept." Correspondingly, the law affirms that a "person who profanes a sacred thing is to be punished by a just penalty" (can. 1369).[37] The clergy and the laity alike are required to give special attention and reverence to any objects and places that have been consecrated.[38]

The following and last canon in this regard talks about exorcism and the norms of its legitimate performance. Canon 1172§1 says: "No one can perform exorcisms legitimately upon the possessed unless he has obtained special and express permission from the local ordinary." The next paragraph adds: "The local ordinary is to give this permission only to a presbyter who has piety, knowledge, prudence, and integrity of life."[39] These numbers make clear that exorcisms can be performed only with the necessary authority. As in the case of Confession, the ability depends on the authority.

All of these aspects will be considered with more detail and practical explanations in the following chapters. However, before getting into these details, having a basic understanding of what the *Code of Canon Law* provides as a solid point of reference on these matters gives an invaluable starting point. Additionally, for the sake of completeness, a few more documents need to be mentioned to complete our points of reference.

In 1990, a new code of canon law was issued for the Eastern Catholic Churches, the 23 *sui iuris* Churches, which are in communion with the pope. This Code of Canons of the Eastern Churches (*Codex Canonum Ecclesiarum Orientalium*, i.e., CCEO), similar to the

---

[36] can. 1171.
[37] John M. Huels, "Part II Other Acts of Divine Worship," 1405. Referring to the former can. 1376.
[38] See chap. 8.
[39] can. 1172 §2. See especially chap. 7.

CIC, deals with sacramentals in chapter 8 of Title XVI (Divine Worship and Especially Sacraments). The discussion of sacramentals comes after a consideration of the Divine Liturgy and the sacraments. The definition offered reflects the definition from the Second Vatican Council. Canon 867§1 determines:

> "Through the sacramentals, which are sacred signs, by which in imitation of the sacraments effects, especially spiritual ones, are signified and obtained through the intercession of the Church, people who are disposed to receive the principal effect of the sacraments and the various circumstances of life are sanctified."[40] In other words, the Eastern tradition defines sacramentals similarly to the Western tradition, in that they see them as sacred signs integrally connected to the sacraments, authorized through the Church herself, and effecting the sanctification of the lives of the people to whom they are administered. However, the canons of the Eastern Church differ from those in the tradition of the West in the following ways. In the East, special emphasis is put on "Sacred Places," "Cemeteries and Ecclesiastical Funerals," "Feast Days and Days of Penance," and "Veneration of the Saints, of Sacred Images and Relics."[41] Additionally, the law grants to the particular Churches greater freedom regarding the norms for sacramentals, saying in can. 876 §2 CCEO: "Concerning the sacramentals the norms of the particular law of the individual Church *sui iuris* should be observed."[42]

Also important to mention is the *Book of Blessings,* published for liturgical use on October 1, 1989, as the mandatory reference point for blessings in the dioceses of the United States. The authors of this book attempted to apply the liturgical reform to the sacramentals as it was decreed by the Second Vatican Council. It was intended to foster a "full, conscious, and active participation of the faithful and that any

[40] CCEO, can. 867 §1.
[41] CCEO, cann. 869–888.
[42] CCEO, can. 867 §2.

elements should be eliminated that in the course of time had obscured the true nature and purpose of sacramentals."[43] The decree of approbation does not explain how to identify these "obscured elements," nor does it explain how "active participation" should be fostered. All this will be analyzed in more detail in chapter 3.

The *Catechism of the Catholic Church* also refers to the definition of sacramentals from Vatican II, saying in paragraph 1667: "Holy Mother Church has, moreover, instituted sacramentals. These are sacred signs which bear a resemblance to the sacraments. They signify effects, particularly of a spiritual nature, which are obtained through the intercession of the Church. By them men are disposed to receive the chief effect of the sacraments, and various occasions in life are rendered holy."[44] Again, location matters: This definition is located after the treatment of the seven sacraments, and it therefore follows the same structure as SC and the CIC. Various forms of sacramentals are mentioned, such as blessings (of persons, meals, objects, and places); certain blessings have a lasting effect, especially when a person, an object, or a place is consecrated to God.[45] Exorcisms are mentioned as well, and it is affirmed that the Church is given power over the evil one: "Jesus performed exorcisms and from him the Church has received the power and office of exorcizing."[46]

Another document that needs to be mentioned in this context is the Apostolic Letter Motu Proprio *Summorum Pontificum*, issued on July 7, 2007, by Pope Benedict XVI. It has special importance for any

---

[43] Congregation for Divine Worship, Decree, in National Conference of Catholic Bishops (ed.), *The Roman Ritual Revised by Decree of the Second Vatican Ecumenical Council and Published by Authority of Pope John Paul II*, (New York: Catholic Book Publishing Corp., 1989), 19.
[44] CCC, 1667.
[45] Cf. CCC, 1672.
[46] CCC, 1673.

consideration regarding the sacramentals, since it tried to reconcile the Church with her own past, granting access to the whole of tradition:

> The Roman Missal promulgated by Pope Paul VI is the ordinary expression of the *lex orandi* (rule of prayer) of the Catholic Church of the Latin rite. The Roman Missal promulgated by Saint Pius V and revised by Blessed John XXIII is nonetheless to be considered an extraordinary expression of the same *lex orandi* of the Church and duly honored for its venerable and ancient usage. These two expressions of the Church's *lex orandi* will in no way lead to a division in the Church's *lex credendi* (rule of faith); for they are two usages of the one Roman rite.[47]

These theological and legal determinations are of great importance, since they granted access to the whole liturgical tradition, including the sacraments and sacramentals. However, on July 16, 2021, Pope Francis issued the Apostolic Letter *Traditiones Custodes*,[48] through which he retracts and limits many of those permissions[49] granted by Pope Benedict — without providing a satisfactory theological explanation. Furthermore, referring to the Second Vatican Council, he contradicts that same council, claiming that there is a "unique expression of the *lex orandi* of the Roman Rite." According to him, only the liturgical books promulgated after the Council are in conformity with the decrees of Vatican II.[50] However, this is simply not possible, for various reasons. In this context, it is only necessary to mention two of these reasons. First, within the Catholic Church, there has always been a plurality, not a uniformity, especially concerning the liturgy. This

---

[47] Benedict XVI, SP.
[48] Francis, Apostolic Letter Motu Proprio *Traditiones Custodes*, July 16, 2021, in https://www.vatican.va/content/francesco/en/motu_proprio/documents/20210716-motu-proprio-traditionis-custodes.html [10.5.2023].
[49] Benedict XVI, SP, Art. 2f.
[50] Cf. ibid., Art. 1.

becomes evident when referring to the different rites within the Church in the West (e.g., the Ambrosian, or Dominican, Rite) and in the East (e.g., the Armenian and Byzantine Rite and the other rites of the Catholic Eastern Churches). If the affirmation made above would be true and put into practice, it would consequently lead to abolish the whole liturgical tradition of the Roman Rite. Second, if there is only one unique expression of the *lex orandi*, the pope would have declared the tradition, of which his office is a part, to be dissolved. Pope Pius V was aware of this when he issued a missal in 1570 that included the whole of the Latin tradition. To protect this treasure, in which the Apostolic Succession is grounded and founded, he decreed that whoever infringes his decree to use this missal in the future "will incur the wrath of Almighty God and of the blessed Apostles Peter and Paul."[51]

However, at this point, it is not necessary to enter further into this discussion — even though it would be worthwhile, since it touches the heart of the Church's tradition. Nevertheless, *Traditiones Custodes* does not make any reference at all to the sacramentals; therefore, it must be affirmed that, at least concerning our topic, the law given by Pope Benedict XVI in *Summorum Pontificum* continues to be valid. Thus also, the use of the older ritual is also valid, which — according to Art. 9 §1 — every priest is allowed to use. It is necessary to mention this, since the administration of some of the sacramentals according to the ancient ritual is more effective than the renewed version. This is due to the nature of the sacramentals, which will be explained in chapter 2.

At this point, it can be concluded that the *Code of Canon Law* of 1917 provided the first important definition of sacramentals,

---

[51] In Latin "Si quis autem hoc attentare praesumpserit, indignationem omnipotentis Dei, ac beatorum Patri et Pauli Apostolorum ejus se noverit incursurum." Pius V, Papal Bull *Quo Primum*, 14.7.1570, in *Missale Romanum, Ex Decreto SS. Concilii Tridentini restitutum Summorum Pontificum cura recognitum*, Editio iuxta typicam, (Thalwil: C. H. Beck, 2012), (7)–(8).

offering concrete norms for their use. It was the result of a development which had started some hundred years earlier. This process corresponds to an organic development, which is also reflected in the modifications from the 1917 *Code of Canon Law* and in the one of 1983. However, one of the key differences consists in the fact that, in 1917, sacramentals were described as "things and actions"; in 1983, they are called "sacred signs." In concert with the Western tradition, the Eastern Code of Canon Law emphasizes the main goal of their use: sanctification. In summary, presently it can be affirmed that sacramentals are sacred signs that bring about spiritual effects through the intercession of the Church. Furthermore, it can be concluded: "Thus, like sacraments, sacramentals are liturgical celebrations that include prayer and often a material sign of some kind."[52]

1.2. The Problem Regarding the Right Hermeneutic

During the latter half of the twentieth century, rationalism and the philosophical paradigm of technical progress became major challenges for the Christian Faith. Already in the 1950s, Joseph Ratzinger had warned in an essay that paganism would spread into the heart of the Church, a statement for which he was criticized at the time;[53] unfortunately, it proved to be prophetic. A new mentality spread, based on an immanent-materialist worldview, which claimed to be "scientific." Meanwhile, it excluded the metaphysical-supernatural dimension that is part and parcel with the Faith. This mentality had a strong impact on Christianity across the board, especially on theologians themselves — they wanted to be considered "scientific" and up to date.

---

[52] John M. Huels, "A Juridical Notion," 350.
[53] Cf. Joseph Ratzinger, "Die neuen Heiden und die Kirche," in *Kirche - Zeichen unter den Völkern. Schriften zur Ekklesiologie und Ökumene*, in JRGS, vol. 8/2, (Freiburg im Breisgau: Herder, 2010), 1143–1158. This process has also affected many priests. Cf. Ralph Weimann, "Die Krise der Kirche als Krise des Klerus," in NOrd 73 (2019): 244–256.

Within this context, the approach toward the sacramentals changed. First, there was a turn toward history, for the "first generation of liturgists were for the most part historians."[54] They claimed to go *ad fontes*, i.e., to be going back to the source and origin of ideas regarding sacramentals. Yet this was often understood as something problematic because it skipped over the value of the living tradition. Such an approach is opposed to the Second Vatican Council, which has affirmed: "The words of the holy fathers witness to the presence of this living tradition, whose wealth is poured into the practice and life of the believing and praying Church."[55] Even though the Council affirmed that the living tradition needed to be respected, quite the opposite happened. On one side, many things which certain "experts" did not recognize as historical were destroyed and abolished. On the other side, entirely new forms were made up, based upon pastoral pragmatism, creativity, and often even banality.[56] In the ensuing decades, this has naturally provoked widespread confusion on all manner of issues, including the understanding, use, and practice of sacramentals. Thus, the clarity on the subject which the Church had attained in the early twentieth century was lost again. This general confusion had a particular impact on sacramentals, because their effects are directly related to and dependent on faith.

As a result, as Antonio Donghi mentioned, much confusion and ignorance regarding the notion of sacramentals remains today.[57] This shows that one must be very careful when theologians claim to be returning to the "original understanding." What do we know about

---

[54] Joseph Ratzinger, Preface, in Alcuin Reid, *The Organic Development of the Liturgy*, 2nd ed., (San Francisco: Ignatius Press, 2005), 9–13, here 12.
[55] DV, 8.
[56] Cf. Joseph Ratzinger, Preface, 12.
[57] Antonio Donghi, "Sacramentali," in Domenico Sartore and Achille M. Trajacca (eds), *Nuovo dizionario di liturgia*, (Rome: Edizioni Paoline, 1988), 1253.

the origin? How can the sources be accessed? What about a true development of doctrine within the Church and through the centuries? In truth, the only way to achieve an authentic development of doctrine is through the living Tradition and within the community of the Church. Whoever refutes a part of this Tradition will provoke a rupture; in such an instance, theology would simply disintegrate.[58]

Since this is an important aspect, especially with regards to the reform of the sacramentals — which also needs to be addressed — it is worth a closer look. Within the Church, there will always be development. However, it *must* lead to a deeper understanding of revelation. The principle *ad fontes* must be understood correctly; it implies that the whole of Tradition is reaching out to the source, which is revelation itself.[59] This excludes skipping parts of Tradition or declaring it as a whole to be non-existent. Rather, it means accessing the source *through* Tradition. Especially after the Second Vatican Council, this was often misunderstood. For that reason, Pope Benedict XVI intervened several times, refuting a "hermeneutic of rupture" and emphasizing a "hermeneutic of reform" in fidelity to the Tradition of the Church.[60] He wrote in his "Letter to the Bishops of the Catholic Church concerning the remission of the excommunication of the four bishops consecrated by Archbishop Lefebvre": "But some of those who put themselves forward as great defenders of the Council also need to be reminded that Vatican II embraces the entire doctrinal history of the Church. Anyone who wants to be obedient to the Council has to accept the faith professed over the centuries

---

[58] Cf. Ralph Weimann, *Dogma und Fortschritt bei Joseph Ratzinger. Prinzipien der Kontinuität*, (Paderborn: Ferdinand Schöningh, 2012).
[59] Cf. DV, 9.
[60] Cf. Benedict XVI, Address to the Roman Curia offering them his Christmas greetings, December 12, 2005, in http://w2.vatican.va/content/benedict-xvi/en/speeches/2005/december/documents/hf_ben_xvi_spe_20051222_roman-curia.html [12.5.2023].

and cannot sever the roots from which the tree draws its life."[61] This hermeneutical principle is of great importance and needs to be respected, especially regarding the sacramentals. Whoever wants to grow in knowledge and wisdom about the revealed truth can never accept a rupture with the past, for continuity with the whole Tradition is the condition for real reform and development.

Actually, during the Protestant Reformation, sacramentals were one of the first things the "reformers" abolished. Of course, there are always aspects that need to be purified and improved, but, as noted, this must always happen in continuity with the Church's tradition. After the Second Vatican Council, the sacramentals were not abolished, but quite a few of the "renewals" were based on principles contrary to the Council and the tradition of the Church. Wherever a hermeneutic of rupture and discontinuity was applied, the reform was doomed to fail. This problem cannot be elaborated here, but it will be taken up and addressed in concrete cases.

Ultimately, the sacramentals have been developed within the living tradition. An inability or refusal to accept and respect this living tradition of the Church would inevitably lead to reinventing the wheel, which cannot be considered as progress but rather as a step backward. This is what has actually happened, especially concerning the sacramentals. Inevitably, the demand for a reform of the reform has arisen by itself.[62]

[61] Benedict XVI, Letter to the Bishops of the Catholic Church concerning the remission of the excommunication of the four bishops consecrated by Archbishop Lefebvre, March 10, 2009, in http://www.vatican.va/content/benedict-xvi/en/letters/2009/documents/hf_ben-xvi_let_20090310_remissione-scomunica.html [12.5.2023].

[62] Cf. Helen Hull Hitchcock, "Pope Benedict XVI and the 'reform of the reform,'" in Neil J. Roy and Janet E. Rutherford (eds.), *Benedict XVI and the Sacred Liturgy*, (Dublin: Four Courts Press, 2011), 70–87. See also Ralph Weimann, "Hermeneutik der Reform als Erneuerung in Kontinuität," in Mitteilungen Institut Papst Benedikt XVI (4/2011): 59–82.

Since the sacramentals are intrinsically related to faith, and faith is, even by many theologians, considered to be "non-scientific," the way in which someone deals with the sacramentals becomes an oath of disclosure; an individual's treatment of them demonstrates whether he really believes his faith. For this reason, it is likely that many have preferred not to address the topic of sacramentals or, if doing so, to use only nebulous phrases in their treatment and discussion of them.[63] In this book, however, a clear stand in the approach toward the sacramentals will be taken, for it is only with precision and clarity that one can move toward a deeper understanding and better application of the sacramentals.

---

[63] Laurence Brett, for example, considers sacramentals as any sign of religious reality. "Like the world, sacramentals are a world of persons, places, times and things. They speak to us about creation, and about that creation as redeemed." Laurence F. X. Brett, *Redeemed Creation: Sacramentals Today*, (Delaware: Pilgrim Reader Books, 1984), 15.

TWO
✣ ✣ ✣
The Theological Notion of Sacramentals

IN THE FIRST CHAPTER, some reference points were provided for the understanding of sacramentals, such as the Second Vatican Council, the codes of canon law of the Western and Eastern Churches, the *Catechism of the Catholic Church* and the Motu Proprio *Summorum Pontificum*, which will — in addition to Sacred Scripture and Tradition — serve to explain the theological notion of sacramentals. Now an explanation of that theological foundation will be provided,[64] which will permit us to come to a correct understanding and use of the sacramentals — for the *lex celebrandi* depends on the *lex credendi*, that is, what is believed in faith will in fact affect and determine how to celebrate and live it out.[65] For that reason, some basic distinctions have to be made.

---

[64] Ralph Weimann, "Die Sakramentalien – Stiefkind der Theologie," in Markus Graulich and Karl-Heinz Menke (eds.), *Fides incarnata*, (Freiburg im Breisgau: Herder, 2021), 391–406.

[65] Cf. The Post-Synodal Apostolic Exhortation *Sacramentum Caritatis* affirms: "The Synod of Bishops reflected at length on the intrinsic relationship between eucharistic faith and eucharistic celebration, pointing out the connection between the *lex orandi* and the *lex credendi*, and stressing the primacy of the *liturgical action*.... The liturgical action can never be considered generically, prescinding from the mystery of faith. Our faith and the eucharistic liturgy both have their source in the same event: Christ's gift of himself in the Paschal Mystery." Benedict XVI, Post-Synodal Apostolic Exhortation *Sacramentum Caritatis*, February 22, 2007, 34, in http://www.

2.1. Basic Distinctions

It is helpful calling to mind briefly the definition of sacramentals, as offered in can. 1166 of the 1983 *Code of Canon Law*: "Sacramentals are sacred signs by which effects, especially spiritual effects, are signified in some imitation of the sacraments and are obtained through the intercession of the Church."[66] This definition helps us understand a common distinction regarding sacramentals:

a) Sacred Signs

Sacramentals are sacred signs, but what does "sacred" mean in a time marked by desacralization and secularism? In recent years, because of the environmental movement and the push for climate protection, an impetus was given to a new form of naturalism, which has also affected theology. According to this view, "nature is the whole of reality."[67] In consequence, the boundary dividing the sacred from the profane is obscured.[68] Thus, all of reality is reduced simply and incorrectly to what can be observed in nature. There are tendencies in theology that go in the same direction. The supernatural is frequently reduced to the natural and, as a result, the distinction between sacred and profane dissolves. In a world where the reference to the supernatural is abandoned, everything mundane is declared sacred and good, even though this would imply the denial of Original Sin and evil.

The German philosopher Josef Pieper (d. 1997) rightly identifies such an approach as depressing and says that it will lead to

---

vatican.va/content/benedict-xvi/en/apost_exhortations/documents/hf_ben-xvi_exh_20070222_sacramentum-caritatis.html [10.5.2023].

[66] CIC, can. 1166.

[67] Jude Patrick Dougherty, "Naturalism," in *New Catholic Encyclopedia*, vol. X, (Washington, D.C.: The Catholic University of America, 1967), 271–274.

[68] James Hitchcock provides an overview, pointing out some of the causes leading to a loss of the sacred. Cf. James Hitchcock, *Recovery of the Sacred*, (San Francisco: Ignatius Press, 1995).

despair, for it would mean "to be imprisoned by a desacralized and entirely 'secular' world, without the possibility of transcending the immediate demands of daily life."[69] In contrast to this secular approach, when the Magisterium of the Church refers to sacred signs, it emphasizes the workings of divine grace, through which persons, places, and things are sanctified. The Constitution on the Sacred Liturgy, *Sacrosanctum Concilium*, says: "Thus, for well-disposed members of the faithful, the liturgy of the sacraments and sacramentals sanctifies almost every event in their lives; they are given access to the stream of divine grace which flows from the paschal mystery of the passion, death, the resurrection of Christ, the font from which all sacraments and sacramentals draw their power. There is hardly any proper use of material things which cannot thus be directed toward the sanctification of men and the praise of God."[70]

In short, then, the Second Vatican Council affirmed that sacramentals are sacred signs directed toward the sanctification of humanity. Any attempt to deny or neglect the difference between the sacred and the profane would necessarily make the sacramentals incomprehensible, or would even lead to a false perception of them as some sort of magic. On the contrary, it is crucial to acknowledge, as Josef Pieper affirmed, the classical principle called *anima forma corporis*, that is, the soul is the life form of the body. While body and spirit belong together, as do nature and grace, they are not the same as each other. An extreme "spiritualism" needs to be avoided just as much as an overemphasis on "naturalism"; neither approach recognizes "the unique opportunity for the individual to transcend the confines of his own subjective self." Pieper concludes, "those who deny the principle of *anima forma corporis* will never understand one of the fundamental concepts in the realm

---

[69] Josef Pieper, *In Search of the Sacred: Contributions to an Answer*, trans. Lothar Krauth, (San Francisco: Ignatius Press, 1991), 45.
[70] SC, 61.

of the sacred: the reality of the *symbol*. They will never realize how entirely normal it is for man to act not merely with a practical goal in mind but also, every now and then, with the intention of setting a sign — be this only the gesture of lighting a candle."[71]

The Italian liturgist and Benedictine priest Cyprian Vagaggini (d. 1999) offers a profound description of how to understand a sacred sign. He states that "sign" is defined as "an instrument which makes some other thing present to the cognitive faculty through the relation it has to the other thing, by the mere fact of being known in this relation."[72] The sign has, therefore, a twofold function: "It reveals the hidden reality and puts us in contact with it."[73] While the indwelling grace of sacred signs is usually hidden to our eyes, it becomes visible through the eyes of faith, and this, in turn, causes spiritual effects.

b) Sacramental Actions

As discussed, the 1917 and 1983 Codes of Canon Law, *Sacrosanctum Concilium*, the *Catechism of the Catholic Church*, and other documents describe the sacramentals in their texts just after they go through the sacraments themselves, indicating that they are similar to the sacraments and ordered toward them. They are intrinsically linked to sacred actions, and these actions are the cause for their own efficacy.

Josef Pieper's small but profound book, *In Search of the Sacred*, provides some helpful insights. He points out that the "sacred action" is the key to understanding the meaning of "sacred," affirming that "only in relation to such action are persons, places, times, and furnishings then also called 'sacred.'"[74] The sacred action follows a distinct logic since it "is never simply 'done' and 'performed' but rather always

---

[71] Pieper, *In Search of the Sacred*, 42.
[72] Cyprian Vagaggini, TDL, 32.
[73] Ambrosius Verheul, *Introduction to the Liturgy. Towards a Theology of Worship*, (Hertfordshire: Anthony Clarke Books, 1972), 105.
[74] Ibid., 25–26.

'celebrated'! A 'sacred action' requires 'celebration.' "[75] He describes the sacred action, which is "furthermore a *physical* event, manifested in visible forms, in the audible language of call and response, in bodily movements and symbolic gestures, in proclamation and song, in the selection of vestments and vessels, and not least in communal silence. In all of this, the 'doing' action of the liturgist corresponds to the analogous, 'contemplating' coaction of the congregation."[76]

In other words, the concept of *the sacred* is always linked to a sacred action.[77] Sacred things are seen through their corresponding actions. Even material things, such as rosaries, crosses, holy water, and the like, become sacred through the sacred actions in which they are used, and they can then contribute to the sanctification of men and women. Blessings are sacred actions par excellence, causing spiritual effects by which graces may be obtained. The decree published in the *Book of Blessings*, by the then-prefect of the Congregation for Divine Worship, says: "The celebration of blessings holds a privileged place among all the sacramentals created by the Church for the pastoral benefit of the people of God. As a liturgical action, the celebration leads the faithful to praise God and prepares them for the principal effect of the sacraments. By celebrating a blessing, the faithful can also sanctify various situations and events in their lives."[78] In other words, the inner center of the sacramentals is a sacred action, which is the efficient cause for producing spiritual fruits. Some authors consider certain acts of piety, such as devotion to the Sacred Heart,[79] as sacramentals; however, it would be more precise to count them among our treasury of sacred actions.

---

[75] Ibid., 26. Thus, Pieper follows Thomas Aquinas. Cf. Thomas Aquinas, STh II–II, q.99, a.1.

[76] Pieper, *In Search of the Sacred*, 26–27.

[77] Cf. Uwe Michael Lang, *Signs of the Holy One. Liturgy, Ritual, and the Expression of the Sacred*, (San Francisco: Ignatius Press, 2015), 56–57.

[78] BoB, 19.

[79] Cf. Ann Ball, *The How-To Book of Sacramentals*, (Huntington: Our Sunday Visitor Publishing Division, 2005), 316ff.

Some of the effects of the sacred actions are of a transient nature, producing graces of sanctification for the moment, as is the case with a common blessing. Others have a lasting character, as in the case of a consecration. In whichever circumstance, however, the sacred action itself is the inner center of any sacramental.[80]

2.2. Four Different Categories of Sacramentals within the Church

There is no complete list of sacramentals in the Church, not even concerning the different types of sacramentals. The Cistercian monk Bernhard Vošicky published a small book on sacramentals, *The Sacramentals of the Church*. He suggests a threefold distinction regarding the different categories of sacramentals: consecrations, blessings, and exorcisms.[81] To these three categories, following the suggestion of Gaspare Lefebvre, a fourth will be added: sacred objects.[82]

2.2.1. Consecrations/Dedications

A consecration is a constitutive blessing that separates the sacred from the profane. The word *consecration* is used to mean the setting apart of persons, places, and objects for the service of God. It derives from the Latin word *consecratio*, which also implies, through its literal translation, an association "with the sacred." Even though *Sacrosanctum Concilium* mentions only the word *consecration* and not *dedication*,[83] soon after the word *dedication* was introduced; its synonymous use has the disadvantage that it weakens the concept of consecration, for a dedication is not in fact the same thing as a consecration. For this

---

[80] See chap. 3.
[81] See Bernhard Vošicky, *Sakraltheologie III. Die Sakramentalien der Kirche*, (Punitz: Hochschule Heiligenkreuz, 1999). Regarding this distinction see also John M. Huels, "A Juridical Notion," 355.
[82] Cf. Gaspare Lefebvre, "XXI. I Sacramentali," in R. Aigrain (ed.), *Enciclopedia Liturgica*, trans. M. Mignone and A. Stella, 2nd ed., (Alba: Edizioni Paoline, 1957), 724–766, here 735.
[83] Cf. SC, 76.

reason, adherence to the concept of *consecration* should be preferred over the use of *dedication*, as the following explanations will show.

Pope Benedict XVI offers a profound insight on this matter, pointing out that the word *consecration* is related to sanctification and holiness, which "in the fullest sense is attributed only to God.... The word 'sanctify' (*qadoš* is the word for 'holy' in the Hebrew Bible) means handing over a reality — a person or even a thing — to God, especially through appropriation for worship."[84] He points out that consecration is a sanctification — that is, something which elevates the person, place, or thing being consecrated "into a new sphere that is no longer under human control."[85] He underlines that consecration includes two dimensions: First, whatever is consecrated belongs to God. Second, because of this belonging to God, it includes "the essential dynamic of 'existing for.' Precisely because it is entirely given over to God, this reality is now there for the world, for men, it speaks for them and exists for their healing."[86] In short, consecrated things belong to God and exist to bring all of humanity to Him.

Pope Benedict's approach is very biblical; he shows that Jesus Christ Himself was consecrated (cf. John, 17:17), and therefore consecration means "that God is exercising a total claim over this man, 'setting him apart' for himself, yet at the same time sending him out for the nations."[87] Persons, places, and objects are consecrated and therefore sanctified in God, and so too in Jesus Christ. "They must be immersed in him; they must, so to speak, be 'newly robed' in him, and thus they come to share in his consecration."[88]

---

[84] Benedict XVI, *Jesus of Nazareth. Part Two: Holy Week. From the Entrance into Jerusalem to the Resurrection*, trans. Vatican Secretariat of State, (San Francisco: Ignatius Press, 2011), 86.

[85] Ibid.

[86] Ibid.

[87] Ibid., 87.

[88] Ibid., 90. According to Benedict, consecration is closely linked to sacrifice, through which sanctification is achieved. See ibid., 86–90.

When a person is consecrated, he or she usually puts on a new robe, as seen in religious orders and the taking on of a new habit. There is an analogous transformation for any building or object consecrated to God.[89] Benedict XVI follows the path indicated in *Sacrosanctum Concilium* that considers "sacredness" as deriving from the liturgical action, from the presence of Christ.[90] However, St. Thomas had already formulated this principle, affirming that "a thing is called 'sacred' through being deputed to the divine worship."[91] It will be helpful to illustrate what this means by presenting some examples of what this looks like in practice on three different levels.

In the first example, the focus will be on the consecration of persons, also referred to as a "special consecration." In 1996, Pope John Paul II published the Apostolic Exhortation *Vita Consecrata* on the consecrated life and its mission in the Church and in the world.[92] The pope speaks about a special consecration, through which one dedicates him or herself to God.[93] He affirms that consecrated life is rooted in God, and that "the entire Christian life bears the marks of the spousal love of Christ."[94] The person is — so to speak — set apart from the profane to live in a unique relationship with God; this life includes participation in the divine mission.[95] *Vita Consecrata* affirms that the baptismal consecration is brought to perfection through the religious profession, which is supposed to lead to a more authentic and explicit configuration. "This

---

[89] See also the more extensive commentary by Uwe Michael Lang, "Sacred Architecture at the Service of the Mission of the Church," in Alcuin Reid (ed.), *Sacred Liturgy: The Source and Summit of the Life and Mission of the Church*, (San Francisco: Ignatius Press, 2014), 198–211, here 197–202.
[90] See SC, 7.
[91] Thomas Aquinas, STh, II–II, q.99, a.1.
[92] John Paul II, Apostolic Exhortation *Vita Consecrata*, March 25, 1996, in http://w2.vatican.va/content/john-paul-ii/en/apost_exhortations/documents/hf_jp-ii_exh_25031996_vita-consecrata.html [12.5.2023].
[93] Cf. ibid., 2.
[94] Ibid., 27.
[95] Cf. ibid., 17–22.

further consecration, however, differs in a special way from baptismal consecration, of which it is not a necessary consequence.... This call is accompanied, moreover, by *a specific gift of the Holy Spirit,* so that consecrated persons can respond to their vocation and mission."[96]

The next aspect is about the consecration of a place. According to ancient tradition, churches and altars are to be consecrated. In 1977, Pope Paul VI promulgated the *Ordo Dedicationis Ecclesiae et Altaris,*[97] which contains the norms and liturgical texts for the blessing and consecration of churches and altars. Regarding the consecration of a church, it says: "Because the church is a visible building, it stands as a special sign of the pilgrim Church on earth and reflects the Church dwelling in heaven. When a church is erected as a building destined solely and permanently for assembling the people of God and for carrying out sacred functions, it is fitting that it be dedicated to God with a solemn rite, in accordance with the ancient custom of the Church."[98] While not getting into the details of the rite of this solemn and inspiring ceremony here, the explanations make clear that it is a consecration performed by a bishop and reserved to him. Through this consecration, the building is raised to a higher order; it is set apart as a sacred place, and the influences of Satan are removed. The Fathers of the Church especially compared the consecration of a church to the consecration of the Jewish Temple. Church and altar are to be consecrated to become the house of God, the gate of Heaven, or — as one of the most famous inscription says in Rome — the *Sancta Sanctorum,*[99] the most holy place, the holiest of holies, sanctified through the grace of God for the presence of God. For that reason, a sacred place is exclu-

---

[96] Ibid., 30.
[97] Paul VI, *Ordo Dedicationis Ecclesiae et Altaris,* (Vatican City: Libreria Editrice Vaticana, 1977).
[98] Ibid., 21.
[99] A reference to the chapel within the church San Lorenzo in Palatio *ad Sancta Sanctorum.*

sively reserved for sacred action; any profane use contrary to the sanctity of the place has to be excluded.[100] Actions, public or private, that are an offense against the sanctity of the church building—namely, anything that uses it in a way that is not sacred—cause scandal to the faithful; as such, they require penitential reparation as prescribed in the *Ceremonial of Bishops*. The rubrics provide precise guidelines for such cases of desecration: "Reparation for the desecration of a church is to be carried out with a penitential rite celebrated as soon as possible. Until that time neither the Eucharist nor any other sacrament or rite is to be celebrated in the church."[101]

In the third and final example, the focus will be on the consecration of things, such as oils, chalices, or patens. For this point, it will be enough to focus briefly on the consecration of chalices. When and how are they and ought they to be consecrated? Some theologians argue that it would be sufficient to use a new and previously unconsecrated chalice for Mass, for, they say, it will be sanctified through its very use. Unfortunately, this way of thinking not only contradicts the living tradition of the Church, but also the inner logic of what is celebrated. Everything that is related to the sacred mystery (that mystery which is God Himself) must be sanctified. It might be helpful to use an allegorical description in order to explain what this means.

When our Lord Jesus Christ came into this world, He was not conceived by a sinful nor by a merely profane person, but by a person who had been consecrated to God and was without the stain of sin. In other words, the Blessed Virgin Mary was holy, consecrated, and

---

[100] Cf. CIC, cann. 562, 1171, 1219, 1228, 1239. See also the commentary provided by Vincenzo Mosca, "I luoghi e i tempi sacri (cann. 1205–1253)," in Gruppo Italiano Docenti di Diritto Canonico (eds), *La funzione di santificare della Chiesa*, (Milan: Edizioni Glossa, 1995), 193–219, here 201.

[101] International Commission on English in the Liturgy (eds.), *Ceremonial of Bishops*. Revised by Decree of the Second Vatican Ecumenical Council and Published by the Authority of Pope John Paul II, (Collegeville: Liturgical Press, 1989), 289.

therefore sanctified. She was the perfect tabernacle. How could it be otherwise, since Jesus Christ is the Holy of Holies?

During the liturgy, the mystery of the Incarnation is made present. Our Lord Jesus Christ, true God and true man, descends on the altar. For that reason, it is necessary to consecrate the vessels ahead of time, those vessels which are going to contain the Most Precious Body and Blood of our Lord Jesus Christ. The new ritual says that this consecration should be done within the Mass and in the presence of the community. Nevertheless, the Mass is not the moment to administer as many sacramentals as possible. The sacredness of the Divine Liturgy can be compromised. Therefore, it was considered a norm in the tradition of the Church not to mix sacraments and sacramentals. For this reason, it would be preferable to do it outside the celebration of the Holy Eucharist.

The new rite of blessings mentions also that any priest may bless the chalice and the paten;[102] however, this is not coherent because it does not do justice to the sacredness and importance of the object. According to the tradition of the Church and until the end of the Second Vatican Council, this rite was exclusively reserved to the bishop, who consecrated the chalice with sacred chrism, making the sign of the cross within the chalice from one edge of the cup to another, spreading the chrism throughout the cup.[103]

In all three of these examples, it can be seen that things such as patens and chalices are consecrated for a permanent purpose; they become sacred through that same consecration.[104] A consecration is also called a

---

[102] Cf. ibid., VII, 125.

[103] The main Latin formula used is: "Conse + crare, et sancti + ficare digneris, Domine Deus, Calicem hunc per istam unctionem, et nostram bene + dictionem in Christo Jesu Domino nostro, qui tecum vivit et regnat in unitate Spiritus Sancti Deus, per omnia saecula saeculorum. R. Amen." *Missale Romanum*, Ex Decreto SS. Concilii Tridentini restitutum Summorum Ponfificum cura recognitum, Editio iuxta typicam, (Thalwil: C. H. Beck, 2012), 304.

[104] Usually, a consecration is characterized using sacred oil. Cf. Heribert Jone, *Gesetzbuch der lateinischen Kirche. Erklärung der Kanones*, vol. II,

constitutive blessing. It signifies the permanent sanctification and dedication of a person, a place, or a thing for a sacred purpose, receiving a sacred character, which transforms it from something that is profane to something that is sacred. This transformation cannot be reversed — except through the authority of the Church — back to a non-sacred use.[105] This is reflected perhaps most clearly in the consecration of persons. When religious brothers and sisters take their final vows, those vows indicate a permanent change. The same has to be said regarding the consecration of a church or a chalice. They become sacred, and, from thence forward, are therefore dedicated only to sacred usage.

2.2.2. Blessings

Common blessings comprise another category of sacramentals. They can be found as early as the biblical account of Creation. God blessed the creatures that came from His hands (cf. Gen. 1:22, 28). Noah received God's blessing (cf. Gen. 9:1). Melchizedek blessed Abram with the words: "Blessed be Abram by God Most High, the creator of heaven and earth; and blessed be God Most High, who delivered your foes into your hand" (Gen. 14:19–20). The importance of blessings is reflected in Jacob's blessing for the favorite son; it secures God's benevolence, protection, and peace. It receives a new and full meaning through Jesus Christ, as affirmed in the Letter to the Ephesians: "Blessed be the God and Father of our Lord Jesus Christ, who has blessed us in Christ with every spiritual blessing in the heavens" (Eph. 1:3). The apostles carried on this pre-Christian tradition in the early Church, which has received its full meaning through Jesus Christ, and was continually practiced in the Church ever since.

2nd ed., (Paderborn: Ferdinand Schöningh, 1952), 406.

[105] The Code of Canon Law says in can. 1222 §1: "If a church cannot be used in any way for divine worship and there is no possibility of repairing it, the diocesan bishop can relegate it to profane but not sordid use."

A decree that was published in the *Book of Blessings* identified them as having a privileged place among all the sacramentals, noting that they are meant to sanctify various situations and events of life,[106] and that it is through blessings that the faithful receive spiritual benefits. The minister implores divine grace to grant some spiritual good. This is realized, for example, when a priest blesses a person, or when a mother blesses her child. The blessing of the sick, or of travelers, or of pilgrims, and so on, are all part of this category of sacramentals. This type of blessing is the most frequent and can be used almost for anything, so long as it does not contradict God's commandment.

Again, Sacred Scripture mentions different forms of blessings.[107] Differing from the consecrations (or constitutive blessings), common and invocative blessings are intended to grant some temporal good, but they do not effect any change of condition as a consecration does.

2.2.3. Exorcisms

There is a third category of sacramentals: the explicit combat against demonic spirits. Through exorcisms, persons, places, and things are freed from the evil one. Further distinctions, such as the difference between minor and major exorcisms, will be made later on.[108] For now, however, it is enough to mention the category as such, as it has an important role to play. This sacramental, above all, reflects the liberating and healing power of Christ in His Church since, as noted, it is through her that people are freed from the influence of the devil.

2.2.4. Sacred Objects and Places

We will call the fourth category of sacramentals sacred objects and places. This includes all other forms of sacramentals that do not belong to consecrations, blessings, and exorcisms. Among them can be counted relics;

---

[106] Cf. BoB, 19.
[107] See chap. 8.
[108] See chap. 7.

the oil of saints, also called *oleum sanctum* (e.g., *Walburgis oleum*); and the use of sacred vestments, such as the blessed vestments destined for the celebration of the Holy Eucharist, but also wedding rings, episcopal rings, scapulars, the Miraculous and St. Benedict Medals, and others. Funeral and burial places are also counted among these sacramentals.

2.3. The Theological Nature of Sacramentals

When considering the theological nature of sacramentals, it is helpful to revisit their definition, since it describes this theological nature: "Holy Mother Church has … instituted sacramentals. These are sacred signs which bear a resemblance to the sacraments: they signify effects, particularly of a spiritual kind, which are obtained through the Church's intercession. By them, men are disposed to receive the chief effect of the sacraments, and various occasions in life are rendered holy."[109] It is worth noting that this definition mentions the spiritual effects of sacramentals — effects which are related to the liturgical action — through which the merits of Christ's redemption become effective. Furthermore, this definition indicates that the institution of sacramentals has to be understood in the context of ecclesiology, i.e., they are instituted through the Church. All of this presupposes their theological background; this is something which needs an explanation, starting with the concept of Original Sin and its consequences. From there, the biblical foundation of sacramentals and the Christocentric character of revelation will be considered — as well as some aspects of ecclesiology — followed by reflections on sacramentals as liturgical actions. The explanation of their theological nature will be concluded with some systematic considerations.

2.3.1. Original Sin and Its Consequence

Through the sin of Adam, the original harmony between God and His creatures was lost. From that moment on, sin has been present in

---

[109] SC, 60.

human history — with destructive consequences. In this sense, Adam is the source of sin, and Christ is the source of grace. The "Original Sin" was an act of disobedience, which wiped away the original holiness. Even though the human person is created in the image and likeness of God, this very image and likeness is distorted through sin. The order of creation was gravely affected in this moment: the harmony was broken, and death made its entrance into human history.[110] This is described in the book of Genesis: "Because you listened to your wife and ate from the tree of which I had forbidden you to eat, 'Cursed be the ground because of you! In toil shall you eat its yield all the days of your life.' ... By the sweat of your face shall you get bread to eat bread, until you return to the ground, from which you were taken; For you are dirt, and to dirt you shall return" (Gen. 3:17, 19).

The damaging consequences of sin did not only affect mankind; they also affected the rest of creation. The original state, in which everything had been created good through God's blessings — the so-called *dona praeternaturalia* — was lost.[111] As a part of this, nature became susceptible to diseases and disorders of every kind. According to Josef Pieper, sin is not only a deficiency; above all, it is an "act." This is because the alignment toward a direction happens by *doing*, and sin is the disturbance of this ordering toward God.[112] In goodness, we move toward God, but in sin, we move away from God.

The Fall did not only leave humanity with the lasting and negative effects of Original Sin, but also exposed to the "ruler of this world" (John 12:31), who has a similarly destructive impact on man and creation. He exercises a harmful influence over nature, affecting persons,

---

[110] Cf. *CCC*, 400. For more detail, see Ralph Weimann, "Die Sakramentalien," 395–396.

[111] Cf. Matthias Scheeben, *Handbook of Catholic Dogmatics. Book One Theological Epistemology*, trans. Michael J. Miller, (Steubenville: Emmaus Academic, 2019), 51.

[112] Cf. Josef Pieper, *Über den Begriff der Sünde*, (Kevelaer: Topos, 2019), 39.

places, and objects (see 1 Pet. 5:8). For that reason, St. Paul acknowledged: "For creation awaits with eager expectation the revelation of the children of God; for creation was made subject to futility, not of its own accord but because of the one who subjected it, in hope that creation itself would be set free from slavery to corruption and share in the glorious freedom of the children of God (Rom. 8:19–21).

If the reality of (original) sin is neglected or rejected, the sacramentals — which God offers to mankind through His Church — will become incomprehensible.[113] They are spiritual means to overcome the consequence of sin and the presence of the devil. Pope John Paul II explained this important aspect from a different perspective in his encyclical letter, *Evangelium vitae*. He referred to "veritable structures of sin" that go against life and create a "culture of death."[114] He affirmed: "Only those who recognize that their life is marked by the evil of sin can discover in an encounter with Jesus the Savior the truth and the authenticity of their own existence."[115] Conversely, this means that if sin and the devil are ignored, then salvation also becomes void, as do all those means that are directed toward salvation. Whenever sin and its devastating consequences are ignored, structures of sin will grow.

Today, there are even many Catholics who do not know what sin is any longer, despite the fact that sin destroys harmony and order and is, therefore, opposed to God and His law. The First Letter of John exhorts each Christian to be realistic in this regard: "If we say, 'We are without sin,' we deceive ourselves, and the truth is not in us" (1 John 1:8). Ignorance concerning sin will also lead to ignorance

---

[113] Some theologians even deny their existence. Cf. Markus Striet, *Ernstfall Freiheit: Arbeiten an der Schleifung der Bastionen*, (Freiburg im Breisgau: Herder, 2018).
[114] John Paul II, EV, 24.
[115] Ibid., 32.

concerning anything — including sacramentals — that is meant to help us in overcoming sin and its consequences.

When considering the lasting effects of Original Sin, it is worth remembering why this moment is called *felix culpa* during the Easter Vigil: Jesus Christ is the new Adam, who through His obedience unto death, even death on a cross (see Phil. 2:8), makes amends for the disobedience of Adam, freeing mankind from the slavery of sin. St. Thomas provided a profound commentary on this elevation of human nature through Christ's willing and divine participation in it: "There is no reason why human nature should not have been raised to something greater after sin. For God allows evils to happen in order to bring a greater good therefrom; hence it is written (Rom. 5:20): 'Where sin abounded, grace did more abound.' Hence, too, in the blessing of the Paschal candle, we say: 'O happy fault, that merited such and so great a Redeemer!'"[116] Christ came into this world to take away the sins of the world and to grant us salvation. He gave His apostles the power to forgive sins by applying the merits of His redemption, especially through the sacraments. From what has been said so far, it becomes clear that sacramentals always include — or should always include — two elements, one to combat the evil that is always seeking to devour us, and one to increase our orientation to God:[117]

1. Apotropaic elements: These aim, through the power of God, to overcome the influences of the devil and the negative consequences of sin. Whenever they are omitted in the use of sacramentals, (original) sin and the existence of the devil is thereby also either rejected or neglected to a proportionate and dangerous degree. This is a very serious

---

[116] Thomas Aquinas, STh III, q.1, a.3.
[117] Cf. Mario Righetti, *Manuale di storia liturgica. I Sacramenti – I Sacramentali*, vol. IV, 2nd ed., (Milan: Ancora, 1998), 474.

issue, for the "reform" of the sacramentals consisted widely in the exclusion of apotropaic elements.[118]

2. Elements of sanctification: The sacramentals are meant to sanctify, bestowing graces on the People of God and creation. This is due to the merits of Christ's redemption. Grace is not only limited to the sacraments but also — even though to a different degree — obtained through the administration of the sacramentals. The first Letter of Paul to Timothy already suggests this interpretation: "For everything created by God is good, and nothing is to be rejected when received with thanksgiving, for it is made holy by the invocation of God in prayer." (1 Tim. 4:4–5)

2.3.2. The Biblical Foundation of Sacramentals

It is important to highlight that all sacramentals are, in one way or another, linked to Sacred Scripture. The Church continuously relates the sacramentals to some sort of biblical basis to assure that they are genuine sacred signs. The *Book of Blessings* emphasized this by relating every blessing to a quotation from Scripture.

Even in the Old Testament, the rites described in the period from Adam's fall to Christ's coming foreshadowed the meaning of the sacramentals. Scripture explains these rites, shedding light on how to understand the sacramentals. In this sense, the Dogmatic Constitution on Divine Revelation says: "God, the inspirer and author of both Testaments, wisely arranged that the New Testament be hidden in the Old and the Old be made manifest in the New."[119] Lest there be any doubt, this affirms that the Old Testament remains of importance. However, it must be underlined that the full meaning of the Old Testament is revealed in Jesus Christ — through His life, His Passion, death, and Resurrection.

---

[118] See chap. 4.
[119] DV, 16.

This affirmation is also significant concerning the sacramentals; a double orientation of Old and New Testament is necessary to understand them properly. To illustrate this, it will be helpful to look at a passage from the Old Testament: "The inhabitants of the city complained to Elisha, 'The site of the city is fine indeed, as my lord can see, but the water is bad and the land sterile.' Elisha said, 'Bring me a new bowl and put salt into it.' When they had brought it to him, he went out to the spring and threw salt into it, saying, 'Thus says the Lord: I have purified this water. Never again shall death or sterility come from it'" (2 Kings 2:19–21). This episode explains the power of God's action over natural elements in the context of the Old Testament. Centuries later, in the New Testament, this specific sacred power will take on a new quality through Jesus Christ. In this sense, it can be said that the sacred actions presented in the Old Testament prefigured what was about to come. But they are not merely about prefigurement; in their own right, they had strong spiritual and sometimes even physical effects and so they are authentic points of reference.

This transformation and deepening of old in the new is also true concerning the power of the priestly blessing, first described in the book of Numbers: "Speak to Aaron and his sons and tell them: This is how you shall bless the Israelites. Say to them: The Lord bless you and keep you! The Lord let his face shine upon you, and be gracious to you! The Lord look upon you kindly and give you peace! So shall they invoke my name upon the Israelites, and I will bless them" (Num. 6:23–27). This is the most popular priestly blessing, and it is one that follows an inner logic. It is God Himself who provides the blessing through the priest, restoring and granting His peace. Sacred Scripture offers numerous forms of blessings, such as when Jesus Christ attended the children and said: "Let the children come to me; do not prevent them, for the kingdom of God belongs to such as these. Amen, I say to you, whoever does not accept the kingdom of God like a child will not enter it. Then he embraced them and blessed them, placing his hands on them" (Mark 10:14–16).

In addition to providing a scriptural foundation for sacramental blessings, Scripture also speaks directly of objects that become sacred. The Acts of the Apostles touches on this, helping in further understanding sacramentals. It mentions that "all the inhabitants of the province of Asia heard the word of the Lord, Jews and Greeks alike. So extraordinary were the mighty deeds God accomplished at the hands of Paul that when face cloths or aprons that touched his skin were applied to the sick, their diseases left them and the evil spirits came out of them" (Acts 19:10–12).

Then, Scripture mentions holy objects, things that were sanctified by physical contact with a saint or with Christ Himself. Among Italian Catholics, at least, this consciousness is still very present. The Capuchins, for example, preserved almost everything that had been in contact with Padre Pio; some of these holy objects, when used with faith, have proven to obtain effects similar to those described in above passage from the Acts of the Apostles.[120] Something else similar is also mentioned in the Gospel of Matthew: "A woman suffering hemorrhages for twelve years came up behind him and touched the tassel on his cloak. She said to herself, 'If only I can touch his cloak, I shall be cured.' Jesus turned around and saw her, and said, 'Courage, daughter! Your faith has saved you.' And from that hour the woman was cured" (Matt. 9:20–22).

The importance of relics — also counted among sacramentals — is likewise present in Scripture. The second book of Kings says: "Once some people were burying a man, when suddenly they saw ... a raiding band. So they cast the man into the grave of Elisha, and everyone went off. But when the man came in contact with the bones of Elisha, he came back to life and got to his feet" (2 Kings 13:21). The Acts of the Apostles describes something similar related to the presence of St. Peter: "Thus they even carried the sick out into the streets and laid them on cots and

---

[120] Cf. Alessandro Gnocchi and Mario Palmaro, *L'ultima Messa di Padre Pio. L'anima segreta del santo delle stigmate*, (Milan: Piemme, 2010), 195–196.

mats so that when Peter came by, at least his shadow might fall on one or another of them. A large number of people from the towns in the vicinity of Jerusalem also gathered, bringing the sick and those disturbed by unclean spirits, and they were all cured" (Acts 5:15–16).

Likewise, the Gospel of John describes the cure of a blind man through sacramentals: "When he had said this, he spat on the ground and made clay with the saliva, and smeared the clay on his eyes, and said to him, 'Go wash in the Pool of Siloam' (which means sent). So, he went and washed, and came back able to see" (John 9:6–7). Similar effects are obtained through the use of sacred oil (cf. James 5:14) and holy water (cf. 2 Kings 5:14).

These few examples show that matter can convey grace and that sacramentals are not unbiblical magical practices, but are frequently mentioned in both Scripture and Tradition.[121] However, to understand the theological meaning more deeply, it will be helpful to provide a systematic explanation.

2.3.3. The "Incarnational Principle"

The New Testament is filled with many concrete examples regarding sacramentals. However, they all reflect the incarnational principle. What does this mean? The Incarnation of Jesus Christ is crucial for any sacramental understanding because "the Word became flesh and made his dwelling among us" (John 1:14). In assuming human nature by the Son of God, this very nature was elevated and filled with divine life. "The Word became flesh" is the concrete way of realizing the divine plan of salvation. There is an inner logic, which can be described as an "incarnational principle," that is also reflected in the sacraments and in the sacramentals. They include natural things, which become effective signs

---

[121] Reiner Kaczynski, "5 Die Benediktionen," in Hans Bernhard Meyer et al. (ed.), *Sakramentliche Feiern II*, vol. 8, (Regensburg: Friedrich Pustet Verlag, 1984), 233–274, here 247–258.

and conduits of divine life.[122] Thus, material realities become "sacred signs" through the power of divine grace, which becomes understandable only in the light of the Incarnation. Similar to the sacraments, the sacramentals point toward God's physical action and presence.

Following the logic of the "incarnational principle," matter can convey grace. Through divine action, persons, places, and objects are sanctified. One of the most outstanding examples is the Mother of God, for she was "full of grace" (Luke 1:28).[123] There were also certain places and objects, such as the Temple in Jerusalem, that were sanctified by the grace of God (cf. Exod. 24:43–44). One of the most outstanding of these holy objects is the shroud of Turin (cf. John 20:6–7); it is now rightfully venerated as an extraordinary relic sanctified by Jesus Christ Himself. This holy object is in itself an instrument for the transmission of grace.

The incarnational principle follows an inner logic. How does this play out? According to Thomas Aquinas, the death of Jesus Christ is the universal cause of our salvation. Nevertheless, a universal cause has to be applied to particular effects. These particular effects are administered by visible signs. St. Thomas concluded in the *Summa Contra Gentiles*: "Now, man's condition is such that he

---

[122] Cyprian Vagaggini called this the "Law of Incarnation," which he defines as follows: "First of all it signifies that God communicates divine life to man through and under the veil of sensible things, which means in turn that man is obliged to pass through these sensible things in order to receive that divine life. In second place, it signifies that what results from that communication is an elevation of man to a divine mode of being and acting, and this not just in the purely moral order in a cognoscitive and affective line, but in the ontological or entitative order and, in this precise sense, in the physical order, so much so that even while the substantial distinction between God and man remains ever intact, man is raised up to a really divine state of being and of acting." Cyprian Vagaggini, TDL, 300.

[123] The language of the Douay-Rheims has been chosen here because the translation offered in the NABRE is inadequate, instead giving "Hail, favored one!" The Vulgate text reads "Ave, gratia plena," and in Greek "Χαῖρε, κεχαριτωμένη."

is brought to grasp the spiritual and intelligible naturally through the senses. Therefore, spiritual remedies had to be given to men under sensible signs."[124]

These considerations help us understand why the Second Vatican Council emphasizes the importance of the incarnational principle,[125] which is related to the sacramental idea. The approach presented in the texts of the Council reflects the realism of the history of salvation, starting with the reality of creation, which is brought to perfection through divine grace. Consequently, the sacramental idea is, on one side, related to creation. On the other side, it transcends the biological sphere through the supernatural reality of God's action. As a result, the human person is not self-sufficient but — according to the constitutional nature of each person — in relation with and toward the divine.[126]

This sacramental idea, taken up in the Second Vatican Council, was further deepened by Joseph Ratzinger, especially in volume 11 of his *Collected Works*.[127] The sacramental idea was supposed to be at the foundation of the liturgical renewal and of the renewal of the Church. It finds its expression in the Constitution on the Sacred Liturgy, *Sacroscanctum Concilium*: "Christ is always present in His Church, especially in her liturgical

---

[124] Thomas Aquinas, *Summa Contra Gentiles*, Book IV, chap. 56, 3, trans. Charles J. O'Neil, St. Isidore e-book library, in https://isidore.co/aquinas/ContraGentiles4.htm [12.5.2023].

[125] The Dogmatic Constitution on Divine Revelation *Dei Verbum* affirmed: "In His goodness and wisdom God chose to reveal Himself and to make known to us the hidden purpose of His will (see Eph. 1:9) by which through Christ, the Word made flesh, man might in the Holy Spirit have access to the Father and come to share in the divine nature (see Eph. 2:18; 2 Pet. 1:4). Through this revelation, therefore, the invisible God (see Col. 1;15, 1 Tim. 1:17) out of the abundance of His love speaks to men as friends (see Exod. 33:11; John 15:14–15) and lives among them (see Bar. 3:38), so that He may invite and take them into fellowship with Himself." DV, 2.

[126] Cf. GS, 36.

[127] Cf. Joseph Ratzinger, TL, 200–214.

celebrations.... By His power He is present in the sacraments, so that when a man baptizes it is really Christ Himself who baptizes. He is present in His word since it is He Himself who speaks when the holy Scriptures are read in the Church. He is present, lastly, when the Church prays and sings, for He promised: 'Where two or three are gathered together in my name, there am I in the midst of them' (Matt. 18:20)."[128] In short, the sacraments, as well as the sacramentals, are based on the order of creation; at the same time, however, they are part of a broader horizon. Therefore, human existence cannot be exhausted or fulfilled merely by biology, for it consists "of a substantial unity between the spiritual form and the physical body."[129] The sacramental idea leads to sound anthropology, a sound understanding of what the human person is who is created in the image of God.[130] Today, especially due to gender ideology,[131] human nature is submitted to tremendous manipulation and ideological colonization, which will — if it continues to spread — also inevitably destroy the necessary conditions for the understanding of the sacramental idea. Whenever human nature is submitted to any false anthropology that so reduces the human person to its material dimension. The sacramental idea — a sanctifying supernatural reality that surpasses the material dimension — is lost and becomes incomprehensible. St. Thomas Aquinas foresaw this and formulated the always valid axiom: "*Gratia non tollit naturam, sed perficit* — Grace does not destroy nature, but perfects it."[132] However, the term "nature" must be understood correctly; human nature essentially includes the spirit.

---

[128] SC, 7.

[129] Ralph Weimann, *Bioethical Challenges at the End of Life. An Ethical Guide in Catholic Perspective*, (Brooklyn: Angelico Press, 2022), 48.

[130] See with more detail: Ibid., 46–52.

[131] See Francis, Post-Synodal Apostolic Exhortation *Amoris Laetitia*, March 19, 2016, 56, in http://www.vatican.va/content/dam/francesco/pdf/apost_exhortations/documents/papa-francesco_esortazione-ap_20160319_amoris-laetitia_en.pdf [12.5.2023].

[132] Thomas Aquinas, STh, I, q.1, a.8.

The incarnational principle sheds light on the importance of material things, things which gain new importance and meaning through divine action; through the power of the spirit, they become sacred signs. The sacramental idea is intrinsically linked to this principle and offers a perspective which necessarily includes a transcending movement toward the supernatural. There is a "sacramental logic, through which God himself gives himself in the sacraments.... Only if Jesus Christ is true God can he reveal to us the face of God. But in that case, sacramental communion with Jesus Christ is sacramental communion with God."[133]

Even though the Second Vatican Council emphasized these essential elements, they were not well understood in the years that followed. Even many theologians adopted a merely horizontal view, failing to account for the necessary transcendent and, one might say, vertical view to the supernatural that is required for a proper understanding of sacramentals. This tendency has, unsurprisingly, often led to forms of naturalism that exclude the supernatural and, consequently, God Himself.[134]

2.3.4. Ecclesiological Considerations

Ecclesiological considerations are another important dimension helpful to understanding the theological nature of the sacramentals. Before the Ascension of our Lord Jesus Christ, He said to His apostles: "All power in heaven and on earth has been given to me. Go, therefore, and make disciples of all nations" (Matt. 28:18–19). As the Father sent Him, He sends the apostles, bestowing upon them all power in Heaven and on earth, provided that they "persevere in the faith, firmly

---

[133] International Theological Commission, "The Reciprocity Between Faith and Sacraments in the Sacramental Economy," March 3, 2020, 18, in http://www.vatican.va/roman_curia/congregations/cfaith/cti_documents/rc_cti_20200303_reciprocita-fede-sacramenti_en.html [10.5.2023].

[134] In 2018 the CDF tried to correct these tendencies. Cf. CDF, Letter *Placuit Deo*, March 1, 2018, 12–14, https://press.vatican.va/content/salastampa/en/bollettino/pubblico/2018/03/01/180301a.html [12.5.2023].

grounded, stable, and not shifting from the hope of the gospel" (Col. 1:23). He gave His apostles the power to cast out demons, to heal the sick, and to administer divine graces. This is affirmed in the Gospel of Luke: "He summoned the Twelve and gave them power and authority over all demons and to cure diseases, and he sent them to proclaim the kingdom of God and to heal [the sick]" (Luke 9:1–2).

In other words, from the very beginning, sacramentals are instituted and administered by the Church. The saving grace of Jesus Christ, the origin of all sacramentality, is transmitted in space and time through the Church.[135] According to a sacramental understanding, the Church was declared to be "in Christ like a sacrament or as a sign and instrument both of a very closely knit union with God and of the unity of the whole human race."[136] Since the Church is *in Christ*, just as a sacrament is, it is her very task to make divine grace accessible to all mankind. This includes the sacramentals, through which those same divine graces can be obtained that order and guide as many people as possible to eternal salvation. Sacramentals produce spiritual effects and divine grace; however, they are obtained through the intercession of the Church.

In times of scandals and abuses, it is difficult for some to understand the essence of what the Church is. Therefore, now more than ever, it is necessary to adopt an approach to our Faith and Church based on the sacramental idea. In his encyclical letter, *Mater et Magistra*, Pope John XXIII called the Church the "Mother and Teacher of all nations."[137] The Church is and remains the "pillar and foundation of truth" (1 Tim. 3:15). To her is entrusted the task to teach and to

---

[135] Cf. International Theological Commission, "The Reciprocity," 78f.
[136] LG, 1.
[137] John XXIII, Encyclical Letter *Mater et Magistra*, May 15, 1961, 1, in http://www.vatican.va/content/john-xxiii/en/encyclicals/documents/hf_j-xxiii_enc_15051961_mater.html [10.5.2023].

guide. While understanding the Church as our Mother, she consists of two components:

> a) A divine element. This is the constitutional and substantial dimension, for Christ, in His divinity, is the head of the Church.[138] It includes, in a broader sense, the Church triumphant in Heaven — the saints and angels.
>
> b) A human element. Particularly today, it is mainly the human element which seems to absorb all of the attention of casual observers. But just as human beings must not be reduced to their biological dimension, so the Church must not be reduced to its human dimension. This reductive view of what the Church is must be avoided. If it is instead embraced, she would be degraded to a political party or a non-profit organization.[139]

The Dogmatic Constitution, *Lumen Gentium*, offers a profound explanation and a type of synopsis of these two elements:

> Christ, the one Mediator, established and continually sustains here on earth His holy Church, the community of faith, hope and charity, as an entity with visible delineation through which He communicated truth and grace to all. But, the society structured with hierarchical organs and the Mystical Body of Christ, are not to be considered as two realities, nor are the visible assembly and the spiritual community, nor the earthly Church and the Church enriched with heavenly things; rather they form one complex reality which coalesces from a divine and a human element. For this reason, by no weak analogy, it is compared to the mystery of the incarnate Word. As the assumed nature inseparably united to Him, serves the divine Word as a living organ of salvation, so, in a similar

---

[138] DV, 7.
[139] Cf. Francis, Homily in *Missa pro Ecclesia*, March 14, 2013, in http://www.vatican.va/content/francesco/en/homilies/2013/documents/papa-francesco_20130314_omelia-cardinali.html [12.5.2023].

way, does the visible social structure of the Church serve the Spirit of Christ, who vivifies it, in the building up of the body.[140]

This explanation provided by the Council is precise since it brings together both elements. However, special emphasis is put on the first dimension since "the Church is *in* Christ." In other words, the Church is first of all God's Church — were it otherwise, she would lose her *raison d'être*, i.e., her whole reason for existence. Even though the human dimension is important, it must be said that the Church remains God's Church primarily in the way that she remains in Christ; the human dimension must be understood as her secondary element, for "Christ is the Light of nations." This light must become visible "on the countenance of the Church."[141] The same can be said analogously concerning sacramentals. They are approved by the Church, their spiritual effects are granted through the intercession of the Church, and they need to be administered in the name of the Church. If making them primarily human-centric instead of Christocentric, they will be corrupted and lose their efficacy.

It is Christ who gave to the apostles the power to bless and to consecrate. "The Church elevates and sanctifies nature by using sensible objects in her worship, in her sacraments, and in her sacramentals."[142] The sacramentals are part of the Church's *munus sanctificandi*, i.e., her duty to provide for the sanctification of the faithful, particularly through her priests acting *in persona Christi*. For that reason, the *Catechism of the Catholic Church* affirms: "Sacramentals are instituted for the sanctification of certain ministries of the Church, certain states of

---

[140] LG, 8.
[141] LG, 1.
[142] Michael Müller, *God the Teacher of Mankind, or Popular Catholic Theology, Apologetical, Dogmatical, Moral, Liturgical, Pastoral, and Ascetical: Sacramentals, Prayer, Vices and Virtues, Christian Perfection, etc.*, (St. Louis: Fr. Pustet & Co., 1888), 2.

life, a great variety of circumstances in Christian life, and the use of many things helpful to man."[143]

Sacramentals are part of the Church's official worship. They are part of the Church's liturgy. Therefore, they must be approved by the authority of the Church.[144]

2.3.5. Sacramentals as Liturgical Actions

In prayer, the Church turns toward Almighty God; accordingly, prayers are part of the Church's liturgical action. Sacramentals "always include a prayer, often accompanied by a specific sign, such as the laying on of hands, the sign of the cross, or the sprinkling of holy water (which recalls Baptism)."[145] At this point, a first and important characteristic of all sacramentals is evident: Sacramentals are, above all, prayer. They are not private or charismatic prayers; rather, they are a liturgical act and, therefore, a prayer of the Church. In consequence, this type of prayer is part of the whole Church, which includes God Almighty, the wellspring of all graces, but it also includes the angels, the saints, and the people gathered together. Contextualized by all of these elements, the sacramentals draw their strength from the supernatural reality.

This affirmation is important concerning the very structure of the prayers used when sacramentals are administered. For that reason, besides the Most Holy Trinity, saints and angels are invoked, since they are a part — the noblest part — of the Church. "Prayer is *Christian* insofar as it is communion with Christ and extends throughout the Church, which is his Body. Its dimensions are those of Christ's love."[146]

This becomes even more comprehensible when the significance of a liturgical action is understood. Considering "the liturgy of the

---

[143] *CCC*, 1668.
[144] See chap. 1.2.
[145] *CCC*, 1668.
[146] *CCC*, 2565.

sacraments and sacramentals," the Constitution on Sacred Liturgy affirms that "they are given access to the stream of divine grace which flows from the paschal mystery of the passion, death, the resurrection of Christ, the font from which all sacraments and sacramentals draw their power."[147] This affirms their place as liturgical actions that lead the faithful to praise God, meaning that, through them, one should be prepared for the principal effects of the sacraments.[148] Inspired by the Liturgical Movement and the Second Vatican Council, the decree for the renewal of the sacramentals offers some principles on how to approach them. In short, as they are part of the treasury of the liturgy, the faithful should seek to participate in them as they participate in all liturgy: "In ordering the reform of the sacramentals, Vatican Council II decreed that in their celebration special attention should be given to the full, conscious, and active participation of the faithful and that any elements should be eliminated that in the course of time had obscured the true nature and purpose of the sacramentals."[149]

In chapter 3, some other elements regarding the participation of the faithful within the administration of the sacramentals are going to be explained. In this context, it is important to affirm that they are considered liturgical actions, and as such they require participation, which is directly linked to their spiritual effects. The best way to participate in the sacramentals and so to benefit from their positive spiritual effects is to remember that both the noblest and the most essential form of participation is prayer.

Sacramentals as liturgical actions usually imply prayers of petition and supplication. This form of prayer is characterized by a humble petition, asking for actual graces through the administration of the Church. The practice of the faithful asking for the blessing of their

---

[147] SC, 61.
[148] Cf. BoB, Decree, 19.
[149] Ibid., 19.

rosaries, medals, and so on naturally reflects this. The prayer of petition is frequently mentioned in the New Testament, as described, for example, in the episode of the Roman Centurion in Matt. 8:5–10:

> When he entered Capernaum, a centurion approached him and appealed to him, saying, "Lord, my servant is lying at home paralyzed, suffering dreadfully." He said to him, "I will come and cure him." The centurion said in reply, "Lord, I am not worthy to have you enter under my roof; only say the word and my servant will be healed. For I too am a person subject to authority, with soldiers subject to me. And I say to one, 'Go,' and he goes; and to another, 'Come here,' and he comes; and to my slave, 'Do this,' and he does it." When Jesus heard this, he was amazed and said to those following him, "Amen, I say to you, in no one in Israel have I found such faith."

The prayer of petition should always accompany the administration of sacramentals, for they are a request to God that He might fulfill a need and grant certain graces. Through this prayer, the person recognizes his dependence on God. At the same time — as can be seen in this story of the centurion — the prayer of petition presupposes faith.[150] However, the prayer of petition is centered not on the wish to fulfill one's own desires, but rather it consists in the search for the Kingdom to come, following and keeping the teaching of Christ. The *Catechism of the Catholic Church* provides a profound explanation for this distinction: "There is a hierarchy in these petitions: we pray first for the Kingdom, then for what is necessary to welcome it and co-operate with its coming. This collaboration with the mission of Christ and the Holy Spirit, which is now that of the Church, is the object of the prayer of the apostolic community. It is the prayer of Paul, the apostle par excellence, which reveals to us how the divine solicitude for all the churches ought to inspire Christian prayer. By prayer every baptized

---

[150] See chap. 4 for more detail.

person works for the coming of the Kingdom."[151] Every need can become the object of petition, which should always accompany the administration of the sacramentals. The prayer of petition is continuously present in all sacramentals, as can be seen in the consecration of a virgin, which is counted among the oldest sacramentals. After renewing the promise of perpetual virginity to God, the virgin is a sacred person; the ceremony is accompanied by prayers of petition. Canon law affirms: "Similar to these forms of consecrated life is the order of virgins who, expressing the holy resolution of following Christ more closely, are consecrated to God by the diocesan bishop according to the approved liturgical rite, are mystically betrothed to Christ, the Son of God, and are dedicated to the service of the Church."[152]

In summary, then, sacramentals are liturgical actions and, at the same time, they are part of the Church's worship, in the center of which is Christ, the head of the Church. In this sense, the specific Christian character of worship is unique and without parallel. It is the actualization and participation in Christ's worship directed toward God the Father and in the power of the Holy Spirit.[153] It belongs to the peculiarity of the liturgical action that it takes place in time, but at the same time transcends time. Thus, three different dimensions of time can be distinguished.

2.3.5.1. Reference to a Past Reality

Each sacramental is somehow linked to a reality within the history of salvation. For this reason, directly or indirectly, each sacramental is linked to the past. For the Church, *the* point of reference is the Incarnation and the Paschal mystery of salvation. When referring to the past, it is important to understand the concept of "history" correctly. There are

---

[151] CCC, 2632.
[152] can. 604 §1.
[153] Cf. Cyprian Vagaggini, TDL, 142.

many misunderstandings and misinterpretations regarding this concept, especially due to the influence of Protestant theology.

This is where the German language has an advantage over the English language, for it has two separate words for *history*: *Historie* and *Geschichte*. There are no real English equivalents to easily translate these distinct terms with their individual meanings. In German, this distinction goes back to the year 1892, in which the theologian Martin Kähler (d. 1912) introduced the so-called *Leben-Jesu-Forschung* (Historical Jesus Research) and published the book *Der sogenannte historische Jesus und der geschichtliche, biblische Christus* (The So-Called Historical Jesus and the Historic, Biblical Christ).[154] Within this work, he presents a distinction between these two different meanings of *history* in German, loosely translated into English as "historical" and "historic." What exactly is the difference?

Kähler was a proponent of liberal theology.[155] He claimed to have discovered a purely historical Jesus, who could be reconstructed by using historical research and historiography. Even though he was convinced that such an approach could not do justice to understanding the mystery of faith, this new approach — based on a positivistic approach toward history as the only possible path for scientific knowledge — became very influential. Theologians who submitted to this methodological approach increasingly undervalued and excluded the divinity of Jesus Christ and any reference to the supernatural. This is a logical consequence of the limits of this methodology. In its extreme forms, it reduces reality only to factual history, excluding any

---

[154] Cf. Martin Kähler, *Der sogenannte historische Jesus und der geschichtliche, biblische Christus: Mit einem Nachwort von Sebastian Moll*, (Berlin: Berlin University Press, 2013).

[155] Liberal theology was inspired by the French Revolution and German idealism, claiming and aiming towards an autonomy of the theologian, and often based on a rationalist approach. Cf. Friedrich Wilhelm Graf, "Liberale Theologie," in LThK, vol. 6, 3rd ed., (Freiburg im Breisgau: Herder, 1995), 884–885.

understanding or admittance of supernatural reality working within it. Given the increasing enthusiasm for scientific methodology at the time, it should come as no surprise that this approach quickly gained traction, since it spoke in terms amenable to the secular academy. More and more, this idea gained currency among theologians, enjoying great popularity; quite a few theologians wanted, like everyone else, to be respected and recognized by secular science.

An approach based only on merely historical (*Historie*) elements corresponds to the modern mentality and the new canon of science, in which the only things considered to be "real" are those which can be examined according to the reductive dimensions of science. The problem becomes apparent when this approach is applied within the context of faith and revelation, for it would exclude belief in any type of supernatural reality or spiritual effects. According to this perspective, apotropaic elements of sacramentals (i.e., as seen earlier, those powerful means against demonic forces) and spiritual effects would be considered non-scientific — and they would therefore be seen as superfluous or even superstitious. Unfortunately, such an approach took its toll, and it is still influential. This approach through the lens of *Historie* not only diminishes an understanding of the power of sacramentals, but it even neglects the divinity of Jesus Christ; for, with such a premise, His divinity could only be considered a hypothesis.

In contrast, the use of the concept of *historic* leads to a deeper, fuller, and more accurate understanding. The so-called biblical Christ was considered a historic figure (*geschichtlich*) since it is a matter of fact that He became man through His Incarnation. However, a broader sense of history leaves room to also include the supernatural reality. The Catholic approach consisted always in an *et ... et*, that is, *both ... and,* making reference to both the natural and the supernatural dimensions, avoiding any ill-conceived reductionisms to one at the expense of the other.

At its heart, this distinction between *Historie* and *Geschichte* involves a profound philosophical question about the relationship between knowledge and faith. According to the modern mentality, knowledge is considered as an objectively verifiable fact, while faith has to do with spiritual reality. This is a widely accepted prejudice, according to which the evidence of faith is relegated to the realm of the subjective. Nevertheless, this approach leads to a reduction of reality through the exclusion of the supernatural. With this background, it becomes even more understandable why the sound approach of *Fides et Ratio* is of great importance: The contemplation of the truth can never be limited only to the realm of reason; on the contrary, "Faith and reason are like two wings on which the human spirit rises to the contemplation of truth."[156]

How does all of this inform our understanding of sacramentals? When referring to "history" or to the "past" in reference to them, both approaches have to be included: *Historie* and *Geschichte* are both reliable sources, but neither is enough on its own. The death of Christ is a historical fact but, at the same time, it surpasses the category of pure *Historie*, for it includes that historic dimension within the supernatural dimension of salvation. Ultimately, sacramentals as liturgical actions are linked to the history of salvation. For this reason, they cannot be limited to a dead history. On the contrary, Jesus Christ is the living source and efficient cause for the fruitfulness of the administration of the sacramentals, because "he is not God of the dead, but of the living, for to him all are alive" (Luke 20:38).

2.3.5.2. Reference to the Present Reality

Sacramentals are visible signs of an invisible reality; given their bridging of these two worlds, they are linked to salvation as well as to the

---

[156] John Paul II, Encyclical Letter *Fides et Ratio*, September 14, 1998, in http://www.vatican.va/content/john-paul-ii/en/encyclicals/documents/hf_jp-ii_enc_14091998_fides-et-ratio.html [12.5.2023].

incarnational principle. If the concept of "history" is correctly understood, it becomes clear that any divine action transcends time. Sacramentals are, therefore, always related to a present reality. They are not magical tools; rather they make God's grace present to us. Similar to the sacraments, they are visible signs containing invisible grace. This aspect is of great significance because all sacramentals are related to the present, i.e., through them, actual graces are obtained in the moment they are practiced. This is due to the presence of God in His Church. Grace is a supernatural gift from God; it is a free and undeserved help that God offers. However, it becomes fruitful when the faithful participate in the life of God; no one can benefit from it without seeking it. In conclusion, the merits of Christ's death and Resurrection are made present in the administration of the sacramentals.

2.3.5.3. Reference to the Future Reality

Sacramentals also make reference to a future reality, for they refer to the heavenly Jerusalem, which corresponds to the vision that is explained in the book of Revelation. "I also saw the holy city, a new Jerusalem, coming down out of heaven from God, prepared as a bride adorned for her husband" (Rev. 21:2). The sacramentals are meant to help us in moving toward the final perfection at the end of time and to the future glory. Their indwelling power surpasses human efforts in increasing the efficacy of sanctifying grace. Meanwhile, the whole work of this sanctification aims toward the future reality, the perfect communion within the Most Holy Trinity. All times, whether acknowledged or not, are directed toward the ultimate times; everything that is done affects the ultimate character of death, judgment, and life in eternity. Sacramentals, as liturgical actions, have to be considered within this broader context, for Christian life is directed toward the final sanctification.[157] Every

---

[157] The Dogmatic Constitution *Lumen Gentium* affirmed: "Therefore in the Church, everyone whether belonging to the hierarchy, or being cared for

person is called to eternal life, which, above all, is a supernatural reality. The sacramentals are related to this supernatural end, which will be fully revealed in the future (cf. Rev. 21:1).

In summary, these three dimensions of time correspond to the structure of Christian prayer. This becomes apparent above all in the celebration of the sacraments, but it is also reflected in the sacramentals. These three dimensions are also present in the eucharistic celebration, especially during the eucharistic prayer. This prayer includes three basic elements: the anamnesis, the epiclesis, and the doxology. While much more could be said about each of them, a brief understanding will serve our purposes here. First, the anamnesis makes reference to the commemoration of the institution that is to God's healing deeds; it looks to the past. The epiclesis is the invocation of the Holy Spirit making present and effective the merits of salvation for today, for the present. Finally, looking to the ultimate end of all things, the doxology refers to the praise of God, "so that God may be all in all" (1 Cor. 15:28).[158]

2.3.6. Systematic Considerations

Sacramentals are a complex reality because many different dimensions must be taken into consideration, especially Christology (doctrine concerning Jesus Christ), pneumatology (doctrine concerning the Holy Spirit), and ecclesiology (doctrine concerning the Church). Even though it is reasonable to distinguish generally among consecrations, blessings, exorcisms, and sacred objects, a certain vagueness and lack of precision will remain in the ordering of particular sacramentals, since they follow a more dynamic concept than the sacraments. Therefore, it must be the task of theology to understand and explain their nature. This requires not a mere intellectual (historical) exercise, nor a sociological

---

by it, is called to holiness, according to the saying of the Apostle: 'For this is the will of God, your sanctification.'" LG, 39.

[158] Cf. Charles Journet, *The Mass: The Presence of the Sacrifice of the Cross*, trans. Victor Szczurek, (South Bend: St. Augustine's Press, 2008), 114.

investigation based on personal experiences, but a reflection on the living faith. In Anselm of Canterbury's *Proslogion* (The Discourse on the Existence of God), the author explains that any theology must be characterized by *"Fides quaerens intellectum,"*[159] faith seeking understanding.

In a similar vein, Joseph Ratzinger affirmed that theology is not a system, nor an ideology, but a reflection on faith: "Theology presupposes faith. It draws its life from the paradoxical union of faith and science. Whoever pretends to abolish this paradox does away with theology and also ought to have the courage to admit it."[160] Without faith, there is no theology. This becomes even more apparent concerning the sacramentals and their use. If, for example, a priest or a bishop would deny certain contents of faith related to the sacramentals, he would not be able to administer them in a proper way, and he certainly would not be able to understand their nature.[161] Teasing such a circumstance out to its natural consequences, it would be absurd for someone who does not believe in the existence of the devil to attempt to perform an exorcism. *Fides quaerens intellectum*, translated to mean that faith which seeks understanding; this faith precedes theology.

From the perspective of faith, some light can be shed on the economy of salvation (God's plan for the salvation of the world), to which the sacramentals are directed. Salvation can only be granted by God, as the Gospel of Matthew affirms: "When the disciples heard this, they were greatly astonished and said, 'Who then can be saved?' Jesus looked at them and said, 'For human beings this is impossible, but for God all things are possible'" (Matt. 19:25–26). The

---

[159] Cf. Anselm, *Proslogion, Proemium,* in F. S. Schmitt (ed.), *S. Anselmi Cantuariensis Archiepiscopi Opera omnia*, (Delhi: Isha Books, 2013), 94.

[160] Joseph Ratzinger, *The Nature and Mission of Theology, Essays to Orient Theology in Today's Debates,* trans. Adrian Walker, (San Francisco: Ignatius Press, 1995), 55–56.

[161] See chap. 4.

Letter to the Romans underlines that the grace of God and personal adherence to Christ are the necessary requirements for salvation: "For, if you confess with your mouth that Jesus is Lord and believe in your heart that God raised him from the dead, you will be saved. For one believes with the heart and so is justified, and one confesses with the mouth and so is saved" (Rom. 10:9–10). It is from this larger perspective that the sacramentals must be understood.

The letter *Placuit Deo*, "To the bishops of the Catholic Church on some aspects of Christian salvation," published in 2018, calls to mind some of the most important elements of salvation, such as the current cultural changes with regards to the meaning of Christian salvation. In Chapter IV, "Christ, Saviour and Salvation," it offers a key for the interpretation of what is called the economy of salvation:

> The Christian faith has illustrated, throughout its centuries-long history, by means of multiple figures, this salvific work of the Son incarnate. It has done so without ever separating the healing dimension of salvation, by which Christ redeems us from sin, from the elevating dimension, by which he makes us sons and daughters of God, participants in his divine nature (cf. 2 Pet. 1:4). Considering the salvific perspective in a descending manner, that is, beginning with God who comes to redeem humanity, Jesus is the illuminator and revealer, the redeemer and liberator, the One who divinizes and justifies the human person. According to an ascending vision, that is, beginning with the human person turning towards God, Christ is the High Priest of the New Covenant, offering perfect worship to the Father, in the name of all humanity: He sacrifices Himself, expiates sins, and remains forever alive to intercede on our behalf. In this manner, an incredible synergy between divine and human action appears in the life of Jesus, a synergy that shows how baseless the individualist perspective is. The descending perspective bears witness to the absolute primacy of the gratuitous acts of God; humility is essential to respond to his salvific love and is required to receive the gifts of God, prior to all of our works. At the same time, the ascending perspective

recalls that, by means of the fully human action of his Son, the Father wanted to renew our actions, so that, conformed to Christ, we are able to fulfill "the good works that God has prepared in advance, that we should live in them." (Eph. 2:10)[162]

The document explains two different dimensions of salvation, both of which are helpful for a theological understanding of the sacramentals. On the one side, salvation consists in freeing the faithful from sin and evil through the merits of Jesus Christ. Mortal sin especially separates us from God and destroys harmony. It is precisely through divine mercy that this harmony with God and neighbor is restored; in short, this harmony is restored because of the salvation obtained for us by Jesus Christ. God therefore not only helps to overcome sin, but He also grants healing that restores our original harmony with Him and elevates the human person to participate in the life of God. God came into this world to redeem humanity (this is called *descending manner*). Individual persons, who seek salvation and forgiveness, turn consequently toward God, who, through His grace, makes man become a participant in His divine nature (this is called *ascending manner*). It is important to affirm that both approaches, both manners, have to be considered to gain a soundly balanced understanding of his interactions with man.[163] This same dual approach is reflected in the nature of sacramentals.

The economy of salvation presupposes a supernatural dimension that transcends the natural. Everything is directed toward the plan of salvation; sacramentals have to be understood as efficient tools that are ordered to this same end. With this context in mind, some conclusions about their trinitarian structure and nature can be drawn.

It is of great relevance, especially regarding the administration of sacramentals. What this means is that, like all Christian prayers, they are directed toward God the Father. Sacramentals have this

---

[162] Cf. CDF, Letter *Placuit Deo*, 9.
[163] Ibid., 8–14.

inner direction, as revealed by the Son (cf. John 14:6–11). He is Father inasmuch as He is the Creator. This profound link between God and creation is important since creation is the "natural foundation" of the sacramentals and nature is directed toward God. Referring to God the Father has a twofold meaning: He is the origin of everything and therefore the supreme authority and — at the same time — He is infinite goodness.[164] The very prayer of the Lord reflects this when addressing God as "Our Father." This is reflected whenever sacramentals are administered, for they start and end "In the name of the Father" and they aim to bring creation to its perfection through divine grace.

In the second part of this trinitarian structure, it becomes clear that sacramentals also have a strong christological nature (cf. incarnational principle). Christ is the eternal Word of the Father. He is the life-giving Word who raised the human race to a higher level by offering divine sonship, which established a new relationship between God and His creatures. The sacramentals reflect this new relationship in particular when a person, place, or object is sanctified through the merits obtained by God the Son. He is the only Son from the Father, "full of grace and truth" (John 1:14).

Finally, the transforming power of the Holy Spirit is also at work in the sacramentals: "It belongs to the Holy Spirit to rule, sanctify, and animate creation, for He is God, consubstantial with the Father and the Son.... Power over life pertains to the Spirit, for being God he preserves creation in the Father through the Son."[165] The sacramentals operate by the power of the Holy Spirit. He makes present the mystery of Christ through His sanctifying grace.

This trinitarian structure is crucial to understanding the theological nature of the sacramentals and should never be omitted. This

---

[164] Cf. *CCC*, 238.
[165] *CCC*, 703.

is reflected, for example, in the rite of blessing and invocation of God over baptismal water:

> O God [the former edition used "Father"], who by invisible power accomplish a wondrous effect through sacramental signs and who in many ways have prepared water, your creation, to show forth the grace of Baptism; … O God, whose Son, baptized by John in the waters of the Jordan, was anointed with the Holy Spirit, and, as he hung upon the Cross, gave forth water from his side along with blood, and after his Resurrection, commanded his disciples: "Go forth, teach all nations, baptizing them in the name of the Father and of the Son and of the Holy Spirit," look now, we pray, upon the face of your Church and graciously unseal for her the fountain of Baptism. May this water receive by the Holy Spirit the grace of your Only Begotten Son, so that human nature, created in your image and washed clean through the Sacrament of Baptism from all the squalor of the life of old, may be found worthy to rise to the life of newborn children through water and the Holy Spirit.[166]

This prayer is directed to God the Father; the spiritual effects are obtained by the merits of the Son, and the divine action becomes present and effective by the power of the Holy Spirit. In this way, the water, sanctified through divine grace, receives a new quality. From this one example, it becomes clear how the sacramentals have an inscribed trinitarian structure; it is the cause of their spiritual effects, and, thus, they usually begin and end in the name of the threefold God.

The Eastern Churches put special emphasis on the action of the Holy Spirit (epiclesis). God the Father is presented as the Almighty, the Creator of all things, who cares for His people. Jesus Christ takes away the sins of the world, obtaining salvation. But, by the power and the descent of the Holy Spirit, sanctification is granted, healing of the sick,

---

[166] *The Roman Ritual. The Order of Baptism of Children*, English trans. according to the Second Typical Edition, For the Use in the Dioceses of the United States of America, (Collegeville: Liturgical Press, 2020), 24–25.

forgiveness of sins, purification, and the expelling of evil spirits. Through the action of the threefold God — called substantial Trinity — divine grace is invoked that Satan and his evil power may be overcome and all temptation of the evil one be resisted. "Eastern Churches witness the exaltation and sanctification of creation, the majestic appearance of God who divinizes us through the transfiguring light of his heavenly grace."[167]

The trinitarian structure reveals that God the Father has renewed and elevated nature, which was corrupted — even though not entirely — through sin. Sin is overcome through Jesus Christ in the power of the Holy Spirit. The biblical narrative, especially as described in the Gospel of John, is evidence of this. In His dialogue with the Samaritan woman, the Lord said to her: "If you knew the gift of God and who is saying to you, 'Give me a drink,' you would have asked him and he would have given you living water" (John 4:10). The evangelist describes an entirely new quality of water, which is related to eternal life: "Everyone who drinks this water will be thirsty again, but whoever drinks the water I shall give will never thirst; the water I shall give will become in him a spring of water welling up to eternal life" (John 4:13–14). Sacramentals, by their nature, are directed toward this new, supernatural dimension.

---

[167] So quoted by Joan L. Roccasalvo, *The Eastern Catholic Churches: An Introduction to their Worship and Spirituality*, (Collegeville: Liturgical Press, 1992), 27.

THREE
✠ ✠ ✠
The Use and the Effects of Sacramentals

THE CRISIS OF FAITH has been growing, and it is not only affecting the laity but also priests. Pope Francis wrote in his first encyclical, *Lumen fidei*, that the crisis of faith is related to the crisis of truth.[168] When the truth of revelation is not recognized anymore, *the* Truth, revealed in Jesus Christ, will also no longer be recognized. However, the "unity of the Church in time and space is linked to the unity of the faith."[169] These basic considerations that he affirmed in his encyclical letter are also of great importance as regards the sacramentals. Pope Francis calls to mind the so-called *nexus mysteriorum*, that is, the interconnectedness of all articles of faith: "Since faith is one, it must be professed in all its purity and integrity. Precisely because all the articles of faith are interconnected, to deny one of them, even of those that seem least important, is tantamount to distorting the whole."[170] These fundamental affirmations are important to understand the use and the effects of the sacramentals.

The sacramentals do not work *ex opere operato*, that is, by the very fact of the actions being performed, as the sacraments do. This

---

[168] Francis, LF, 25.
[169] Ibid., 47.
[170] Ibid., 48.

marks the fundamental difference between sacraments and sacramentals. The efficacy of the sacraments is guaranteed by God, regardless of the holiness of the minister or the recipient; it is the power of Jesus Christ that acts through the Holy Spirit. In contrast, the effectiveness of the sacramentals depends on three additional factors: the spiritual disposition of the celebrant, the spiritual disposition of the recipient, and the intercessory power of the Church. They do not work *ex opere operato*, but *ex opere operantis*. This distinction will be explained further in the following paragraphs.

3.1. *Ex Opere Operantis Ecclesiae* in Contrast to *Ex Opere Operato*

Crucial for the understanding of the sacramentals and their effects is a clear comprehension of what *ex opere operantis* means. The literal meaning of this axiom is "from the work of the doer." In consequence, this means that the effectiveness of sacramentals does not depend primarily on their inherent grace-conferring power (as in the case of the sacraments), but on the moral condition of the persons who are receiving and administering the sacramental graces. Sacramentals are similar to the sacraments in that they consist of outward signs or sensible elements, but, unlike the sacraments, they are mostly of ecclesiastical origin, rather than being instituted directly by Christ Himself.[171] It is because of this that they do not infuse grace of their own power. For this reason, they have to be used devoutly to produce spiritual effects.

Especially in the thirteenth century, important theological clarifications were made regarding sacramentals; these clarifications serve as a basis to understand them today. In that period, it was common for theologians to distinguish between the Mosaic rites and the sacraments, but these Mosaic rites were put on a level similar to that of the sacramentals. In this context, the principle *ex opere operantis*

---

[171] See chap. 2.3.4.

Ecclesiae developed. St. Thomas affirmed that in the sacraments — he referred above all to the Eucharist — the priest acts "in the person of Christ."[172] However, the sacramentals refer to acting "in the person of the Church."[173] This emphasizes the importance of the ecclesiological dimension, namely, the role of the Church. The minister of a sacramental is a minister of the Church; therefore, he is, in a special way, part of the "person of the Church." This identification corresponds to a sacramental understanding, which becomes most visible in personal holiness.[174] In short, the sacramentals are different from the sacraments because they confer grace to the extent that the persons involved respond to that grace through their faith and moral dignity. Much depends, then, on the disposition and personal holiness of the recipient and minister.

Unfortunately, certain Protestants particularly misinterpreted this principle; they related it falsely to the sacraments. For that reason, the Council of Trent (1545–1563) confirmed some centuries later what St. Thomas had already said concerning Baptism: "For the sacrament is not perfected by the righteousness of the minister or of the recipient of Baptism, but by the power of God."[175] In consequence, the Council of Trent declared that the seven sacraments work *ex opere operato*; they are not the result of the *ex opere operantis Ecclesiae*. Canon 8 of Session VII states: "If anyone shall say that by the said sacraments of the New Law, grace is not conferred from the work which has been worked [*ex opere operato*], but that faith alone in the divine promise suffices to obtain grace: let him be anathema."[176] However, the Council of Trent did also affirm that the disposition of

---

[172] Thomas Aquinas, STh III, q. 82, a. 6.
[173] Ibid., III, q. 82, a. 7.
[174] Cf. LG, 39–42.
[175] Thomas Aquinas, STh III, q. 68, a. 8.
[176] Canons and Decrees of the Council of Trent, Session VII, can. 8, 263. Council of Trent (1547), DS 1608.

the recipient and the minister are of particular importance; the very nature of sacraments and sacramentals in this regard is different. Joseph Ratzinger offers a helpful explanation regarding the right understanding of this aspect. He expounds that, in Medieval theology, the original formula "was not *ex opere operato*, but *ex opere operato Christi*. This means the sacraments now no longer work by foreshadowing and asking; rather, they are effective as a result of what has already happened."[177]

At the same time, the sacraments are no magical practices. While grace is present in them through their origin in Christ, they do still require the correct disposition in those persons who approach them to obtain spiritual fruits. Christ does not force Himself on us, either through sacramentals or sacraments. As the First Letter to the Corinthians admonishes: "Therefore whoever eats the bread or drinks the cup of the Lord unworthily will have to answer for the body and blood of the Lord. A person should examine himself, and so eat the bread and drink the cup, or anyone who eats and drinks without discerning the body, eats and drinks judgment on himself" (1 Cor. 11:27–29).

The *ex opere operato* refers only to the way in which the sacraments function; it does not refer to the fruits, which are bound to certain requirements and dispositions. Their effects — their spiritual fruits — will always depend on how their recipient cooperates and is disposed to receive them. Padre Pio of Pietrelcina said that if one attended only a single celebration of the Holy Eucharist in the right disposition, he would be entirely sanctified because of what it contains. What graces are available, if only the faithful would dispose themselves to receive them! And, even though the sacraments work *ex opere operato*, this does not mean that the love and faith of the minister are irrelevant to their efficacy. Prof. Michael Schmaus affirmed:

---

[177] Joseph Ratzinger, TL, 180.

He who is charged with the office of dispensing the sacraments will carry out his work in the right way only if he tries to live more and more in community with Christ and with the Holy Spirit, which means living out of faith and out of love for God. Thus, to keep the language of the Council of Trent, the *opus operantis* is combined with the *opus operatum*.[178]

According to a Catholic understanding, participation, transformation, and sanctification correspond to the fruitful reception of the sacraments. This understanding is evident in the Gospel of John: "Amen, amen, I say to you, unless a grain of wheat falls to the ground and dies, it remains just a grain of wheat; but if it dies, it produces much fruit" (John 12:24). It is necessary for a Christian to "put on the new self, created in God's way in righteousness and holiness of truth" (Eph. 4:24). These basic considerations are helpful to come to a better understanding of the *ex opera operantis Ecclesiae*, which, though distinct, is nonetheless linked to the *ex opera operato Christi*.

In 1947, in his Encyclical Letter *Mediator Dei*, Pope Pius XII explained in more detail how this works. He spoke about Sacred Liturgy and explained the efficacy of the sacraments, which "derives first of all and principally from the act itself (*ex opere operato*). But if one considers the part which the Immaculate Spouse of Jesus Christ takes in the action, embellishing the sacrifice and sacraments with prayer and sacred ceremonies, or if one refers to the 'sacramentals' and the other rites instituted by the hierarchy of the Church, then its effectiveness is due rather to the action of the church (*ex opere operantis Ecclesiae*), inasmuch as she is holy and acts always in closest union with her Head."[179] He distinguishes between objective piety, which is related to

---

[178] Michael Schmaus, *Dogma: The Church as Sacrament*, vol. 5, (Maryland: Rowan & Littlefield, 1975), 15.

[179] Pius XII, Encyclical Letter *Mediator Dei*, November 20, 1947, 27, in http://www.vatican.va/content/pius-xii/en/encyclicals/documents/hf_p-xii_enc_20111947_mediator-dei.html [3.5.2023].

the effective reality of sanctifying grace, and subjective or personal piety. Consequently, there should be no opposition "between the action of God, who pours forth His grace into men's hearts so that the work of the redemption may always abide, and the tireless collaboration of man, who must not render vain the gift of God."[180]

Especially with regards to the sacramentals, it is important to keep these two dimensions (the work of God and the collaboration of man) in mind. On one side, sacramentals are actions of the Church (the objective part); on the other side, the recipient and minister will receive grace inasmuch as he lives in close union with Christ (the subjective part). Jesus Christ had assured that the treasure of divine grace entrusted to the Church is operative; however, as seen above, graces are obtained by individuals through the moral dignity and the holiness of their lives. At this point, the comparison with a vessel may be helpful. The properly disposed Christian is open to divine grace. Meanwhile, the one who is not disposed cannot receive grace because the vessel is closed. In other words, these two elements must be taken into consideration, particularly when talking about sacramentals: a) the rites instituted by the Church cause effects by the objective performance of the rite, which corresponds to the so-called *opus operatum*; b) the spiritual effects correspond to the "general laws which regulate the hearing of prayer."[181]

Pope Pius XII was very keen to reconcile both dimensions. For that reason, he affirmed in *Mediator Dei*:

> No more can the efficacy of the external administration of the sacraments, which comes from the rite itself (*ex opere operato*), be opposed to the meritorious action of their ministers of recipients, which we call the agent's action (*opus operantis*). Similarly, no conflict exists between public prayer and prayers in private,

---
[180] Ibid., 36.
[181] Cyprian Vagaggini, TDL, 113.

between morality and contemplation, between the ascetical life and devotion to the liturgy.[182]

The call for holiness, addressed in Chapter 5 of the Dogmatic Constitution *Lumen Gentium*, shows that the last council continued in the same direction that Pope Pius XII had taken it; indeed, his writings were the most quoted source during the Second Vatican Council. The developments after the conclusion of the Council, however, were quite contrary to his initial direction. The call for holiness remained widely unheard, and the *ex opere operantis* with its twofold dimension was no longer understood. This is also due to the misunderstanding of the so-called *participatio actuosa*, a guiding principle for the liturgical reform, which is intrinsically linked to the subjective dimension.

3.2. *Participatio Actuosa*: Devout Participation

Pope Pius XII had developed the concept of *"participatio actuosa,"* that is, devout participation,[183] with more precision than would be done during the Second Vatican Council. However, the concept, as such, was not new. The term was first coined by Pius X in 1903 in his Motu Proprio "Tra le Sollecitudini" on sacred music. The term was used first in Italian: *partecipazione attiva ai sacrosanti misteri e alla preghiera pubblica e solenne della Chiesa*.[184] It was rendered in the Latin edition differently, first as *participatio divinorum mysteriorum atque*

---

[182] Pius XII, Encyclical Letter *Mediator Dei*, 36.
[183] When Pope Pius XII explains the meaning of this concept, which he calls *actuosa singulorum participatione* (the English translation is far more than a mere translation, "active and individual participation"), he refers to the participation in the mystery of salvation "to obtain the salutary fruits." Encyclical Letter *Mediator Dei*, 78.
[184] Pius X, Motu Proprio *Tra Le Sollecitudini*, in ASS 36 (1903–1904): 329–339, here 331. Own translation: "active participation in the sacred mysteries and in the public and solemn prayer of the Church."

Ecclesiae communium et solemnium precum.[185] In a second edition, issued through a decree by the Sacred Congregation of Rites, the Latin formula was changed: *hoc est ex actuosa cum sacrosanctis Mysteriis, publicis solemnibusque Ecclesiae precibus communicatione.*[186]

Using the Latin cognates from this *Motu Proprio* — namely, participation in the divine mysteries (from the first edition) and communication with the sacred mysteries (from the second edition) — the term was taken up by Dom Lambert Beauduin in 1909; it soon became a central concept within the so-called Liturgical Movement.[187] The general idea was widely welcomed, even though it corresponded more to an intuition than to a precise concept. However, the concept needed further clarification and precision. Discussions started about a dialogical Mass and other theories, but the concept was ambiguous and not clearly defined. The discussions about a right understanding were interrupted by the Second World War and finally treated by Pius XII in *Mediator Dei*, in which he affirmed an "active and individual participation" as an essential and primary means of sanctification.[188]

The Second Vatican Council embraced this fundamental principle of the Liturgical Movement. The Constitution *Sacrosanctum Concilium* introduced the *participatio actuosa*, officially translated into

[185] Pius X, Motu Proprio *De Musica Sacra*, in ASS 36 (1903–1904): 387–395, here 388. Own translation: "participation in the divine mysteries and in the public and solemn prayer of the Church."

[186] Pius X, Motu Proprio *De Musica Sacra*, in Congregationis Sacrorum Rituum (ed.), *Decreta authentica*, Collecta, vol. VI, (Rome: Typis Polyglottis Vaticanis, 1912), 29–38, here 30.

[187] Cf. Juan Javier Flores, "La partecipazione liturgica punto di partenza del movimento liturgico," in Agostino Montan – Manlio Sodi (eds.), *Actuosa Participatio. Conoscere, comprendere e vivere la Liturgia*, (Vatican City: Libreria Editrice Vaticana, 2002), 229–245, here 231.

[188] Cf. Pius XII, Encyclical Letter *Mediator Dei*, 78. In Latin, however, he used the word "actuosa."

English as "active participation";[189] unfortunately, this is in fact a poor translation, which means that widespread misunderstandings were inevitable. A more accurate approach is presented by Cyprian Vagaggini, who offers a profound insight into the correct understanding of this concept. First, he affirms that the end of every pastoral work "is to guide and conduct the people to Christ and Christ to the people."[190] For its realization, an internal encounter of the soul with God is necessary. He calls this a "plenary participation." Vagaggini explains that the focus should be on conducting an individual in a church "so that he may in one way or another participate in the liturgy, but creating in him of an internal moral attunement with the liturgical reality as sanctification in Christ and worship of God in Christ."[191] The explanation of this Benedictine monk is very helpful since it presents a precise description of this *participatio actuosa*, even though not a definition. In short, it is not about reordering the liturgy to make it easier for any given individual, but rather about reordering that individual's interior disposition, that he might more readily orient himself to the sacred.

The concept of *participatio actuosa* aims toward a devout participation in the mystery of salvation — not to the performance of some action.[192] German scholar Johannes Nebel profoundly explored this in one of his articles, writing that "True *participatio actuosa* experiences its deepest realization in the *participatio Dei*, the communion with God."[193] Ultimately, participation is about sharing in God; therefore, the believer

---

[189] Paul Gunter presents a critical analysis. Cf. Paul Gunter, "Active Participation in the Renewal and Promotion of the Liturgy of Vatican Council II," in ibid. (ed.), *Sacrosanctum Concilium. Sacred Liturgy and the Second Vatican Council*, (London: Carrigboy, 2015), 126–141.

[190] Cyprian Vagaggini, TDL, 838.

[191] Ibid., 838.

[192] Cf. SC, 14.

[193] Ralph Weimann, "Verschiedenheit der Formen und die Einheit in der Liturgie, *Lex celebrandi* als Spiegelbild der *lex credendi*," in M. Graulich (ed.) *Zehn Jahre Summorum Pontificum. Versöhnung mit der Vergangenheit – Weg in die Zukunft*, (Regensburg: Friedrich Pustet, 2017), 86–116, here 110.

does not make the divine his own, but he participates in that which is above him. This is made especially clear in the Offertory Prayer of the Mass, when the priest mixes the water into the wine. At this moment, the prayer is that we may "share in the divinity of Christ."[194]

These commentaries aside, because the conciliar document itself failed to provide a clear definition of *participatio actuosa*, the concept remained ambiguous. This is clear in the text of the Council itself: "With zeal and patience, pastors of souls must promote the liturgical instruction of the faithful, and also their active participation in the liturgy both internally and externally, taking into account their age and condition, their way of life, and standard of religious culture."[195] The use of the concept without a precise definition of terms, lacking in clarity, left wide leeway for interpretation and application. It was almost inevitable that after the conclusion of the Council, a process would erupt to provoke confusion and misunderstanding. In the years since, this has caused great damage to the liturgy; mundane arbitrariness and "creativity" have encroached on and obscured the divine mystery more and more, often leading to banality and self-destruction.[196]

Aware of this problem, Pope John Paul II tried to correct misinterpretations and misapplications of the term, first through the instruction *Ecclesiae de Mysterio* in 1997,[197] and again in 2004 through *Redemptionis*

---

[194] Johannes Nebel, "Die *participatio plena et actuosa* im Lichte der *sacra potestas*. Klärungsversuche zur Sinnerhellung christlicher Liturgie," in Forum katholische Theologie 32 (2016): 1–22, esp. 2.

[195] SC, 19.

[196] This was brought into evidence in his critical analysis by Klaus Gamber, *The Reform of the Roman Liturgy: Its Problems and Background*, trans. Klaus D. Grimm, (Harrison, NY: Una Voce Press, 1993).

[197] It was affirmed that the goal of participation is holiness and that the Church's structure and nature must be respected. "This happens when all participants, with faith and devotion, discharge those roles proper to them." CDF et al., *Ecclesiae de Mysterio*, August 15, 1997, Art. 6 §1, in http://www.vatican.va/roman_curia/pontifical_councils/laity/documents/rc_con_interdic_doc_15081997_en.html [3.5.2023].

Sacramentum, an instruction that was published by the Congregation for Divine Worship and the Discipline of the Sacraments.[198] However, the problem wasn't solved.

Joseph Ratzinger, later Pope Benedict XVI, came to a profound understanding of this topic. Contemporary Polish theologian Mariusz Biliniewicz summarizes his position: "active participation" consists first of all in an "internal, spiritual encounter with the mystery of the Eucharist. External, bodily participation is also needed (singing, answering, bodily gestures, and the like) but [this] is subordinated to that inner attitude of reception of God's gift."[199] Something similar was also echoed in Pope Benedict's 2007 Apostolic Exhortation, *Sacramentum Caritatis*. He wrote that "some misunderstanding has occasionally arisen concerning the precise meaning of this participation." He affirmed: "In fact, the active participation called for by the Council must be understood in more substantial terms, on the basis of a greater awareness of the mystery being celebrated and its relationship to daily life."[200] After all this explanation and contextualization, it can be offered what would have been a good, original English translation of *participatio actuosa*: devout or authentic participation — markedly more acute in character and intensity than a simple "active participation." At this point, however, any new translation that might be adopted would make sense only if accompanied by a precise definition and catechesis

---

[198] For example, the instruction invites us to correct "widespread superficial notions and practices" and "to instill anew in all of Christ's faithful that sense of deep wonder before the greatness of the mystery of faith that is the Eucharist." Congregation for Divine Worship and the Discipline of the Sacraments, Instruction *Redemptionis Sacramentum*, March 25, 2004, 40, in https://www.vatican.va/roman_curia/congregations/ccdds/documents/rc_con_ccdds_doc_20040423_redemptionis-sacramentum_en.html [3.5.2023].

[199] Mariusz Biliniewicz, *The Liturgical Vision of Pope Benedict XVI. A Theological Inquiry*, (Bern: Peter Lang, 2013), 98–99.

[200] Benedict XVI, *Sacramentum Caritatis*, 52.

to prevent misunderstandings, leading the faithful instead to a correct understanding and therefore to sanctification.

While the discussion of a proper disposition of the faithful for liturgical participation has largely focused on commentary and development within the twentieth century, the concept is in fact far from novel. As far back as the fourth century, St. Augustine provided a profound explanation of this concept in his commentary on the Tractates on the Gospel of John. He wrote:

> If you sit down to supper at the table of a ruler, consider wisely what is set before you; and so put to your hand, knowing that you are bound to make similar preparations. For what is the table of the ruler, but that from which we take the body and blood of Him who laid down His life for us? And what is it to sit thereat, but to approach in humility? And what is it to consider intelligently what is set before you, but worthily to reflect on the magnitude of the favor? And what is it, so to put to your hand, as knowing that you are bound to make similar preparations, but as I have already said, that, as Christ laid down His life for us, so we also ought to lay down our lives for the brethren? For as the Apostle Peter also says, Christ suffered for us, leaving us an example, that we should follow His steps (1 Pet. 2:21). This is to make similar preparations. This it was that the blessed martyrs did in their burning love; and if we celebrate their memories in no mere empty form, and, in the banquet whereat they themselves were filled to the full, approach the table of the Lord, we must, as they did, be also ourselves making similar preparations.[201]

More recently, the *Book of Blessings* also took up these principles and invited Catholics to attend the celebration of the sacramentals with a "full, conscious, and active participation."[202] At this point, it is helpful to understand the principle of *ex opere operantis*, which could be loosely

---

[201] Augustinus, *Tractatus in Joannis Evangelium*, 84, 1–2, PL 35, 1846ff. English translation, in http://www.newadvent.org/fathers/1701084.htm [22.2.2023].
[202] BoB, 19.

translated as: participation in the divine action that renders fruitful the spiritual effects of that divine action.

This idea has been further developed by Johannes Nebel.[203] In one of his articles, he made a significant subdivision that helps to approach this complex subject. In what follows, his explanations are continued and modified insofar as they are relevant to the sacramentals.[204]

The principle of *ex opere operantis* embraces the whole Church at all times. It signifies man's sharing in Christ's prayer to the Father. This includes the Church Militant on earth, the Church Suffering in Purgatory, and the Church Triumphant in Heaven. In this constant prayer, the Church participates in the *nunc stans* of God (i.e., in God, there is no past nor future, but only presence, which is also called eternity); it connects the Church through all time with its origin. St. Basil makes clear that the Fathers of the Church were not primarily doctrinal authorities, but "witnesses to the prayer of the Church" of earlier ages. Through their witness and example, the orthodoxy of faith is guaranteed only when there is unanimity with the prayer of the Fathers — that is, when the faithful pray today as they used to pray before: "What our fathers said, we also say."[205]

In other words, the Church on earth joins the greater whole of the community that transcends the centuries. In this sense, the exhortation of the Apostle Paul must be understood, who urged the Romans: "Do not conform yourselves to this age" (Rom. 12:2). Thus, it would be extremely problematic if the Church today would not be able or allowed to pray in the way in which previous generations prayed. Such a circumstance would mean that the living

---

[203] Cf. Johannes Nebel, "Die *participatio plena et actuosa,*" 1–22.

[204] Johannes Nebel mentions as a fourth level, with regard to the Eucharist, the concrete liturgical form of the word, and the degree of precision in the interplay of word and gesture.

[205] Basilius, Spir. 16. Quoted in Michael Fiedrowicz, *Theologie der Kirchenväter. Grundlagen frühchristlicher Glaubensreflexion*, 2nd ed., (Freiburg im Breisgau: Herder, 2010), 262.

tradition had been interrupted. It would be compromised by this disruption to its constancy. But, in the face of such possibilities, and despite all diversities and strife, the principle of *ex opere operantis* holds orthodoxy together. Prayer, common and transcending the times, establishes unity. It is a participation in the liturgical memory (*amnesis*) of the Church, through which the grace of God is bestowed.[206] From this, much can be deduced for the sacramentals, which must be part of this very same *memoria*, for anything rooted in the Church's living tradition shares in this indwelling power.

Besides the time-transcending element, the personal adherence to the Creed of the Church is another precondition to obtain devout participation; it includes a twofold sense: a) acceptance of the revealed truth (*fides quae*), referring to the objective-ecclesial dimension, that which is revealed as certain and undeniable through the Church; and b) confidence in God (*fides qua*), referring to the subjective-personal dimension, that is the proper act of faith. When it comes to the reception of grace through the sacramentals, the degree of grace received will be dependent not just on Church teaching, but also on how the individual puts his faith into action. It makes a big difference whether "baptized pagans" are the ones who are participating in a sacramental, or if the people involved really believe what they're about.[207]

To reiterate this point, the actual *devotio* (and holiness) of those participating in the sacramental is of great importance.[208] However, no one can judge the holiness of another, and yet actual devotion (holiness) and the efficacy of sacramentals are mutually dependent. For, without the right disposition of all parties involved, the effects of the sacramentals will not be able to unfold. Separated from Christ we can accomplish nothing, as John's Gospel puts it in a nutshell (cf.

---

[206] Cf. Nebel, "Die *participatio plena et actuosa*," 18.
[207] Cf. ibid., 12.
[208] Ibid., 16.

John 15:5); this applies to the participation of the faithful in the sacramentals as much as it does to every other sphere of our lives.

Considering sacramentals as liturgical actions implies that they are in fact related to the mystery of the Most Holy Trinity and, in a special way, to the Incarnation, death, and Resurrection of Jesus Christ.[209] Therefore, the sacramentals must be administered and received in such a way that they become acceptable to the *Logos*, namely, to Jesus Himself. Also in this regard, sacramentals are similar to the sacraments, as can be seen in the Mass. In the Roman Canon of the Mass, the priest asks that the sacrifice be *acceptabilem*.[210] Whenever the liturgical action is acceptable to God, it is most effective; this acceptability and consequent efficacy are the very heart of *participatio actuosa*.

3.3. Participated Effects of the Sacramentals

Since the sacramentals aim toward sanctification, participation of those involved in their practice is of crucial importance. As seen above, in as much as the minister and recipient are correctly disposed, they will obtain spiritual effects. The personal sanctification of the minister and recipient are therefore of great value. The words of the Gospel of St. Matthew become true: "For to everyone who has, more will be given and he will grow rich; but from the one who has not, even what he has will be taken away" (Matt. 25:29). Also, the parable of the talents could be considered within this context (cf. Matt. 25:6–30). And the Gospel of John affirms: "I am the true vine, and my Father is the vine grower. He takes away every branch in me that does not bear fruit, and everyone that does he prunes so that it bears more fruit" (John 15:1–2).

---

[209] See chap. 2.3.3.
[210] The Roman Canon says: "Quam oblationem tu Deus in omnibus quaesumus benedictam, adscriptam rationabilem *acceptabilem que* facere digneris." In English, "Be pleased, O God, we pray, to bless, acknowledge, and approve this offering in every respect; make it spiritual and *acceptable*."

Opposed to any spiritual fruitfulness is sin. Mortal sin destroys the relationship with God, since it "results in the loss of charity and the privation of sanctifying grace, that is, of the state of grace. If it is not redeemed by repentance and God's forgiveness, it causes exclusion from Christ's kingdom and the eternal death of hell, for our freedom has the power to make choices for ever, with no turning back."[211]

In the current times, the consequences of sin are often neglected, with serious ramifications. Frequently, even the consciousness of sin is no longer present, even among Catholics. It must be affirmed that whoever lives in mortal sin cannot receive any spiritual fruit; this of course also affects the administration and reception of the sacramentals. A priest, a religious, or even a bishop who lives in mortal sin is deprived of sanctifying grace. Such men would become, as Scripture says, "blind guides (of the blind). If a blind person leads a blind person, both will fall into a pit" (Matt. 15:14). Some might think that this is exaggerated, but it is only a logical consequence, as affirmed by Scripture. "Whoever is not with me is against me, and whoever does not gather with me scatters" (Matt. 12:30). Either someone is with God — or not. There is no grey zone or neutral area in spiritual life. This becomes even more evident when considering the sacramental idea, which essentially implies a relationship with the living God. Therefore, St. Francis de Sales writes: "The first purification to be made is that of sin."[212]

Because the spiritual effects of the sacramentals depend on the relationship with God, the spiritual effects and power of the sacramentals result in a participated effect: the receiver participates in the effects of Christ's redemptive work and in the intercession of the Church. Any spiritual power is a participatory power. The worst form of clericalism consists in not recognizing that a priest is "only"

---

[211] *CCC*, 1861.
[212] Francis de Sales, *Philothea or An Introduction to the Devout Life*, (Charlotte, North Carolina: TAN Books, 2010), 16.

an administrator of divine grace, as St. Paul said: "We hold this treasure in earthen vessels, that the surpassing power may be of God and not from us" (2 Cor. 4:7). Therefore, clericalism can be defined as acting against the divine commandment and teaching accordingly.

For this reason, living faith is a critical element in effecting grace through sacramentals. Of course, grace is always a free and unmerited gift of God, but faith has an indwelling power. "When one has faith merely the size of a little mustard seed, mountains can be moved. As Simon the Magician found out, any grace that is imparted must be in conformity with God's will and cannot be manipulated solely by human means."[213]

Sacramentals depend upon faith, which opens the door to divine grace.[214] If the right dispositions are present, the greatest miracles can happen. To better understand this, a look to the example of sacred icons, images, and statues will be helpful; they are all sanctified through blessings, and, by these blessings, they become like open windows that give us views of divine reality. However, the window serves only if the glass remains clean, if it permits the sun to penetrate its structure. If the window is closed and covered by dirt, light cannot enter. It is the reality of sin that it does not permit the light to get in. Sacred images — as all sacramentals — will obtain grace to the degree that the person looking at them is orienting himself to receive divine grace. They are related to supernatural realities and require participation in the divine. The Second Council of Nicaea (AD 787) presented the subsequent definition of sacred images:

> We, continuing in the regal path, and following the divinely inspired teaching of our Holy Fathers, and the tradition of the Catholic Church ... define in all certitude and diligence that as the

---

[213] Cf. Stephen J. Rossetti, *The Priestly Blessing. Rediscovering the Gift*, (Indiana: Ave Maria Press, 2018), 44.

[214] See Francis, LF, 31.

figure of the honored and life-giving Cross, so the venerable and holy images, the ones from tinted materials and from marble as those from other material, must be suitably placed in the holy churches of God, both on sacred vessels and vestments, and on the walls and on the altars, at home and on the streets, namely such images of our Lord Jesus Christ, God and Savior, and of our undefiled lady, or holy Mother of God, and of the honorable angels, and, at the same time, of all the saints and of holy men.[215]

The spiritual effects of the sacramentals depend primarily on the participation in divine grace, which becomes even more evident when considering the nature of sacramentals. Their spiritual quality is elevated to a higher degree through grace and by the means of a blessing or consecration. Consequently, a person, place, or object is sanctified through the grace of God. This is reflected in Sacred Scripture: "For creation awaits with eager expectation the revelation of the children of God; for creation was made subject to futility, not of its own accord but because of the one who subjected it, in hope that creation itself would be set free from slavery to corruption and share in the glorious freedom of the children of God" (Rom. 8:19–21). Divine grace grants a new spiritual quality due to the sacred action that is producing the fruits of sanctification. Nevertheless, those fruits presuppose collaboration with divine grace.

3.4. Importance of the Formula

In addition to devout participation, the formula used is also of great importance to achieve the desired spiritual effects of the sacramentals. It was said that sacramentals are liturgical actions and that they are instituted by the Church. They are, therefore, part of the Church's heritage, which includes the richness of the Church's tradition. At the same time, they receive their effectiveness through the Church's

---

[215] Council of Nicaea II, 787, in DS, 302.

intercession.[216] All of this is at work in their various particular formulas, formulas which express it and are an essential element of their rites. However, it is not enough to pronounce their formulas like some sort of a magical practice; sacramentals must be accompanied by faith and love to achieve positive spiritual effects.

One example can help illustrate this. Some parts of the traditional blessing of the St. Benedict Medal go back to the writings of St. Gregory the Great (d. 604). The blessing includes an exorcism against Satan and his influence, since St. Benedict is the patron saint of the exorcists. Even though the medal came into existence only centuries after his death, it is still linked to the life of this saint, and includes a rich tradition. The formula is supposed to reflect this linkage, aiming to bring forth spiritual effects, which are related to the past, present, and future. It follows that the medal is blessed in a certain way that must contain these elements. The following part of the benediction prayer reflects all of this:

> In the name of God the Father + almighty, who made heaven and earth, the seas and all that is in them, I exorcise these medals against the power and attacks of the evil one. May all who use these medals devoutly be blessed with health of soul and body. In the name of the Father + almighty, of the Son + Jesus Christ our Lord, and of the Holy + Spirit the Paraclete, and in the love of the same Lord Jesus Christ who will come on the last day to judge the living and the dead, and the world by fire. Amen.[217]

Like this prayer, many benedictions were reserved to monks, religious, or bishops until the Second Vatican Council. Through the liturgical reform, it was attempted to ease access to these blessings. Now, indeed, every

---

[216] See chap. 2.3.4.
[217] RR, 494–595. English translation from: The Order of Saint Benedict, The Medal of Saint Benedict, in https://www.osb.org//gen/medal.html [22.3.2023].

priest can bless according to the given formula. This is without any doubt a positive achievement. However, there are two limiting factors to mention at this point: first, a large number of priests today are no longer aware of these blessings; second, the formula has been fundamentally and substantially changed, which will be discussed in more detail later on.

Another aspect of sacramental formulas to consider regards the language in which they are spoken. To facilitate so-called "full and conscious participation" of the faithful, the language was changed from Latin to the vernacular. This also suited many priests, and continues to suit an increasing number of them, as fewer and fewer are able to understand or speak Latin. It must be underlined that it is important for the minister of the sacramentals to understand the content in order to perform the prayers in the power of faith. Yet, the mysteries of faith are not primarily understood through a comprehensible language, but through living faith. This fact was widely forgotten and obscured in the years following the Second Vatican Council. Intelligibility and acceptance in faith are two fundamentally different concepts.

In this context, another aspect of sacramental formulas, this one with even more far-reaching consequences, must be mentioned; it has led to changing not only the language but the very nature of blessings. The decree accompanying the *Book of Blessings* says:

> In ordering the reform of the sacramentals, the Vatican Council II decreed that in their celebration special attention should be given to the full, conscious, and active participation of the faithful and that any elements should be eliminated that in the course of time had obscured the true nature and purpose of sacramentals. The Council further decreed that the number of reserved blessings should be limited, with reservation made in favor only of bishops or Ordinaries, and that provision should be made for qualified laypersons to impart some blessings, at least in certain circumstances and at the discretion of the Ordinary.[218]

[218] BoB, 19.

These instructions are very ambiguous. This can be seen in that, on the one hand, participation is encouraged, but on the other hand, it says that any "elements should be eliminated that in the course of time had obscured the true nature and purpose of sacramentals." For some working on the liturgical reform, this number was pretext enough to leave behind major parts of the Church's tradition. In consequence, many of the most powerful formulae were abolished and, consequently, sacramentals lost their effectiveness. As a result, the *Book of Blessings*, within its almost *nine hundred* pages, does not even include a specific blessing of the medal of St. Benedict! The general instruction to the *Book of Blessings*, in fact, may even increase confusion:

> In the adaptation of celebrations a careful distinction must be made between matters of less importance and those principal elements of the celebrations that are here provided, namely, the proclamation of the word of God and the Church's prayer of blessing. These may never be omitted even when the shorter form of a rite is used. For the planning of a celebration these are the foremost considerations:
>
> a. in most cases a communal celebration is to be preferred, and in such a way that a deacon, reader, cantor or psalmist, and choir all fulfill their proper functions;
>
> b. a primary criterion is that the faithful are able to participate actively, consciously, and easily;
>
> c. provision should be made for the particular circumstances and persons involved, but with due regard for the principles of the liturgical reform and the norms laid down by the responsible authority.[219]

Some of these instructions are understandable, since the liturgical reform intended to link everything to the incarnational principle. For this reason,

---

[219] Ibid., 27f.

special importance was given to the Word of God. At the same time, this instruction does not correspond to the sacramental idea, nor does it explicitly refer to their trinitarian structure, which is essential for the valid administration of any sacramental. Instead, a Protestant understanding paves its way, when "in most cases communal celebrations" are requested. This corresponds to the tendency to replace the sacramental character (divine origin) with communal celebrations (human origin). At the same time, such an emphasis on communal celebration is simply not feasible in practice. One might wonder if the "experts" who came up with this instruction — in contrast to the tradition of the Church — developed this at their desks with little or no practical experience to inform their sweeping ideas. Imagine, for example, someone asking a priest to provide a simple blessing for a rosary or a medal. According to these instructions, the priest would need to call the congregation and the church choir together, proclaim the Word of God, and then perform a blessing that, in point of fact, is not even a blessing — as will be shown. At this point, the limits and even the failure of the liturgical reform are sadly undeniable.

The Dogmatic Constitution *Lumen Gentium* presents an approach almost contrary to this type of understanding, emphasizing that the ministerial priest acts with divine power being, however, interrelated to the common priesthood of the faithful.[220] Furthermore, an "easy participation" is alien to the understanding of Catholic liturgy. It's not supposed to be *easy*; it never was. It's supposed to be linked to the sublime sacrifice of Our Lord Jesus Christ on the Cross. There is nothing easy about that,

---

[220] The Constitution affirms: "Though they differ from one another in essence and not only in degree, the common priesthood of the faithful and the ministerial or hierarchical priesthood are nonetheless interrelated: each of them in its own special way is a participation in the one priesthood of Christ. The ministerial priest, by the sacred power he enjoys, teaches and rules the priestly people; acting in the person of Christ, he makes present the Eucharistic sacrifice, and offers it to God in the name of all the people. But the faithful, in virtue of their royal priesthood, join in the offering of the Eucharist." LG, 10.

and to pretend that there could be is to undermine the very nature and identity of the liturgy itself. Moreover, the special emphasis in this instruction that is placed on the particular circumstances of individual situations opens the doors to liturgical arbitrariness. When individual sympathies and desires become the measure of a liturgical action, rather than adherence to set and proscribed rites given by the Church herself, the sacramentals will be rendered ineffective, for they cause them to be administered in a way that is separated from the authority of the Church. This is actually happening today, for there is in fact no ordinary administration of the sacramentals; almost every priest feels empowered to handle matters according to his own understanding and ideas.

Additionally, these criteria set out in the instruction for the *Book of Blessings* contradict *Sacrosanctum Concilium*, which says: "Finally, there must be no innovations unless the good of the Church genuinely and certainly requires them; and care must be taken that any new forms adopted should in some way grow organically from forms already existing."[221] It must be acknowledged that most of the so-called "renewed sacramentals" are actually *new* sacramentals. They were mostly invented by professors and academics applying a hermeneutic of rupture (as opposed to the hermeneutic of reform in continuity with the one subject Church; this distinction means that what they did was breaking with Church tradition instead of encouraging a natural growth that was a logical and organic development, that was built on and upheld tradition). The break with tradition was justified by making use of a liturgical archaeologism combined with pastoral pragmatism.[222] It was said that they wanted to return to the

---

[221] SC, 23.
[222] Joseph Ratzinger affirms: "Because it is often all too obvious that historical knowledge cannot be elevated straight into the status of a new liturgical norm, this archaeological enthusiasm was very easily combined with pastoral pragmatism: people first of all decided to eliminate everything that was not recognized as original and was thus not part of the 'substance', and then they supplemented the 'archaeological remains', if these still seemed insufficient, in accordance with 'pastoral insights.'" Joseph Ratzinger, TL, 593.

original forms, but they in fact ignored the living tradition. This became the pretext to let the practice become the new criterion. Thus the traditional sacramentals were abandoned in favor of the spirit of the times. This *petitio principii*, a type of circular reasoning, was the underlying problem regarding the realization of the liturgical reform of the sacramentals, accomplished by so-called experts.[223] Subsequently, the living faith of the people and organic growth as guiding criteria were abandoned.

Thus, almost all the formulas of the sacramentals were changed and lost their importance because the new instructions allowed for a creative and arbitrary application. This has led to devastating consequences. Today, most priests and bishops are no longer familiar with the basic principles underlying the sacramentals. They are mostly insecure when they need to impart any type of blessing. It was in fact when I asked a priest for his first blessing after his ordination, and he didn't know how to do it, that I realized that I needed to write this book. And it is not just new priests who are lacking such essential priestly knowledge; even bishops are usually uncertain about sacramentals. This situation is quite serious precisely because it does concern a priest's basic office.

Today, many of the sacramentals are deprived of their effectiveness. There are several reasons for this: on the one hand, uncertainty on the part of the minister leads to the fact that he does not administer them with strong faith; his uncertainty leads to doubt. On the other hand, the new formulas are often quite ineffective, because essential elements have been neglected in their revisions: sacred signs have been abandoned (for example, the sign of the cross itself), and apotropaic elements have been omitted (as a reminder, these are the elements that were originally included in all sacramentals that were specifically ordered to combat

---

[223] Cf. Ralph Weimann, "Verschiedenen Formen und die Einheit in der Liturgie. *Lex celebrandi* als Spiegelbild der *lex credendi*," in M. Graulich (ed.) *Zehn Jahre Summorum Pontificum. Versöhnung mit der Vergangenheit – Weg in die Zukunft*, (Regensburg: Friedrich Pustet, 2017), 86–116.

demonic powers and influences).[224] These difficulties associated with liturgical reform are widespread, but they are nowhere more evident than in the sacramentals. One example is enough to illustrate this.

In 2000, the new rite of exorcism was published by so-called experts. The former chief exorcist, Fr. Gabriele Amorth, said in an interview about it: "This long-awaited Ritual has turned into a farce. An incredible obstacle that is likely to prevent us acting against the demon."[225] Fr. Amorth's reaction, given the fact that he had more practical experience in battling demons than almost anyone in the Church at the time, makes one wonder if the authors of this new rite had any practical experience in exorcisms at all.

There is a lot of talk about the pastoral practice of exorcisms, but it is all too often just empty talk, with little or no actual pastoral practice. Today, even doctoral theses on this subject are written by people who have never even participated in an exorcism. Fr. Amorth has some particular criticisms of the rite that are painfully enlightening:

> Point 15 [of the new ritual] treats of evil spells and how one should behave when dealing with them. An evil spell is an evil brought about on a person by means of recourse to the devil. It can be accomplished under a variety of forms like spells, curses, the evil eye, voodoo and macumba. The Roman Ritual used to explain how one should confront it. The New Ritual on the other hand, categorically declares that it is absolutely forbidden to perform exorcisms in such cases. Absurd. Evil spells are by far the most frequent causes of possessions and evil procured through the demon: at least 90% of cases. It is as good as telling exorcists they can no longer perform exorcisms.[226]

---

[224] See especially chap. 4–7. See also chap. 3.2. It was shown that the formulae, if rooted in the Church's living tradition, have an indwelling power.

[225] Gabriel Amorth, Interview with Father Amorth, Exorcist, on the Reform of the Rite of Exorcism after Vatican II, in https://www.fisheaters.com/praeternaturalworldamorth.html [4.5.2023].

[226] Ibid.

In conclusion, then, the formulas of the sacramentals are of great importance for several reasons. Since the sacramentals are performed in the "person of the Church" (*ex opere operantis*), they cannot be reinvented in isolation from the living Tradition of the Church. In them, the whole Church prays with her intercessory prayer. Even more, as the new sacramentals were made up according to the ambiguous criteria of so-called "experts" and often based on meaningless content, they *cannot* produce the intended spiritual effects. The living tradition should instead designate the way, and the criterion of organic growth needs to be respected. Not all renewed formulas are bad or useless, but they need to correspond to the nature of sacramentals. Josef Andreas Jungmann (d. 1975), *peritus* (expert, who assists and advises the hierarchy) at the Second Vatican Council, confirmed these limitations. He underlined that special attention was devoted to the blessings "for persons, articles and situations of life, which have been incorporated in large numbers in the Roman Ritual. As they are of the most different origins, their liturgical form not only often shows the lack of a sense of form, but also an exuberance here and a poverty there, which stands in no relation to the importance of the object."[227]

In this context, the value and importance of Pope Benedict's 2007 Motu Proprio, *Summorum Pontificum*, becomes even more evident. When understood and applied correctly, it not only reconciles the present with the past, but it makes the traditional forms available once again. Thus, a priest trained in the new form can use the sacramentals according to the old form. Pope Benedict wrote: "For that matter, the two forms of the usage of the Roman Rite can be mutually enriching."[228]

---

[227] Josef Jungmann, "Constitution on the Sacred Liturgy," in Herbert Vorgrimler (ed.), *Commentary on the Documents of Vatican II*, vol. 1, 2nd ed., (New York: Herder, 1967), 1–87, here 54.

[228] Benedict XVI, Letter to the Bishops on the Occasion of the Publication of the Apostolic Letter "Motu Proprio Data" *Summorum Pontificum*, July, 7, 2007, in http://www.vatican.va/content/benedict-xvi/en/letters/2007/documents/hf_ben-xvi_let_20070707_lettera-vescovi.html [11.5.2023].

The Church did not start at the Second Vatican Council nor with the liturgical reform; rather, she has a living Tradition. The venerable *vetus* form must be considered the *princeps analogatum* (valid point of reference), and the new form must be measured according to the living Tradition of the Church. This is apparent in the formula of each sacramental, which, when said properly, is a prayer of the Church of all times.

3.5. Essential Characteristics of the Revised *De Benedictionibus*

As was already said, one can reasonably suspect that parts of the liturgical reform were inspired by making use of liturgical archaeologism combined with pastoral pragmatism. The valid principle *ad fontes* (as a reminder, this principle implies that the whole of Tradition is reaching out to its source — revelation itself) was frequently misused to justify the break away from an organic development.

One reason for this can be found in the Constitution on Sacred Liturgy, *Sacrosanctum Concilium*, which made such wrongful application possible through ambiguous formulations regarding the renewal. The document states: "The sacramentals are to undergo a revision which takes into account the primary principle of enabling the faithful to participate intelligently, actively, and easily; the circumstances of our own days must also be considered. When rituals are revised, as laid down in Art. 63, new sacramentals may also be added as the need for these becomes apparent."[229]

These indications led to problematic consequences, for the reasons described above. From then on, it was possible to declare the wishes and ideas of the people to be the new point of reference and the measure of all things. If a renewal would have been based on the faith of the simple, this might still have been justifiable somehow. But in reality, the "renewal" was put into the hands of so-called experts,

---

[229] SC, 79.

who were given authority to elaborate the reform. As a result, for the first time in Church history, the liturgy was subjected to the arbitrariness of experimentation. While this overly complex situation is too vast in scope to be explained in detail here,[230] a few of the more pertinent facts will be mentioned.

Annibale Bugnini (d. 1982), the chief architect of the liturgical reform, affirms that the experts "carried the burden of the reform in their study and research; they were the architects, craftsmen, and specialized workers."[231] Already, the wording indicates something problematic,[232] a very deep underlying problem concerning the "reform." In contrast to what Bugnini describes, it has been the living faith in past centuries that has led to reforms. Historically, this was the case precisely because true *reform* consists in better understanding the true *form* (Christ) and in following Him. But here, all of a sudden, it is the experts who undertake this task, acting according to criteria that are not transparent, often based only on the light of reason, not of faith. Even worse, experiments were carried out by these experts, experiments which had to give way to arbitrariness. By contrast faith conveys security, the opposite of arbitrary change.[233] And, once the experts started experimenting with their reforms, there was no principle of authority to which they could make recourse to monitor the experiments of everyone else.

It was for sure the worst mistake within the liturgical reform that the experts were given permission for a process of testing, submitting the

---

[230] For more detail, see: Ralph Weimann, "Verschiedenheit der Formen," 86–116.

[231] Annibale Bugnini, *The Reform of the Liturgy 1948–1975*, trans. Matthew J. O'Connell, (Collegeville: Liturgical Press, 1983), 932. It is even more problematic when Bugnini praises the special role of the observers within the liturgical reform, who often were not even Catholic. Cf. ibid.

[232] Agostino Marchetto affirms that especially Bugnini and Vagaggini used substantially new concepts but a traditional vocabulary. Cf. Agostino Marchetto, *Il Concilio Ecumenico Vaticano II. Contrappunto per una storia*, (Vatican City: Libreria Editrice Vaticana, 2005), 68.

[233] Cf., Francis, LF, 4.

liturgy to a period of two years of experimentation. Bugnini indicates twelve regulations, which were supposed to guarantee a sound application; however, even some of these regulations were more than arbitrary, as, for example, number three: "In each diocese in which an experiment is conducted, someone is appointed, again with the consent of the local Ordinary, to see to the pastoral and ritual preparation in that place and, bearing in mind the concrete circumstances, to decide on that which the Ordo leaves to the determination of the conferences of bishops.... The collaboration of the laity in all this will be very profitable."[234]

Consequently, as the indicated principles were arbitrary in and of themselves, they could not but produce liturgical abuses, a fact that was affirmed even by Bugnini himself.[235] However, if the "Church draws her life from the Eucharist,"[236] provoking such consequences is outrageous. Subsequently, creativity, totally foreign to the nature of the liturgy, was and is widely accepted. James Hitchcock is right when he affirms that "the only half-recognized (but ultimately logical) goal towards which liturgical change has been moving ... is the complete suppression of ritual ... and its replacement by home-made, semi-spontaneous celebrations in which each community chooses the readings it finds most relevant to its needs and composes its own prayers, making anything short of that seem compromising."[237]

To illustrate this, it will be helpful to compare the previous form of the *Rituale Romanum* with the new edition. A simple comparison of the opening formulas of the general blessing (*Benedictio ad omnia*)

---

[234] Ibid., 264.
[235] Ibid., 264–265.
[236] John Paul II, Encyclical Letter *Ecclesia de Eucharistia*, April 17, 2003, 1, in http://www.vatican.va/holy_father/special_features/encyclicals/documents/hf_jp-ii_enc_20030417_ecclesia_eucharistia_en.html [10.5.2023].
[237] James Hitchcock, "Continuity and disruption in the liturgy: a cultural approach," in Neil J. Roy and Janet E. Rutherford (eds), *Benedict XVI and the Sacred Liturgy*, (Dublin: Four Courts Press, 2011), 88–97, here 93.

is quite illuminative. Such a blessing does not exist anymore in the very extensive *Book of Blessings*, although it includes seventy-one chapters of specific blessings.

Previous edition	New edition
℣: Adjutorium nostrum in nomine Domini. [Our help is in the name of the Lord.]	V. In the name of the Father, and of the Son, and of the Holy Spirit.
℟. Qui fecit caelum et terram. [Who made heaven and earth.]	47. A minister who is a priest or deacon greets those present in the following or other suitable words, taken mainly from sacred Scripture.
℣. Dominus vobiscum. [The Lord be with you.]	V. The grace and peace of God our Father and the Lord Jesus Christ be with you all.
℟. Et cum spiritu tuo. [And with your spirit.][238]	49. In the following or similar words, the minister prepares those present for the blessing.[239]

The previous form usually starts with a dialogue between the priest — who would ordinarily be the minister of the rite — and the assembly or the server as representative of the people. Then, the minister says the proper prayer and blessing, which is always accompanied by making the sign of the cross over the person, place, or object that is to be blessed. Finally, he sprinkles the person, object, or place with holy water, which is sometimes followed by an incensation.

The new rite consists mainly of two parts that imitate the structure of the revised liturgy of the sacraments. The general instruction establishes the following two elements as guiding principles: "First, the proclamation of the word of God, and second, the praise of God's

[238] RR, 368.
[239] BoB, 36–37.

goodness and the petition for his help."²⁴⁰ The first part of the celebration can begin with a suitable song, and it usually includes the sign of the cross, a liturgical greeting, and a response, but creativity is always suggested, according to changing and individual circumstances. This is followed by a reading from Scripture, a responsorial psalm or song, and the opportunity "for any exhortation or homily that may be given, as occasion suggests."²⁴¹ The second part is supposed to be a praise of God and can include intercessions before or after the prayer of blessing as its center. The possibility of a shorter rite is also offered, which has to include necessarily two elements: "The proclamation of the word of God and the Church's prayer of blessing. These may never be omitted even when the shorter form of a rite is used."²⁴²

If, for example, a priest would be asked to bless a rosary or a Miraculous Medal, first he would need to proclaim the Word of God, which has almost nothing to do with the blessing. If he would follow the indicated instructions, he would cause profound perplexity among the faithful, who just asked for a simple blessing. The evidence of the artificial character of the new rite in this exclusion of essential elements and inclusion of futile elements becomes clear. In actual practice, almost no priest ever applies this rite.

At this point, it will be helpful to turn to some of the research and results presented by Uwe Michael Lang from the Oratory of London. He describes the sad progression from *Sacrosanctum Concilium* to *De benedictionibus*.²⁴³ According to his research, it was above all the French Dominican liturgist, Pierre-Marie Gy (d. 2004), who worked out the first draft for *De benedictionibus*. This Dominican was part of the

---

[240] General Introduction, §20, in BoB, 27.
[241] Ibid., §21, in BoB, 27.
[242] Ibid., §23, in BoB, 28. An immensely helpful commentary is provided by Uwe Michael Lang, "Theologies of Blessing: Origins and Characteristics of *De benedictionibus* (1984)," in Antiphon 15.1 (2011): 27–46, especially 38.
[243] Lang, "Theologies of Blessing," 27–46.

so-called *Nouvelle théologie*; Lang lays out the theological principles on which Gy's revision was to be built: "At the very beginning, he notes the difficulties of this task, because the contemporary world is marked by an increasing tendency towards desacralization and secularization. This means that, while in some parts of the world, including rural regions in Europe, but above all Africa and Latin America, blessings are still firmly rooted in the lives of the faithful, in other parts, especially in the developed and industrialized countries of Europe and North America, the use of blessings has diminished significantly."[244]

According to Gy, the renewed sacramentals had to respond to this changed situation. To this end, he defined two criteria that gave him the greatest possible room for any type of change. The sources for the liturgical reform concerning sacramentals were to be based on Sacred Scripture and on the early Church. Thus, what was previously described as liturgical archaelogism is elevated to the authoritative criterion, even in contradiction to *Dei Verbum*.[245] What about the *living* Tradition of the Church? Why should more than 1,500 years of organic development and natural precedent be skipped over and disregarded? Since our knowledge of the early Christian period is limited, "pastoral necessities" took the place of the living Tradition. And this is how the liturgical reform of the sacramentals took place, leading to a twofold structure of the sacramentals: they are conceived as acts of thanksgiving and praise of God for the good gifts of creation.[246] The Jewish *berakah*, as described by the prophet Daniel, served as a model for the sacramental reform: "Blessed are you, and praiseworthy, O Lord, the God of our ancestors, and glorious forever is your name" (Dan. 3:26). It is an ancient blessing, often repeated in the Old Testament, in which God is praised for His goodness and

---

[244] Ibid., 33.
[245] Cf. DV, 9.
[246] Pierre-Marie Gy, "Labores coetum a studiis: De benedictionibus," in *Notitiae* 7 (1971): 123–132, here 124.

care. This very structure is also reflected in the new eucharistic prayers, especially in the prayers used during the Offertory.

To reiterate, the reform of the sacramentals was based on a twofold reference point: Scripture and the early Church. Although Gy admitted that the early Church would use blessings, which would fall under the category of "constitutive blessings," whatever blessings might have been used so many years ago had to be revised and changed. Here, too, it becomes clear how incoherent was the reform that was put into practice. One example comes to mind that is particularly illuminating. On the feast of St. John the Evangelist, there had been a traditional blessing of wine, expressed in the formula *"benedicere et consecrare digneris."*[247] This type of formula, which was often used in the early Church, was rejected since it did not correspond to Gy's ideas of the twofold reference point. Also, according to the new premises, blessings should be invoked primarily on persons rather than on things or places. Gy was of the opinion that this was necessary to combat superstition. However, even in the New Testament, the use of blessings of objects and places is clearly described; for just one example of this, Sacred Scripture describes Jesus as having blessed the fish and the bread used to feed the multitudes (cf. Mark 8:7).[248] As so often happened during the implementation of liturgical reform, it was not primarily a matter of going back to the sources (*ad fontes*), but of projecting one's own ideas onto the past. In doing so, one relied on an archaelogism, which, however, was used selectively. Things that fit into one's own concept were included — others were omitted.

All of this becomes even more clear when considering the reform's exclusion of apotropaic elements. According to the Tradition of the Church, most of the sacramentals had included these anti-demonic elements, intended to combat evil influences through the power of God. The blessing of many objects, such as holy water, salt,

---

[247] Lang, "Theologies of Blessing," 35.
[248] For more detail see ibid.

oil, and the like, first included a purification, which was in fact a type of exorcism. Gy interpreted *Sacrosanctum Concilium* in such a way that these elements were to be eliminated, claiming that it would assist in avoiding superstition. Their place was filled with readings from Scripture, preaching, catechetical instructions, chants, acclamations, and other communal elements. These are of course potentially all good things, but none of them carry the specific intrinsic weight or serve the particular purpose of apotropaisms.

The minimizing relegation of apotropaic blessings cannot be attributed to a lack of biblical reference; rather, it is related to parts of modern theology and its premises. At the risk of oversimplifying matters, this problem will be discussed briefly. The preparatory work for this had been done by theologians "such as Edward Schillebeeckx OP (1914–2009) and Karl Rahner SJ (1904–1984), who considered the whole created world already endowed with or permeated by divine grace."[249] They extended the notion of "sacramentality" to the whole creation and "so the specific nature of the sacraments is lost: the sacraments and, by consequence, the sacramentals are mere manifestations that make explicit what already takes place."[250] Uwe Michael Lang points out that "unlike classical theology, Rahner no longer takes the sacraments as signs that confer the grace they signify, or instrumental causes of grace *extra nos*, but rather as visible manifestations of the inner event of grace that already occurs in man, and is not necessarily linked with Christian Revelation."[251] The consequences with regard to the sacramentals cannot be underestimated; at least partially, it would render them invalid or degrade them to empty characters.

There are more problematic consequences related to this approach concerning the sacramentals. Original Sin and its

---

[249] Ibid., 44.
[250] Ibid., 45.
[251] Lang, "Sacred Architecture," here 197–198.

consequences,²⁵² as well as the mysterious work of the devil, are denied or, at the very least, obscured by it. The decision to no longer bless any places or inanimate objects, but instead only persons, makes this clear. If, for example, there is a place or a house where strange and even abnormal things happen (e.g., the place could be described as haunted or cursed or was once used for satanic practices, etc.), according to the reforms, the priest is no longer supposed to bless it. Such an attitude leads consequently to the abolishing of exorcisms, of prayers of liberation, and of apotropaic elements in general. This caused a break with the Tradition of the Church, and it even contradicted Sacred Scripture, which states: "We know that we belong to God, and the whole world is under the power of the evil one" (1 John 5:19). Also, it is worth noting that the *Apostolic Tradition* contains numerous blessings of milk, fruits, food, and so forth. The earliest sacramentaries contained various such prayers, which demonstrates just how inconsistent and thin the supposed return to the traditions of the early Church actually was in these reforms.²⁵³

Uwe Michael Lang affirms: "The texts of the prayers are for the most part newly composed, even though they are modeled on or contain elements of ancient euchological [Eastern Orthodox ritual] sources. According to the principle already presented in Gy's *relatio* of 1970, with things and places, the actual blessing is invoked not on the objects themselves, but on the persons who use them."²⁵⁴

This is clearly illustrated in the blessing of candles on the feast of the Presentation of the Lord (Candlemas, February 2). It says in the second option (from two):

---

[252] Cf. chap. 2.3.1.
[253] Cf. Lang, "Theologies of Blessing," 45.
[254] Ibid., 39.

Latin	English
Deus, lumen verum, aeternae lucis propagator et auctor, cordibus infunde fidelium perpetui luminis claritatem, ut, quicumque in templo sancto tuo splendore praesentium luminum adornantur, ad lumen gloriae tuae feliciter valeant pervenire. Per Christum.	O God, true light, who creates light eternal, spreading it far and wide, pour, we pray, into the hearts of the faithful the brilliance of perpetual light, so that all who are brightened in your holy temple by the splendor of these candles may happily reach the light of your glory.[255]

It is already surprising that the minister can choose between two prayers. The prayer corresponding to the second option requires not even the sign of the cross and is, therefore, no prayer of blessing at all, since the candles are not blessed. The prayers adopted in *De benedictionibus* follow the same "logic." It was a frequent practice after the reforms that often even the sign of the cross was omitted in so-called blessings. It is, however, *the* sign for any Christian blessing, and it is always obligatory in the older *Rituale Romanum*. It took almost twenty years for the Congregation for Divine Worship and the Discipline of the Sacraments to take note of this great omission. In September 2002, a decree was issued indicating that a blessing, when given by sacred ministers (a bishop, priest, or deacon), must always be accompanied by the sign of the cross. The decree, signed by Cardinal Medina Estévez, says:

> Since, from the established usage, the liturgical custom has always been in force that in the rites of blessing the sign of the cross is employed by being traced by the celebrant with the right hand over the persons or things for whom mercy is implored, this Congregation for divine worship and the discipline of the sacraments, in order to dispel any doubts, has established that, even if the text

---

[255] *The Roman Missal*, 3rd Chapel Edition, (New Jersey: Catholic Book Publishing, 2011), February 2, The Presentation of the Lord, 667.

of the part of the Roman ritual entitled "The Book of Blessings" remains silent about the sign itself or lacks an express mention of the appropriate time for this action, nevertheless the sacred ministers should adopt the aforementioned sign of the cross as necessary when carrying out any blessing. Without a mention, however, the appropriate time should be regarded as when the text of the blessing uses the words *blessing, to bless*, or similar or, lacking these words, when the prayer of blessing itself is concluded.[256]

From a purely practical point of view, the *Book of Blessings* was both problematic and resulted in insufficiencies. For one thing, the book is physically too extensive and heavy; a priest could hardly carry it around with him. And then there is the consideration that there are far too many choices included, not providing clarity in how to give a blessing. For example, it offers for the blessing of religious articles (such as rosaries) a short formulary, similar to the *Benedictio ad omnia* of the old ritual. It says: "May this (name of article) and the one who uses it be blessed, in the name of the Father, and of the Son, + and of the Holy Spirit."[257] This is preceded by five pages of explanations on

---

[256] Congregation for Divine Worship and the Discipline of the Sacraments, *Decree*, Unofficial English Translation in http://notitiae.ipsissima-verba.org/show/135 [14.5.2023]. "Cum ex usitato more semper liturgica viguisset consuetudo, ut in ritibus benedictionis signum crucis adhiberetur, id dextera manu a celebrante super personas aut res describendo, pro quibus misericordia impetratur, haec Congregatio de Cultu Divino et Disciplina Sacramentorum ad dirimenda dubia statuit, ut, etiam si textus illius partis Ritualis Romani cui titulus *De Benedictionibus* silentio signum ipsum praetereatur vel expressa in eo careat mentione temporis opportuni huius actionis, attamen tamquam necessarium in quavis benedictione sacris ministris peragenda supradictum signum crucis usurpetur. Hac vero absente mentione, tempus opportunum habeatur cum textus benedictionis verba *benedictio, benedicere* vel similia praebeat vel his deficientibus verbis, cum concluditur ipsa oratio benedictionis." Congregation for Divine Worship and the Discipline of the Sacraments, *Decretum*, in AAS 94 (2002): 684. See also Uwe Michael Lang, "Theologies of Blessing," 39–40.

[257] BoB, 624.

how a blessing is to be given in imitation of the sacraments, with a reference to Sacred Scripture, including intercessions, and a prayer of blessing — which explicitly does not foresee the blessing of the object.[258] At this point, it can be seen what the unhappy consequences are of those so poorly conceived principles of reform, principles which were stringently applied to the "renewal" of the sacramentals.

The Congregation for Divine Worship and the Discipline of the Sacraments recognized this indirectly. The above-mentioned decree, signed by Cardinal Estévez, was meant to correct the renewed form at least regarding the sacred sign of the cross. The *Catechism of the Catholic Church* seems to have anticipated this already: "Among sacramentals *blessings* (of persons, meals, objects, and places) come first. Every blessing praises God and prays for his gifts. In Christ, Christians are blessed by God the Father 'with every spiritual blessing.' This is why the Church imparts blessings by invoking the name of Jesus, usually while making the holy sign of the cross of Christ."[259] With this statement, the *Catechism* succeeded in pointing out that direction which, reconciled with the past, can lead to a renewed understanding of the sacramentals. It would be desirable if more theologians would follow this path.

3.6. Importance of the Signs

One last aspect needs to be mentioned in this context. Together with the formulas, the signs of sacramentals have special importance. There is a tendency today to reduce sacred signs to a minimum, due at least in part to what was stated in *Sacrosanctum Concilium*: "The rites should be distinguished by a noble simplicity; they should be short, clear, and unencumbered by useless repetitions; they should be within the people's powers of comprehension, and normally should not require

---

[258] Ibid., 617–622.
[259] CCC, 1671.

much explanation."²⁶⁰ This affirmation was often used as a pretext to abolish most of the sacred signs; simplicity was requested and "useless repetitions" were to be avoided. Pope John Paul II did address these "erroneous applications," but he did not, unfortunately, manage to reverse this predominating tendency.²⁶¹

Yet the effectiveness of sacramentals depends also on the sacred sign, and especially repetitions of these signs have proved to bear spiritual effects if done with the proper attitude. This becomes clear when considering the blessing of a priest and of a bishop. The bishop, with the fullness of the sacramental power, makes the sign of the cross three times when he blesses. This is not simply a repetition; rather, it is the exterior expression of the sacramental grace. This logic had been applied to the sacramentals until the liturgical reform — a logic that presupposed a sacramental understanding. It seems that some of the main architects of the liturgical reform were inspired by a different approach. They made reference to the ambiguous texts, quoted above, to abolish what was part of a genuinely Catholic tradition.

In 1922, Romano Guardini had published an excellent little book, *Sacred Signs*. If his explanations and arguments had been understood,

---

[260] SC, 34.

[261] The pope said: "Side by side with these benefits of the liturgical reform, one has to acknowledge with regret deviations of greater or lesser seriousness in its application. On occasion there have been noted illicit omissions or additions, rites invented outside the framework of established norms; postures or songs which are not conducive to faith or to a sense of the sacred; abuses in the practice of general absolution; confusion between the ministerial priesthood, linked with Ordination, and the common priesthood of the faithful, which has its foundation in Baptism." John Paul II, Apostolic Letter *Vicesimus Quintus Annus*, December 4, 1988, 13, in http://www.vatican.va/content/john-paul-ii/en/apost_letters/1988/documents/hf_jp-ii_apl_19881204_vicesimus-quintus-annus.html [4.5.2023]. Regarding this topic see also Nicola Bux, *Benedict XVI's Reform. The Liturgy between Innovation and Tradition*, trans. Joseph Trabbic, (San Francisco: Ignatius Press, 2012), 62–67.

respected, and referenced during the liturgical reforms, their outcome would have been much different. In his introduction, he writes:

> The liturgy is not a matter of ideas, but of actual things, and of actual things as they now are, not as they were in the past. It is a continuous movement carried on by and through us, and its forms and actions issue from our human nature. To show how it arose and developed brings us no nearer to it, and no more does this or that learned interpretation. What does help is to discern in the living liturgy what underlies the visible sign, to discover the soul from the body, the hidden and spiritual from the external and material. The liturgy has taken its outward shape from a divine and hidden series of happenings. It is sacramental in its nature.[262]

Cardinal Ratzinger expressed hope that Guardini's basic understanding of sacred signs might be taken up again by liturgists. He affirmed: "To liturgy belong both speech *and* silence, singing, the praise of the instruments, the visual image, the symbol, and the gesture that corresponds to the word."[263] Sacred signs have multiple meanings; it is through them that spiritual effects are to be produced, and this understanding needs to be rediscovered: they are an essential element of the sacramentals.

Therefore, sacred signs, such as the sign of the cross, the imposition of hands, and so on, have particular value; they are not only signs of salvation, but are in fact visible signs that cause invisible effects.[264] Through them, creation is elevated. As a result, material things, such as medals, scapulars, crosses, images, and also places and persons, are sanctified. Therefore, it is part of time-honored tradition that priests, and even more so bishops, should give blessings. A priest — and even more so a bishop — should always give a blessing at the end of a

---

[262] Romano Guardini, *Sacred Signs*, trans. Grace Branham, (St. Louis: Pio Decimo Press, 1956), 9.
[263] Joseph Ratzinger, TL, 326–327.
[264] See SC, 33.

meeting because invisible grace is thereby bestowed upon the faithful who are disposed to it. By doing this, they pass on what they themselves have received (see 1 Cor. 11:23).

Sacred signs help to rediscover, as Romano Guardini wrote, the soul from the body — in other words, the invisible from the visible. Whenever these signs are given and attended on with faith and love, people will obtain through them invisible grace. Like the sacraments, sacramentals are supposed to sanctify daily life. The Constitution on the Sacred Liturgy says that these sacred signs "bear a resemblance to the sacraments: they signify effects, particularly of a spiritual kind, which are obtained through the Church's intercession. Thereby one is disposed to receive the chief effects of the sacraments, and various occasions in one's life are rendered holy."[265]

In conclusion, sacred signs should not be omitted or reduced to a minimum. This tendency must be overcome for the sake of the graces that might be obtained through them. The Church encourages us to make frequent use of sacred signs in everyday life. They are not magical practices, but efficient signs of a greater reality. Through the use of sacred signs — especially the sign of the cross — the same effects may be obtained as through prayer. The sign is a sacred action through which God is glorified and graces are obtained.[266]

3.7. Conclusion

To recap the ground this chapter has covered, spiritual effects are obtained in sacramentals through participation in the action of the Church (*ex opere operantis Ecclesiae*), insofar as the Church *is* in Christ. For that reason, devout participation is necessary to obtain the spiritual fruits that sacramentals offer. Besides the christological dimension, the ecclesiological dimension is also of great importance because the effectiveness of the

---

[265] SC, 60.
[266] Regarding a practical application see chap. 6.

sacramentals comes through the intercessory power of the Church, which necessarily includes the whole of the living Tradition. As a result, it is through the authority of the Church that rites are instituted, and they must be recited by authorized persons with the intention to do what the Church does. Thus, "some effects are also obtained infallibly by the objective performance of the rite, and therefore by a certain *opus operatum*, as it were."[267] Approved prayers, formulas, and signs, as a fruit of the living Tradition of the Church, form an essential element of the rite. However, the effects depend also on the moral dignity (living faith) and disposition of the one receiving the sacramentals; this is *the* determining factor.

By making use of sacramentals, the faithful direct themselves toward the Most Holy Trinity, from which all graces flow. The Church is the Mystical Body of Christ and, therefore, ever pleasing in the sight of God. In establishing the sacramentals, the Church grants to them, and through them, an intercessory power; whoever makes devout use of these sacred things and actions with the right disposition will receive spiritual benefits. Finally, four chief effects of the sacramentals can be enumerated:

1. Through them, the faithful belongs to God and is under His protection. Whenever the rite is validly performed and objectively received, it "produces infallibly the spiritual effect, which consists in the fact that God accepts the object or person as reserved for His exclusive use."[268] Whenever a chalice, a church, or an altar is consecrated to God, it is set apart and reserved exclusively for Him; the same can be said about someone who consecrates his or her life to God. The Apostle Paul had expressed this as follows: "Yet I live, no longer I, but Christ lives in me" (Gal. 2:20).

---

[267] Cyprian Vagaggini, TDL, 112.
[268] Ibid., 113.

2. Any kind of actual grace can be received. Depending on the supernatural acts of faith accompanying the administration of the sacramentals, actual grace can be received. Unlike the sacraments, the sacramentals do not have the power of directly conferring sanctifying grace; nevertheless, "By means of these actual graces, the recovery or increase of sanctifying grace can be achieved."[269] If, for example, a Christian who is not in the state of grace uses holy water devoutly, he may receive an actual grace, which would enable him to make an act of (perfect) contrition. An actual grace may also prevent someone from losing sanctifying grace through mortal sin. Also for this reason, the use of sacramentals is recommended when someone is tormented by temptations; it can be a powerful help not to fall into sin, or to obtain from God the remission of (venial) sins, or the grace of conversion. It is also lawful to use sacramentals to obtain temporal favors such as good health and success in studies, business, and the like.

3. Sacramentals provide liberation from evil spirits and influences. All sacramentals are supposed to include apotropaic elements to prevent any diabolical influence over persons, places, and things. This is not limited only to exorcisms, but is an integral part of all sacramentals. For this reason, the administration of all sacramentals must include the sign of the cross.

4. Sacramentals are a powerful help to eternal life and spiritual growth. The primary end of the sacramentals is eternal life and, therefore, the spiritual good of the soul. Sacramentals can be a great help in growing in the spiritual life and preparing for eternal life.

---

[269] Ibid.

FOUR
✠ ✠ ✠

The Minister and the Recipient

4.1. Introduction

WHEN CONSIDERING THE MINISTER and the recipient of sacramentals, it is necessary to reflect on several aspects of importance, such as divine action, authority, participation, and spiritual effects. Canon law provides a basic orientation, first in defining the minister of any sacramental, providing an objective foundation for the rest of the discussion: "The minister of sacramentals is a cleric who has been provided with the requisite power. According to the norm of the liturgical books and to the judgment of the local ordinary lay persons who possess the appropriate qualities can also administer some sacramentals."[270]

Consequently, the ordinary minister of sacramentals is the cleric, not the layperson. Nevertheless, the cleric must be ecclesiastically authorized to administer them, and he must not be prevented from the exercise of his power. If a priest, for example, is suspended from his priestly ministry, he will have difficulties obtaining fruits of holiness through the administration of the sacramentals. However, there is a common understanding that sacramentals administered by a priest from the priestly Society of Saint Pius X unfold spiritual power nevertheless, because those priests have been validly ordained

---

[270] can. 1168.

and they usually use the traditional formulas and signs, which are part of the heritage of the Church.

The *Code of Canon Law* also gives a clear regulation regarding persons who are excommunicated: "An excommunicated person is forbidden to celebrate the sacraments or sacramentals and to receive the sacraments."[271] Both the administration and the reception of the sacraments themselves are forbidden to anyone excommunicated, but an excommunicated person may still receive sacramentals (though an excommunicated cleric may not administer them). Regarding the ministers, this prohibition to celebrate the sacraments and sacramentals affects the liceity, but not the validity of such an administration. In simple terms, this means that they are not allowed to celebrate them, but, should they break that law and celebrate them anyway, they are in fact still valid. The Code admits two exceptions from this rule. One regards the minister:

> If a censure prohibits the celebration of the sacraments or sacramentals or the placing of an act of governance, the prohibition is suspended whenever it is necessary to care for the faithful in danger of death. If a *latae sententiae* [a canonical penalty that is inflicted automatically, at the very moment a law is contravened] censure has not been declared, the prohibition is also suspended whenever a member of the faithful requests a sacrament or sacramental or an act of governance; a person is permitted to request this for any just cause.[272]

Regarding the recipients, the Code states: "If a penalty prohibits the reception of the sacraments or sacramental, the prohibition is suspended as long as the offender is in danger of death."[273] In both cases, the administration or reception in danger of death is not only valid but also licit. With these basic points from canon law in place, it is

---

[271] can. 1331 §1, no. 3.
[272] can. 1335.
[273] can. 1352 §1.

possible to move on to consider the spiritual fruits of the sacramentals with regard to the minister and the recipient.

4.2. Spiritual Fruits Obtained by the Minister and the Recipient

The *Code of Canon Law* addresses the question of validity and liceity, but it does not address the question of spiritual benefit; this is to be inferred by theology. Some important aspects of this have already been discussed in the previous chapter; however, in this new context, some further reflections are required.

It is exceedingly difficult to answer whether a priest or a bishop, living in the state of mortal sin, can fruitfully administer the sacramentals. Since he is validly ordained, he can still be an instrument to achieve spiritual effects (see: *opus operatum*)[274] if the recipient is well prepared. And yet, moral dignity is of great importance with regard to the participated effects.

The difficulty concerning this question becomes more evident when looking specifically at exorcisms. If a priest or a bishop performs an exorcism, even though living in mortal sin and, therefore, separated from Christ — the source, from which all spiritual power flows — his attempts at the exorcism would be limited, and not effective. Even more, it would be extremely dangerous and, above all, irresponsible. To confront spiritual beings whose nature is superior to human nature is hopeless if it is done without the requisite power — power which can only come from God and, therefore, depends on the moral dignity of the minister, through which he remains united to God.

Still, it is difficult to answer the question of whether or to what degree the holiness or sinfulness of a person affects the administration of the sacramentals. The whole debate on the heresy of Donatism does not need to be repeated (but see the note for some

---

[274] Cf. chap. 3.1.

context).[275] Nevertheless, the attempt will be made to provide some general indications through a simplified scheme and some principles, which might be helpful, and through drawing a distinction between the minister and the recipient concerning the spiritual fruits.[276] The following explanations refer above all to the supernatural virtue of faith and the spiritual fruits related to it.

Minister → holiness of life → abundance of spiritual fruits

Among other presuppositions mentioned above, spiritual fruits are achieved through the personal action of the minister. Since he administers the sacramentals, his instrumental function is of great importance. A "good instrument" will obtain better results than a poor instrument. The minister is bound to the intercessory power of the Church, which becomes effective to the degree that the minister participates in the Church's holiness. A minister living a holy life will obtain plenty of spiritual fruits. This is especially evident in the lives of the saints.

Minister → mediocre lifestyle → some spiritual fruits

Some spiritual fruits are obtained through a minister living a mediocre lifestyle. The book of Revelation passes harsh judgment on such ministers: "I know your works; I know that you are neither cold nor hot. I wish you were either cold or hot. So, because you are lukewarm, neither hot nor cold, I will spit you out of my mouth" (Rev. 3:15–16). In other words, moral dignity has an impact on the spiritual fruits obtained through the personal action and instrumental function of the minister.

---

[275] Donatists "assumed that the part played by the minister in the administration of the Sacraments was substantial and not merely instrumental; therefore, they maintained that a minister without grace could not confer the Sacraments." Denis Faul, Art. "Donatism," in *New Catholic Encyclopedia*, vol. IV, (Washington, D.C.: The Catholic University of America, 1967), 1001–1003, here 1002.

[276] The other important elements of sacramentals concerning the fruitfulness, such as the rite, the formulae, and signs will be left aside. See chap. 3.

Minister → separated from God → no spiritual fruits

No spiritual fruits are obtained through the personal action of a minister who is in the state of mortal sin. Sacred Scripture affirms: "Whoever remains in me and I in him will bear much fruit because without me you can do nothing" (John 15:5). Since the minister has an instrumental function and the instrument only works if connected to the one using it (Jesus Christ), no personal fruits can be obtained through the personal action of someone who is separated from God. Living faith is animated by charity, which excludes mortal sin.[277] As the priest, when administering sacramentals, speaks not only in his own name, but through the Church, graces can nevertheless be obtained — through the intercession of the Church.

Recipient → holiness of life → abundance of spiritual fruits

The same scheme can be applied with regard to the recipient. The spiritual fruits obtained by the recipient depend on his moral disposition. This disposition may be compared to a vessel, which is about to be filled. If there are no obstacles, it may be filled to the brim. The intercessory power of the Church becomes effective if the recipient is himself open to grace. This is affirmed in the Gospel: "For to everyone who has, more will be given and he will grow rich; but from the one who has not, even what he has will be taken away" (Matt. 25:29).

Recipient → mediocre lifestyle → some spiritual fruits

Similar to what has been described above, the spiritual fruits will diminish through a mediocre lifestyle. "No one can serve two masters" (Matt. 6:24). Mediocrity proves to be just as detrimental to spiritual effect as doubting. Thus, the Letter of James affirms: "For the one who doubts is like a wave of the sea that is driven and tossed about by the wind. For that person must not suppose that he will receive

---

[277] Cf. Reginald Garrigou-Lagrange, *The Theological Virtues. Volume One: On Faith*, trans. Thomas a Kempis Reilly, vol. 1, (Binghamton: Herder, 1965), 367.

anything from the Lord, since he is a man of two minds, unstable in all his ways" (James 1:6–8). Doubts are often described as a good thing today, as even faithful are encouraged to question everything. But, in reality, they have a corrosive effect in terms of spiritual fruits, which depend on the devout participation of the recipient in the mystery of God.

Recipient → separated from God → no spiritual fruits

Charity, as a supernatural virtue, animates faith. Whenever it is missing, no spiritual fruits can be obtained, for the reasons explained above. Since the recipient will achieve spiritual effects to the degree in which he participates in the mystery, he cannot receive any if he does not participate, that is, if he is in the state of mortal sin. The spiritual fruits depend on the disposition of the receiver and follow the principle *ex opere operantis*.

4.3. The Spiritual Effects of Consecrations and Blessings

The question arises: what does this mean concerning consecrations? For example, how should the consecration of a virgin be understood in terms of the relationship between the minister and recipient? Does the lifestyle of the minister have an impact on the recipient? To answer this question, something similar could be said about the consecration of places or things. First, it must be taken into consideration that, of all sacramentals, consecrations have the greatest proximity to the sacraments, which produce spiritual effects following the principle of *ex opere operato*. Thus, consecrations do not primarily depend on the holiness of the minister, but on the disposition of the receiver. Even though they are not sacraments, they do have an indwelling efficiency similar to the sacraments because they produce permanent effects, due to the intercessory power of the Church. Thus, in consecrations, spiritual fruits are granted to the recipient without doubts regarding the validity or invalidity of their administration.

It must be affirmed that the efficacy of constitutive blessings is above all ensured by the prayer of the Church (rite).[278] If a person receives a constitutive blessing with faith and the right disposition, spiritual fruits will be obtained. In this sense, the explanation provided by Avery Dulles concerning the fruitfulness of the sacraments is also valid concerning the sacramentals: "The fruitfulness of sacraments depends on the faith and devotion of the recipients, in the sense that their good dispositions permit the sacraments to achieve their effect. The power of Christ is operative in us through faith, whereby we unite ourselves with his Passion."[279]

4.4. The Minister of Sacramentals

According to the previous editions of the *Rituale Romanum*, the minister of the blessings is any priest (*presbyter*), except in cases of those blessings that are reserved for bishops, priests of specific religious orders, congregations, and the Roman Pontiff. Deacons and lectors can give certain blessings that are expressly permitted to them. The *Code of Canon Law* from 1917 stated that the legitimate minister of the sacramentals is the cleric, putting special emphasis on the ecclesiological dimension.

---

[278] The *Catechism of the Catholic Church* says: "Certain blessings have a lasting importance because they consecrate persons to God, or reserve objects and places for liturgical use. Among those blessings which are intended for persons — not to be confused with sacramental ordination — are the blessing of the abbot or abbess of a monastery, the consecration of virgins and widows, the rite of religious profession, and the blessing of certain ministries of the Church (readers, acolytes, catechists, etc.). The dedication or blessing of a church or an altar, the blessing of holy oils, vessels, and vestments, bells, etc., can be mentioned as examples of blessings that concern objects." CCC, 1672. Cf. Uwe Michael Lang, "Theologies of Blessing," 34.

[279] Avery Dulles, "The Theology of Worship: Saint Thomas," in Matthew Levering and Michael Dauphinais (eds.), *Rediscovering Aquinas and the Sacraments: Studies in Sacramental Theology*, (Chicago: Hillenbrand Books, 2009), 1–13, here 7.

The *Code of Canon Law* from 1983, as also reflected in *De benedictionibus*, takes a different approach. It relates the ministry of blessing to the exercise of the priesthood of Jesus Christ, which is (secondly) reflected in an ecclesiological ordering. The general principle is the same, since every blessing is linked to the source of any blessing: Jesus Christ.

However, no special attention is granted to the ontological difference (that is, the difference in nature) between a cleric and a layperson. Nevertheless, it does affirm the hierarchical order. The bishop is the first minister of blessings; for this reason, certain blessings may be reserved to him, such as the consecration (blessing) of abbots, virgins, the blessing of churches, cemeteries, oratories, and usually all articles for use in connection with the altar, such as chalices, patens, holy oils, and so on. Some of these blessings can be delegated to priests.[280] The explanation of the office of the bishop is given through a communal perspective, since it is of special significance for the entire diocesan community.

A priest can celebrate all blessings included in *De benedictionibus*, unless a bishop is present, as a bishop will always take precedence; or unless the blessing is reserved to the bishop. This is also reflected in can. 1169 §2: "Any priest can impart blessings, except for those reserved to the Roman Pontiff or to Bishops." The blessings reserved to the pope are usually the blessing of the *pallium* for archbishops (a liturgical vestment worn over the chasuble), the *Agnus Dei* (a disc of wax, impressed with the image of a lamb and blessed by the pope traditionally made from the wax of the Paschal Candle), and especially the *Urbi et Orbi* (special papal blessing given on particular solemn holy days, such as Easter, Christmas, and after the election of a newly elected pope).

---

[280] BoB, General introduction, 26.

Although a deacon can give those blessings indicated for him in the *De benedictionibus*, according to the order of hierarchy, when a priest is present, the blessing should be carried out by the priest. The *Code of Canon Law* affirms: "A deacon can impart only those blessings expressly permitted by law."[281]

The fourth hierarchical group that may impart blessings is acolytes and readers. They are not considered clerics, even though nowadays they are a kind of "leftover" from the minor orders.[282] By formal institution, "this special office in the Church is rightly preferred over another layperson as the minister designated at the discretion of the local Ordinary to impart certain blessings."[283] Finally, the general introduction in the *Book of Blessings* states:

> Other laymen and laywomen, in virtue of the universal priesthood, a dignity they possess because of their baptism and confirmation, may celebrate certain blessings, as indicated in the respective orders of blessings, by use of the rites and formularies designated for a lay minister. Such laypersons exercise this ministry in virtue of their office (for example, parents on behalf of their children) or by reason of some special liturgical ministry or in fulfillment of a particular charge in the Church, as is the case in many places with religious or catechists appointed by decision of the local Ordinary, after ascertaining their proper pastoral formation and prudence in the apostolate. But whenever a priest or a deacon is present, the office of presiding should be left to him.[284]

---

[281] can. 1169 §3.
[282] Paul Bradshaw defines them as follows: "In addition to the orders of bishops, presbyter, and deacon, ... the early Church also knew of other permanently appointed officials designated to exercise certain liturgical functions — what later centuries would come to call the minor orders." Paul F. Bradshaw, *Ordination Rites of the Ancient Churches of East and West*, (New York: Liturgical Press, 1990), 93.
[283] BoB, General introduction, 26.
[284] Ibid., 26.

De benedictionibus respects and emphasizes the importance of the hierarchical order, which is a participation in the "sacred origin." Unfortunately, it is precisely this understanding that has been largely lost today; a functional, practical attitude has become more and more prevalent.

As can be seen above, the general introduction emphasizes the importance of the participation of the faithful, referring to the concept of the common priesthood. The faithful who have been marked with the seal of Baptism and so consecrated to God are called a "kingdom of priests" (Exod. 19:6). This concept expresses the dignity of being a child of God, but it is distinct from the actual ministerial priesthood "in essence."[285] Nonetheless, this very dignity of the faithful is the reason why laypeople "may celebrate certain blessings, as indicated in the respective orders of blessings, by use of the rites and formularies designated for a lay minister."[286] They act in virtue of their proper office, for example, when parents bless their children; moreover, they may exercise an extraordinary ministry, which is usually related to the liturgy; or they may exercise particular offices in the Church, such as catechists. In any case, the general rule must be respected: whenever a bishop, priest, or deacon is present, the blessing should be imparted by them, and in that order of hierarchy.

Today, because of the overly practical attitude that has been adopted, the reality is quite different from this hierarchical ideal; in short, a functional perspective takes more and more precedence over a sacramental perspective. It happens frequently that "lay ministers" preside over all types of celebrations, even when priests or bishops are present. Some of the laity consider that it would be a humiliation if they were to step down and give what would in fact be proper deference to a priest. And, what is even worse, all too often they do not come to participate in the celebration for the sake of the graces available, but only

[285] LG, 10.
[286] Ibid.

because they are there to perform a function. Should they then be asked not to perform it, they find themselves betrayed, for their focus has been off the mark from the start. In many parts of Germany, Switzerland, and other countries, it is not uncommon for these lay ministers to complain to the Ordinariate as soon as a priest insists that the actual rule of hierarchy be observed.

Above all, this is reflected when laypeople distribute Holy Communion even when there are enough priests present. This is a strong contradiction to a proper sacramental understanding. In some countries, it is even common that laypeople administer not only all kinds of sacramentals, but even invalidly administer the sacraments, such as the Anointing of the Sick.[287] The same logic is followed by the Protestant communities in Germany, which introduced a blessing robot in 2017. This robot gives blessings in five languages, with its hands shining brightly.[288] This shows how far a functional understanding has paved the way over the correct sacramental understanding. Concerning the Catholic Church, these problems are also rooted — to a certain degree — in *De benedictionibus*. Uwe Michael Lang pointed out: "Thus *De benedictionibus* roots the liturgical ministry of blessings not in the ordained priesthood, but in the common priesthood of the baptized. Nonetheless, the place of the blessings within the life of the people of God leads to a hierarchical ordering of the liturgical ministry of blessing, which will always be assumed by the ordained minister of the highest rank, who is present."[289]

[287] This is practiced in Switzerland, for example, as described here Raphael Rauch, Ausländerstimmrecht, Krankensalbung durch Frauen, Dreikönig: Was diese Woche wichtig wird, January 4, 2021, in https://www.kath.ch/newsd/auslaenderstimmrecht-krankensalbung-durch-frauen-dreikoenig-was-diese-woche-wichtig-wird/ [12.5.2023].
[288] Harriet Sherwood, "Robot priest unveiled in Germany to mark 500 years since Reformation," May 30, 2017, in https://www.theguardian.com/technology/2017/may/30/robot-priest-blessu-2-germany-reformation-exhibition [12.5.2023].
[289] Lang, "Theologies of Blessing," 41.

With the emphasis in *De benedictionibus* being placed on the common priesthood, it was easy to misunderstand and disregard the sacramental structure of the ordained priesthood. Actually, Martin Luther (d. 1546) rejected the ordained priesthood in favor of the common priesthood; this unfortunate rejection has not, sadly, been contained within Lutheranism, but has infected Catholics as well, leading to the functional understanding of this office that is now all too prevalent.[290] For this reason, it is very problematic to create a new ritual based on a principle that is easy to misunderstand.

A similar position was assumed in the *Catechism of the Catholic Church*: "Sacramentals derive from the baptismal priesthood: every baptized person is called to be a 'blessing,' and to bless. Hence laypeople may preside at certain blessings; the more a blessing concerns ecclesial and sacramental life, the more is its administration reserved to the ordained ministry (bishops, priests, or deacons)."[291]

Uwe Michael Lang observes a certain tension between the *Code of Canon Law* (from 1983) and *De benedictionibus* (from 1984). The 1983 *Code of Canon Law* "follows the indications given in *Sacrosanctum Concilium*, but it retains much of the structure and contents of the older code and, in fact, like the older *Rituale Romanum*, considers the ordained cleric the minister of blessings."[292] The starting point seems to be different: in *De benedictionibus*, the starting point is the common priesthood; in the *Code of Canon Law*, it is the ontological presence of Jesus Christ, namely, the fact that Jesus Christ is present in the priest who acts *in persona Christi*. Canon 1168 affirms: "The minister of sacramentals is a cleric who has been provided with the requisite power."[293] And can. 1169 confirms: "Those marked with

---

[290] Cf. Anton Ziegenaus, *Die Heilsgegenwart in der Kirche. Sakramentenlehre*, vol. VII, (Aachen: MM Verlag, 2003), 495.
[291] *CCC*, 1669.
[292] Lang, "Theologies of Blessing," 42.
[293] can. 1168.

the episcopal character and presbyters permitted by law or legitimate grant can perform consecrations and dedications validly."[294] In other words, every priest is an ordinary minister of those blessings which are not reserved to the pope and the bishop. But the underlying problem and inconsistency remains unresolved. Nevertheless, it should be clear that only a sacramental perspective can facilitate the correct understanding of the sacramentals.

4.5. The Common or Ministerial Priesthood

When considering the common priesthood (that is, the priestly dignity in which all baptized participate), it is helpful to return once again to canon law. Canon 1168 affirms: "According to the norms of the liturgical books and to the judgment of the local ordinary, lay persons who possess the appropriate qualities can also administer some sacramentals."[295] This affirmation clearly expresses the previously mentioned tension. The number highlights "appropriate qualities," which is not at all a theological notion, and dismally allows even more for a functional emphasis and understanding.

And this led to a paradoxical situation. On the one hand, laypeople have taken things out of the priests' hands, things to which the laypeople are not entitled. On the other hand, a sound practice and use of sacramentals has been largely abandoned. This becomes clear in a look at common practice before the Second Vatican Council. Mothers and fathers were used to blessing their children before they left home, or even on ordinary mornings. The sprinkling with holy water, accompanied by a prayer and the sign of the cross, was a frequent practice among the faithful, as a sacred sign of protection and devotion. It was also common that, after evening prayers, and before the children went to bed, parents made the sign of the cross

---

[294] can. 1169 §1.
[295] can. 1168.

on the forehead of their children. Scapulars were widespread, as was the wearing of the Miraculous Medal, and the like. Most of these sacramentals — which were even more widely applied in the monasteries by the superiors, abbesses, and abbots — were abandoned after the conclusion of the Second Vatican Council. Some considered them to be a leftover of past times, rooted in a feudal understanding of submission. Others considered them simply superstitious. Undoubtedly, rationalism has contributed to this development, which tends to exclude the supernatural, adopting that tiresome functional view, and degrading a faith-based understanding.

Religious communities, until this time fervent dispensers of sacramentals (cf. St. Benedict's Medal, etc.), abandoned their use to a great extent. Religious went so far as to refuse the blessing of their monastery or convent, especially when associated with apotropaic elements. On the other hand, they have had no problems in welcoming practices which are contrary to the Faith and even against the first commandment. Not a few religious communities adopted esoteric practices, such as pendulums, yoga, reiki, and others. To put it mildly, there is a certain relationship between the abandoning of the sacramentals and the acceptance of those practices which are at odds with Catholic teaching.

This confusion, which had a deep impact on religious life, has also affected the laity. As priests and other clerics and religious abandoned the practice of so many of these things, laypeople moved in to fill the void, imparting blessings and performing rites that are properly reserved to an ordained minister. While it is true that laypeople can bless certain things and obtain spiritual fruits, especially if the particular layperson lives a holy life, he may only give a blessing by the merits of his personal sanctity; in contrast, an ordained minister gives blessings and so imparts grace by the merits of his ontological configuration with Christ, that is, by virtue of the fact that, through his ministerial office, he is acting as Christ. Consequently, there is a profound difference concerning these two distinct administrations of the sacramentals, which must be taken into consideration. Therefore, a layperson may bless certain things or persons, but in a different way than an ordained minister. The priestly blessing with the gesture of the sign of the cross ought to be reserved to the ordained minister.[296]

Whenever the sacramental idea is misunderstood,[297] abandoned, or not accepted, any consideration of the sacramentals will be deficient. Sacramentals and their spiritual effects cannot be understood from a functional perspective. For that reason, sacramentals (and sacraments as well) must have as their starting point the sacramental idea — which includes the supernatural — otherwise, they will become incomprehensible. Disregarding this fundamental principle has led to a development in which the laity is clericalized and the clergy is secularized; this process is increasing continuously, causing gradually more confusion. According to a sacramental understanding, there is a fundamental difference between the common and the hierarchical priesthood, as affirmed in the Dogmatic Constitution *Lumen Gentium*:

> Though they differ from one another in essence and not only in degree, the common priesthood of the faithful and the ministerial or hierarchical priesthood are nonetheless interrelated: each of them in its own special way is a participation in the one priesthood of Christ. The ministerial priest, by the sacred power he enjoys, teaches and rules the priestly people; acting in the person of Christ, he makes present the Eucharistic sacrifice, and offers it to God in the name of all the people. But the faithful, in virtue of their royal priesthood, join in the offering of the Eucharist. They likewise exercise that priesthood in receiving the sacraments, in prayer and thanksgiving, in the witness of a holy life, and by self-denial and active charity.[298]

---

[296] Cf. BoB, 16–18.
[297] See chap. 2.3.3.
[298] LG, 10.

The difference "in essence" refers to an ontological distinction (a distinction in nature) of great importance. The priest is consecrated; however, this consecration cannot be compared to a constitutive blessing, for it marks in him an ontological difference that makes him a sharer in Christ's priesthood. Federico Suárez writes: "He is a priest continuously, internally, invisibly; he is a priest always and at every moment, whether he is performing the highest and most sublime office or the most vulgar and humble action of his ordinary life.... A priest is another Christ. This is so by virtue of the nature of the priesthood itself, which is a participation and continuance of Christ's priesthood on the cross, where he died to redeem man from the slavery of sin."[299]

Columba Marmion explains that the priest has no power which is not part of Christ's. "He is the one source of the whole priesthood which glorifies God in the manner conceived by Him."[300] This was brought into evidence by the Dogmatic Constitution *Lumen Gentium*. The ministerial priesthood differs in essence; it is a gift for the People of God since the priest acts in the person of Christ, making Him and His divine power present.

Lumen Gentium affirmed, therefore, that even though both forms are different by essence, they are interrelated, and "each of them in its own special way is a participation in the one priesthood of Christ."[301] However, the way of participation is entirely different, which can be summarized as follows:

[299] Federico Suárez, *About Being a Priest*, (Dublin: Scepter Publishers, 1997), 8–9. Highly recommended and profound are Cardinal Manning's remarks concerning the priesthood, in his work of lasting relevance. Cf. Henry E. Manning, *The Eternal Priesthood*, a reprint of the 8th ed., (New York: Catholic Publications Society Co., 2014).

[300] Columba Marmion, *Christ – The Ideal of the Priest. Spiritual Conferences*, trans. Matthew Dillon, (St. Louis: Herder, 1952), 20. In the same direction aim the remarks of Marc Ouellet, *Amici dello sposo. Per una visione rinnovata del celibato sacerdotale,* (Siena: Cantagalli, 2019), esp. 34–41.

[301] LG, 10.

Common Priesthood of the Faithful	Ministerial/Hierarchical Priesthood
Participating in and receiving Christ's priesthood (receiving character)	Giving and administrating Christ's priesthood (giving character)
Joining in the offering and receiving of divine grace	Carrying a sacred power
Offering prayer and thanksgiving	Acting divinely in the Person of Christ
Witnessing a holy life	Teaching and ruling the priestly people

Within the context of the affirmation "difference in essence," the sentence "*a laici congruis qualitatibus pareditis*" ("laypersons who possess the appropriate qualities") has provoked some debates among the participants of the Second Vatican Council. The former *peritus* and expert in liturgical matters, Josef Andreas Jungmann (d. 1975), a prominent Jesuit priest from Innsbruck and a supporter of the Liturgical Movement who was involved in the preparation of the conciliar text, provides an interesting commentary:

> The last sentence is to be traced to a resolution from mission bishops in the assembly of the Council. It means that suitable laypeople, who are in the service of the Church, like catechists, lay brethren, helpers in pastoral work, can bless and say prayers in an official capacity. In this way the Christianization of a frequent custom could be greatly facilitated in mission lands. Such a proposal signifies an innovation at the most ... in comparison with present-day notions. The proposal was accepted, but not without strong resistance (1637 affirmative and 607 negative votes), which found expression also at the final voting on the chapter in 184 modi which were either of a negative nature or asked for reservations, and even on 21 November 1963, after the

explanation of the relator to justify the proposal (yes), in 132 negative votes.[302]

The Commission declared that according to current canon law (from 1917), sacramentals were not by nature reserved to clerics; moreover, it was confirmed that even a lector could bless fruits and bread, and not every blessing was necessarily bound to the sacred power of the ministerial priesthood.[303] It will be helpful to briefly follow this line of argumentation, because it provides some insights for the understanding of the sacramentals and their renewed use.

According to this line of reasoning, a sacramental understanding (of the minister) was obscured, and therefore the role of the minister was soon understood according to a functional perspective. Pierre-Marie Gy suggested that, under certain circumstances and according to pastoral opportunities, blessings could be administered by a priest or by a layperson. It was even concluded that it "should be clear that the liturgical celebration is not just that of the priest who blesses."[304] Of course, the celebration of a liturgical action is always a celebration of the whole Church; however, the concept "celebration" must be correctly understood. Johannes Nebel pointed out that, in the years following the Council, there was a truncated understanding of the sacramental action. The *actio*, that is, the divine action in which the believer participates, came to be understood as the *celebratio* of the congregation. In the process, the latter was increasingly understood in functional terms. Therefore, in the end, it is no longer the divine mystery in which the believer participates, but the celebration (*celebratio*)

---

[302] Josef Jungmann, "Constitution on the Sacred Liturgy," 55.
[303] Cf. Francisco Gil Hellín, *Constitutio de sacra liturgia, Sacrosanctum Concilium. Concilii Vaticani II synopsis in ordinem redigens schemata cum relationibus necnon patrum orationes atque animadversiones*, vol. 5, (Vatican City: Libreria Editrice Vaticana, 2003), 241.
[304] So quoted in Lang, "Theologies of Blessing," 36.

as such.[305] A few experts have contributed significantly to this fundamental shift. It is surprising how influential singular experts have been during the realization of this "reform," and how they applied certain criteria which did not correspond to the Second Vatican Council nor to the Tradition of the Church, but to the premises of modernity.

Above all, there are two considerations which would argue in favor of extending the use of the rites of blessings to laypeople:

> First, the New Testament concept of blessing as giving thanks and praise to the Creator for his good gifts of Creation, and, secondly, the need to promote the use of blessings in an increasingly secularized world. This being said, the Congregation's Plenary Assembly held that laypeople should not pronounce blessings in the presence of a priest or deacon, and that the laity's use of blessing should be restricted to the context of the family, such as parents blessing children, yet not when for instance a priest is visiting the families of his parish. From the brief text recorded in Notitiae, it would appear that extending the rites of blessings to laypeople was met with reserve by the cardinals and bishops who were then members of the Vatican dicastery.[306]

Today, a certain parallel to the time of the Protestant reformation can be affirmed: the difference between the common and the ministerial priesthood is often no longer understood, or the distinction is even neglected. But if this meaning and correct understanding are lost — a meaning and understanding which can only be comprehensible when approaching the topic from a sacramental perspective — the sacramentals will also become incomprehensible. The minister of the sacramentals is an instrument of Christ, "so as to make room for the Logos himself and, through fellowship with the human Jesus, to draw people into

---

[305] Cf. Johannes Nebel, "Die *participatio plena et actuosa*," 20.
[306] Ibid., 36–37.

fellowship with the living God."[307] Therefore, he does not act of his own volition. Pope Benedict explained something similar during a homily at the conclusion of the year for priests: "The priesthood, then, is not simply 'office' but sacrament: God makes use of us poor men in order to be, through us, present to all men and women, and to act on their behalf. This audacity of God who entrusts himself to human beings — who, conscious of our weaknesses, nonetheless considers men capable of acting and being present in his stead — this audacity of God is the true grandeur concealed in the word 'priesthood.'"[308]

4.6. Theological Considerations

Before concluding the fourth chapter and, therefore, the first part of this book, it will be helpful to summarize some theological considerations concerning the ministers and recipients of sacramentals; these considerations provide the background for the practical application of sacramentals, since the *lex celebrandi* (the law of celebration) must reflect the *lex credendi* (the law of belief, or faith) and vice versa.[309] The problem of the renewal of the sacramentals lies in the way it was brought about. As seen above, it was not done according to the principle of organic growth, as was directed in *Sacrosanctum Concilium*,[310] but by applying a hermeneutic of rupture.[311] Whenever this is done, it is opposed to real reform; this is because authentic reform leads to the rediscovery of the original form, and

---

[307] Joseph Ratzinger, *Pilgrim Fellowship of Faith. The Church as Communion*, trans. Henry Taylor, (San Francisco: Ignatius Press, 2005), 160.
[308] Benedict XVI, Homily in Conclusion of the Year for Priests, June 11, 2010, in http://www.vatican.va/content/benedict-xvi/en/homilies/2010/documents/hf_ben-xvi_hom_20100611_concl-anno-sac.html [12.5.2023].
[309] Cf. Hector Scerri, *Koinonia, Diakonia and Martyria. Interrelated Themes in Patristic Sacramental Theology as expounded by Adalbert-G. Hamman*, (Malta: University of Malta, 1999), 159–165.
[310] Cf. SC, 23.
[311] Cf. chap. 1.3.

is, therefore, possible only according to organic growth.[312] The German writer and novelist Martin Mosebach affirmed: "In the ancient world, if a ruler broke a tradition he was regarded as having committed an act of tyrannis."[313] Mosebach's judgment is remarkable, for he relates this statement primarily to the liturgical reform.

De benedictionibus was influenced by a hermeneutic of rupture with the living Tradition of the Church. This is due especially to the methodology by which it was developed, which considered only Scripture and the early Church as sources for renewal. Blessings were primarily conceived as acts of thanksgiving and praise of God. The act of blessing "consists above all in the recognition and proclamation of the goodness of created things and of the loving care of their Creator. The apotropaic aspect of blessing, that is, to protect against the influences of evil — and of the Evil One, is largely absent."[314]

The general principles for the renewal of the sacramentals, as proposed by Gy, were applied, often causing confusion, especially with regard to the understanding of the fundamental difference between the common priesthood of the laity and the ministerial priesthood. The Jesuit Father Mario Lessi-Ariosto, then undersecretary of the Congregation for Divine Worship and the Discipline of the Sacraments, affirmed in 1986 that the content of *De benedictionibus* "is practically all new."[315] This does not only — as said above — concern the *lex orandi* and the *lex celebrandi* but necessarily affects the *lex credendi*. It gives rise to several questions regarding the underlying theology of such reforms.

[312] Cf. Ralph Weimann, *Dogma und Fortschritt*.
[313] Martin Mosebach, *The Heresy of Formlessness. The Roman Liturgy and Its Enemy*, trans. Graham Harrison, (San Francisco: Ignatius Press, 2006), 24.
[314] Lang, "Theologies of Blessing," 44.
[315] Cf. Mario Lessi-Ariosto, Linee interpretative dell'iter redazionale del *De benedictionibus*, in Rivista liturgica 73 (1986): 214–230, here 214. See also Reiner Kaczynski, "Blessings in Rome and the Non-Roman West," in Anscar J. Chupungco (ed.), *Handbook for Liturgical Studies*, vol. 4, *Sacraments and Sacramentals*, (Collegeville: Liturgical Press, 1997), 393–410, here 393–394.

These considerations touch on a key question, which was addressed by Pope Benedict XVI in his Christmas address to the Roman Curia of 2005. He explained that there are two different hermeneutics:

> On the one hand, there is an interpretation that I would call 'a hermeneutic of discontinuity and rupture'; it has frequently availed itself of the sympathies of the mass media, and also one trend of modern theology. On the other, there is the 'hermeneutic of reform', of renewal in the continuity of the one subject-Church which the Lord has given to us. She is a subject which increases in time and develops, yet always remaining the same, the one subject of the journeying People of God. The hermeneutic of discontinuity risks ending in a split between the pre-conciliar Church and the post-conciliar Church.[316]

Thus, it must be concluded that the process of revision of the sacramentals did not fulfill the positive criteria described by Pope Benedict of an organic growth within a hermeneutic of reform in continuity with the one subject Church. The intervention of the Congregation for Divine Worship and the Discipline of the Sacraments in 2002 supports this position,[317] as does Daniel Van Slyke, who says that the "present Order is in no way derived from the previous Order; it is not a revision, but an entirely new work."[318] Stephen Rossetti summarizes these problems in his book, *The Priestly Blessing*, stating that the revision was criticized by some theologians because of the lack of "such words as 'bless,' 'consecrate,' or 'sanctify' in addition to the deletion of an apotropaic function."[319] This has led to a real dilemma. On the one hand, sacramentals are instituted by the Church and must be faithfully observed. On the other hand, the renewed sacramentals were composed based on a hermeneutic of rupture, which rendered them ineffective. Whenever there is confusion, a basic criterion remains the living Tradition

---

[316] Benedict XVI, Address to the Roman Curia.
[317] See chap. 3.5.
[318] Daniel G. Van Slyke, "The Order for Blessing Water: Past and Present," in Antiphon 8:2 (2003): 12–23, here 17.
[319] Stephen J. Rossetti, *The Priestly Blessing*, 79.

of the Church. In other words, there is a need for further studies, which must include the richness of the living Tradition and must consider it as its *princeps analogatum* (the principle by which all other principles are measured). This might even lead to a "reform of the reform,"[320] one that could correct some or even all of the erroneous developments that have come about because of a foundation on this hermeneutic of rupture.[321]

The living Tradition of the Church is a vital force; this is especially true of the sacramentals. Therefore, it is important to draw from their flow and to bring forth "the new and the old" (Matt. 13:52). A sacramental perspective requires such a hermeneutic. Blessings, consecrations, exorcisms, and sacred objects cannot be understood from a functional perspective; they must instead be related to the ontological reality of Jesus Christ being present in His Church. Sacramentals work *ex opere operantis Ecclesiae*; they require devout participation in Christ's action to obtain spiritual fruits.

The minister, provided with the requisite power, and following the appropriate rite (one that includes the designated formulas and sacred signs) serves like an instrument. Unlike the sacraments, spiritual fruitfulness does not depend solely (*ex opere operato*) on the efficacy of the sacramentals, even though the formulas are also of particular importance. Nevertheless, it is the moral dignity (holiness) of the minister and the recipient that are also fundamental to achieving spiritual fruitfulness. Therefore, the minister cannot be

---

[320] Joseph Ratzinger explained this concept in a conference, affirming that it refers to the new form: "If, by means of such a 'reform of the reform', we could get back to a faithful, ecclesial celebration of the liturgy, then this would in my opinion be itself an important step, because the *ecclesial dimension* of the liturgy would once more be clearly apparent." Joseph Ratzinger, TL, 565.

[321] Important landmarks from a canonical perspective on this path are provided by the work of Fernando Palacios Blanco, *El Romano Pontífice y la liturgia. Estudio histórico-jurídico del ejercito y desarollo de la potestad del Papa en materia litúrgica*, (Toledo: Instituto Teológico San Ildefonso, 2018). From a theological perspective see my work, *Dogma und Fortschritt*.

reduced to merely fulfilling a certain function, since he also participates as a believer (recipient) in the administration of the sacramentals. There is a great need for this to be rediscovered in today's Church, especially concerning the priests who administer the sacramentals. Their prayer life, their sacrifices, and their personal holiness can all contribute to unfolding a spiritual power concerning the sacramentals. What this means for practical implementation becomes particularly clear with regard to exorcisms.[322]

---

[322] Cf. chap. 7.

SECOND PART

Pastoral Considerations of the Sacramentals

✠ ✠ ✠

THE SECOND PART OF this book is going to be more practical. Nevertheless, the theological foundation of the sacramentals, which was considered in the first part, is of primary importance, as it allows their correct and therefore fruitful application. This is underlined above all by the fact that the *lex celebrandi* (the practical application) must correspond to the *lex credendi* (the Faith of the Church). However pastoral a concrete application may be, it will produce spiritual fruit only if it is an expression of good theology, which in turn follows the *regula fidei* (the rule of faith). To be very clear, there can be nothing that is separate from dogma that is an authoritative affirmation of revelation. Any pastoral application requires a grounding in the living Faith of the Church, a certain disposition on behalf of the faithful. It must reflect the Faith of the Church since it is done in the name of the Church; otherwise, it would lose its effectiveness. Sacramental grace comes from God and is transmitted through the Church, in which the faithful participate.

Spiritual fruits of the sacramentals are obtained through the intercession of the Church, and thus they correspond to the Faith of the Church, which is contained in the *lex credendi*. Sacred Scripture and the living Tradition, as well as the authentic Magisterium of the Church, are indispensable markers along the way. For that reason, it is important to embrace the Faith of the Church in all its purity and integrity.[323]

As discussed already, faith consists essentially of two dimensions.[324] On the one side, there is an objective and cognitive element of faith (*fides quae*). Faith in God implies the revealed content (the dogmas of faith), namely, that which is believed. The acceptance of revelation is the first step to belief. However, this is not only an academic exercise of some abstract truth, but the acceptance of Jesus Christ, true God, and true man, as He becomes accessible to us through Sacred Scripture and Tradition. Therefore, faith requires also the personal acceptance and assimilation of the revealed objective truth; it requires a personal act of faith (*fides qua*).[325] "There can be no subjective understanding of faith alone (*fides qua*), which is not linked to the authentic truth of God (*fides quae*), handed down in revelation and preserved in the Church. There is, therefore, 'a profound unity between the act by which we believe and the contents to which we give our assent.' "[326]

The sacramentals become effective according to the principle of *ex opere operantis*. Consequently, the *lex vivendi* (the life of the Church, the manner of living) should never contradict the *lex credendi*. Whenever someone does not live what he believes, he will turn into an unbeliever. If Christianity is first and foremost a way of life, it becomes clear how inseparable these two dimensions are. St. Paul made this point in his Letter to the Hebrews: "For it is impossible in the case of those who have once been enlightened and tasted the heavenly gift and shared in the Holy Spirit and tasted the good word of God and the powers of the age to come, and then have fallen away, to bring them to repentance

---

[323] Cf. Francis, LF, 48.
[324] Cf. chap. 3.2.
[325] Cf. International Theological Commission, "The Reciprocity," 4.
[326] Ibid., 51.

again, since they are recrucifying the Son of God for themselves and holding him up to contempt" (Heb. 6:4–6).

The actual crisis in the Church is indeed a crisis of faith because some — even shepherds — have left the path of faith. It is important not to forget the Lord's words: "If you keep my commandments, you will remain in my love, just as I have kept my Father's commandments and remain in his love" (John 15:10). Keeping God's commandments is the necessary precondition to receiving divine grace. Robert Dodaro made this clear in the debate over divorce and remarriage, which reflects fundamentally the relationship of *lex vivendi* and *lex credendi*. He wrote: "These are not a series of rules made up by the Church; they constitute divine law, and the Church cannot change them.... God's mercy does not dispense from following his commandments."[327]

Since sacramentals are no magic practices, they require a "devout participation," a life according to God's commandments and His grace. This is — as has been shown — important regarding the minister and the recipient. Understanding should be opened up through appropriate catechesis, guiding the faithful to proper participation. From this perspective, it becomes understandable, why sacramentals include a "missionary dimension." They offer great opportunities to guide people toward the sacraments, to change their lives, and to grow in friendship with Jesus Christ, from whom sacramentals draw their spiritual power. They are a continuous reminder that the source of all grace is God.

Priests are especially supposed to be dispensers of grace, to participate in the Church's work of sanctification. For this reason, they need a mentality that emphasizes and favors a life of holiness. The Dogmatic Constitution on the Church encourages this path: "Therefore, all the faithful of Christ are invited to strive for the holiness and

---

[327] Robert Dodaro, "The Argument in Brief," in ibid. (ed.), *Remaining in the Truth of Christ. Marriage and Communion in the Catholic Church*, (San Francisco: Ignatius Press 2014), 11–35, here 35.

perfection of their own proper state. Indeed they have an obligation to so strive. Let all then have care that they guide aright their own deepest sentiments of soul. Let neither the use of the things of this world nor attachment to riches, which is against the spirit of evangelical poverty, hinder them in their quest for perfect love."[328]

Personal holiness makes the sacramentals more effective and fruitful; this happens whenever the personal lifestyle corresponds to divine grace. Scripture says: "The person who is trustworthy in very small matters is also trustworthy in great ones" (Luke 16:10). Little does not mean unimportant: The little things within life often have great effects or lead to great consequences. It was always part of the Catholic tradition to pay special attention to the details; it is through them that many things are revealed. Faith becomes manifest not only in the supreme act of martyrdom, but must become manifest in daily life. All of this is important regarding the practical application of the sacramentals, to which the further explanations will be dedicated.

---

[328] LG, 42.

FIVE
✥ ✥ ✥

Invocations of the Name of Jesus Christ

IN THIS CHAPTER, THE focus will be on two elements, both of which are an integral part of each of the sacramentals: the invocation of the name of Jesus Christ and the sign of the cross. The *Catechism of the Catholic Church* also emphasizes these two elements as an integral part of any blessing: "The Church imparts blessings by invoking the name of Jesus, usually while making the holy sign of the cross of Christ."[329] Although both are of such fundamental importance, many people today are unaware of them. Today, it is common that Catholics talk about Jesus as "our brother" and "our friend," which is undoubtedly correct. And yet it is limited, for much more is associated with the name of the Savior Jesus Christ. His name is not "just" like any other name; it signifies a mission, and it has an inherent power.

This aspect of Jesus Christ's name will become more comprehensible when sacramentals are approached with "devout participation," which in turn requires a basic knowledge of the subject matter. For this reason, it will be helpful to dedicate one chapter to discovering the meaning and significance of the invocation of the name of Jesus Christ.

[329] CCC, 1671.

5.1. The Biblical Foundation of Invocations

The etymological meaning of the name *Jesus* is described in the Gospel of Matthew, as He who "will save his people from their sins" (Matt. 1:21). *Jesus* signifies "God saves." For that reason, a devout reverence is presupposed for everyone who wants to invoke His name, as described in St. Paul's Letter to the Philippians: "God greatly exalted him and bestowed on him the name that is above every name, that at the name of Jesus every knee should bend, of those in heaven and on earth and under the earth, and every tongue confess that Jesus Christ is Lord, to the glory of God the Father" (Phil. 2:9–11). In the name of Jesus, demons will be driven out, the faithful will speak new languages (cf. Mark 16:17–18), and miracles will occur (cf. Acts 9:34).

The saving character related to His name becomes even more evident since *Jesus* is usually combined with the title of honor: Christ. The word *Christ* derives from the Greek χριστός (*chrīstós*), and it signifies the anointed. Anointing had a special importance in the Old Testament since the prophets, the kings of Israel, and the high priests were anointed (e.g., 1 Kings 19:15–16). In the case of Jesus Christ, this must be understood in a new sense, as St. Thomas explained. The word "Christ" signifies "both the Godhead anointing and the manhood anointed."[330] He is the one who has been anointed (by the Father) and who anoints mankind. His very name characterizes His mission to bring salvation, to which all sacraments and sacramentals are ordered. Therefore, His name expresses both: identity and mission.[331] Already the testimony of the apostles shows that, when His name is invoked with faith, spiritual benefits are obtained, since His person (identity) is intrinsically linked to His mission (salvation). The apostles, however, had seen His mighty deeds when they invoked His name, and they associated it with His presence. Just

---

[330] Thomas Aquinas, STh III, q.16, a.5.
[331] Cf. *CCC*, 430.

as when they were gathered at Pentecost and He miraculously entered through the locked doors (cf. John 20:19), His saving power becomes present when His name is invoked with living faith.

Thus, the name of *Christ* is also a profession of faith, as seen when St. Peter confessed: "You are the Messiah [Christ]" (Mark 8:29). The title *Christ* indicates His identity, as Peter affirmed on various occasions (see Luke 9:20), and as described in the Gospel of Matthew: "You are the Messiah [Christ], the Son of the living God" (Matt. 16:16). Joseph Ratzinger comments on these passages: "What it means to call Jesus 'Christ' is explained: namely, that he is the 'Lord,' that he himself is God from God and not merely a man favored by God."[332] This is not the place to give a full explanation of the christological and soteriological (relating to salvation) significance of His name; for the purposes of our discussion, it is sufficient to point out that the invocation of the name of *Jesus Christ* has a strong biblical foundation, which allows us to draw conclusions about its use in the sacramentals.

5.1.1. Salvation

A Christian becomes a Christian when he or she accepts Jesus Christ in faith, which includes the *fides qua* and the *fides quae*, His humanity and divinity. This is affirmed in the First Letter of John: "Who is the liar? Whoever denies that Jesus is the Christ. Whoever denies the Father and the Son, this is the antichrist. No one who denies the Son has the Father, but whoever confesses the Son has the Father as well. Let what you heard from the beginning remain in you. If what you heard from the beginning remains in you, then you will remain in the Son and in the Father. And this is the promise that he made us: eternal life" (1 John 2:22–25). The faith in Jesus Christ becomes operative

---

[332] Joseph Ratzinger, *On the Way to Jesus Christ*, trans. Michael J. Miller, (San Francisco: Ignatius Press, 2005), 57.

through Baptism through which the faithful are reborn as sons of God and freed from sin.

The invocation of the name of Jesus Christ can never be only an abstract affirmation; it implies the acceptance of God who reveals Himself. Consequently, salvation is linked to this name. Whoever accepts the path of salvation will accept Jesus Christ. What is more, he or she will be baptized in His name and becomes a bearer of His name. Accordingly, the disciples are called Christians (cf. Acts 11:26), and they are anointed for eternal life.

Salvation is related to this name, for there "is no salvation through anyone else, nor is there any other name under heaven given to the human race by which we are to be saved" (Acts 4:12). For that reason, the Letter to the Romans says: "Everyone who calls on the name of the Lord will be saved" (Rom. 10:13). This is also affirmed in the book of Revelation. Those chosen for eternal life have written on their foreheads the name of Jesus Christ (cf. Rev. 14:1). The heavenly vision, as described by the Apostle John, shows that the elected "will look upon his face, and his name will be on their foreheads" (Rev. 22:4). These few examples show that salvation is correlated to the "one mediator between God and the human race, Christ Jesus, himself human, who gave himself as ransom for all (1 Tim. 2:4–6)."[333]

5.1.2. Purification, Sanctification, and Justification

The First Letter to the Corinthians begins with the following words: "Paul, called to be an apostle of Christ Jesus by the will of God, and Sosthenes our brother, to the church of God that is in Corinth, to you who have been sanctified in Christ Jesus, called to be holy, with all those everywhere who call upon the name of our Lord Jesus Christ, their Lord and ours" (1 Cor. 1:1–2). For the apostles, the name of

---

[333] CDF, Declaration *Dominus Iesus*, August 6, 2000, 13, in https://www.vatican.va/roman_curia/congregations/cfaith/documents/rc_con_cfaith_doc_20000806_dominus-iesus_en.html [12.5.2023].

Jesus Christ is intrinsically linked to His presence. They assemble in His name (cf. 1 Cor 5:4), and they are aware that by invoking His name with faith, His divine power becomes effective, granting fruits of purification, sanctification, and justification.

His Word purifies, as the Gospel of John affirms: "You are already pruned because of the word that I spoke to you" (John 15:3). Also, St. Paul wrote to the Corinthians: "Now you have had yourselves washed, you were sanctified, you were justified in the name of the Lord Jesus Christ and in the Spirit of our God" (1 Cor. 6:11). This brings to light a basic condition of being human and injured by Original Sin. Every person is in need of purification of sins, which only God can give and which He has provided through Jesus Christ, "who gave himself for us to deliver us from all lawlessness and to cleanse for himself a people as his own, eager to do what is good" (Titus 2:14).

Purification is a basic dimension concerning the practical application of all sacramentals since it is the precondition for sanctification. The eternal Son of the Father came into this world to redeem us from sins, offering forgiveness and purification and leading to sanctifying grace. The Letter to the Hebrews especially underlines the importance of sanctification, which corresponds to the divine will because "we have been consecrated through the offering of the body of Jesus Christ once for all" (Heb. 10:10). Sanctification is obtained in Jesus Christ and, for that reason, all Christians are "called to be holy, with all those everywhere who call upon the name of our Lord Jesus Christ, their Lord and ours" (1 Cor. 1:2).

At the same time, sanctification is linked to justification, and both are obtained through faith in Jesus Christ. The Letter to the Romans affirms that it is through faith in Jesus Christ that Christians "are justified freely by his grace through the redemption in Christ Jesus, whom God set forth as an expiation" (Rom. 3:24–25). The invocation of the name of Jesus Christ is, consequently, a powerful means, through which fruits of purification, sanctification, and justification can be obtained.

5.1.3. Healing

The gift of healing is also related to the invocation of the name of Jesus Christ. Precisely in His name, the sick are healed. St. Peter justifies the healing of a cripple to the elders and leaders of the people, saying: "If we are being examined today about a good deed done to a cripple, namely, by what means he was saved, then all of you and all the people of Israel should know that it was in the name of Jesus Christ the Nazorean whom you crucified, whom God raised from the dead; in his name this man stands before you healed" (Acts 4:9–10). In this case — and in several other cases — the grace of healing is granted through the invocation of the name of Jesus Christ. The apostles had received the authority to cure diseases (cf. Luke 9:1–2), and this is accomplished by invoking the name of Jesus Christ; Peter makes this very clear: "'In the name of Jesus Christ the Nazorean, (rise and) walk.' Then Peter took him by the right hand and raised him up, and immediately his feet and ankles grew strong. He leaped up, stood, and walked around, and went into the temple with them, walking and jumping and praising God" (Acts 3:6–8). On this point, it is important to underline that the graces granted by invoking the name of Jesus presuppose that inner attitude (devout participation) which was discussed at length in the first part of this book.

5.1.4. Protection and Liberation against Demonic Actions

Since the name of Jesus Christ is "above every name" (Phil. 2:9), this invocation also has a strong apotropaic (anti-demonic) dimension. Nothing is more sublime than the name of Jesus Christ. It contains an overall surpassing power, which becomes fruitful in those who believe in Him. It is a power "far above every principality, authority, power, and dominion, and every name that is named not only in this age but also in the one to come" (Eph. 1:21). Every spirit and every spiritual creature must submit to the name of Jesus Christ, both because

His name surpasses any other name and also because His name expresses His identity and mission.

Therefore, the invocation of the name of Jesus Christ is a powerful means to liberate houses, objects, or persons from any evil influence. Jesus Christ is the truth (cf. John 14:6) and this truth will set us free (cf. John 8:32). It is Jesus Christ who liberates from evil; He is the one who frees from any evil influence (cf. Gal 5:1). When His name is invoked in confidence, anything becomes possible. The Acts of the Apostles bears witness to this in various places; for example, when St. Paul was "annoyed," as Scripture says, by a slave girl with an oracular spirit. Finally, he turned to the spirit in her and said: "'I command you in the name of Jesus Christ to come out of her.' Then it came out at that moment" (Acts 16:18).

5.1.5. Do Everything in the Name of the Lord Jesus

Finally, there is a general admonition for every Christian to live a life that corresponds to the dignity of a Christian. This will be possible only if the following is respected: "And whatever you do, in word or deed, do everything in the name of the Lord Jesus, giving thanks to God the Father through him" (Col. 3:17). The effectiveness of the invocation of the name of Jesus Christ depends, as in the case of all sacramentals, on the *ex opere operantis Ecclesiae*. In other words, the name of Jesus Christ must be glorified in us (cf. 2 Thess. 1:12) to obtain spiritual fruits. This fact has to be rediscovered, especially in our day, which is often dominated by rationalism, materialism, and relativism. Only then will the word of the Lord become true: "Amen, I say to you, if you have faith the size of a mustard seed, you will say to this mountain, 'Move from here to there,' and it will move. Nothing will be impossible for you" (Matt. 17:20).

The apostles considered themselves to be sent in the name of the Lord. Through the apostolic succession, sacramentals, in similarity to the sacraments, are administered in His name. Sacred Scripture testifies to the indwelling power of this invocation and its practice in the early Church. Thus it should always be present when the sacramentals are used.

5.2. Invocations: Practical Application

As just demonstrated, because the name of Jesus is above every name, its invocation has a particular importance for the practical application of sacramentals. The name has an indwelling power to obtain spiritual fruits relevant for all types of sacramentals.

The invocation of the name of Jesus Christ is and can be considered a sacred sign. As is true for all signs, it can be perceived through the senses. It is sacred because the name of Jesus Christ is above every name, before which "every knee should bend" (Phil. 2:10). To obtain spiritual fruits, the invocation of His name must be made with due reverence and respect, for even the angels and evil spirits tremble and bow their knees before Jesus Christ. Furthermore, the sign of the invocation of His name is sacred because it expresses His mission and identity.

Until the liturgical reform, it was obligatory that, whenever the holy name of Jesus Christ was mentioned in the liturgy, in readings, or other liturgical texts, the priest would bow his head to emphasize the importance of this name and the reverence due to it. This practice could and should be revived today. It is a sad reality that many of these emblematic elements of the former liturgy were abandoned. In some parts it is still a custom that when the Gloria or the *Salve Regina* are recited today, some faithful still bow their head when the name *Jesus* is invoked. This is a "leftover" of a general rule, which was previously applied everywhere. However, it is not only this exterior sign of deference and respect that matters, as the internal disposition of honor due to Jesus Christ must also be properly oriented. Nevertheless, these small external gestures are important because they remind us of the indwelling power associated to the name of Jesus Christ; the physical should mirror and make visible the spiritual and invisible. A "new" consciousness must be revived, not focusing only on the exterior, but also with this emphasis that one correctly expresses the interior disposition through exterior signs.

The Gospel of John affirms: "Whatever you ask in my name, I will do, so that the Father may be glorified in the Son. If you ask anything of me in my name, I will do it" (John 14:13–14). This quotation from Sacred Scripture can serve as a key to use correctly the name of Jesus Christ in the context of the sacramentals. Since they are related to some type of petition — spiritual graces are invoked — this must be kept in mind whenever sacramentals are administered. Therefore, each petition is not only related to the name of Jesus Christ in some vague way, but they are in fact actually administered in His name, by the power of His name. The underlying theological reality of all of this is the Incarnation. As shown before, whenever the incarnational principle is respected and taken into consideration, particular graces may be received, as described in the Gospel of Mark: "These signs will accompany those who believe: in my name, they will drive out demons, they will speak new languages. They will pick up serpents (with their hands), and if they drink any deadly thing, it will not harm them. They will lay hands on the sick, and they will recover" (Mark 16:17–18). Yet the effectiveness of the invocation of the name of Jesus Christ depends on the living faith of the recipient, on the devout participation of that recipient.[334] To invoke His name signifies calling upon His presence; it signifies welcoming the Son of God.[335]

The *Catechism* presents a list of synonyms for the name of *Jesus Christ*, such as "Son of God," "Word of God," "Lord," "Savior," "Lamb of God," "King," "Beloved Son," "Son of the Virgin," "Good Shepherd," "our Life," "our Light," and so on; to each of these is attributed the same indwelling power that is within the name *Jesus Christ*

---

[334] Cf. chap. 3.
[335] Cf. CCC, 2666.

itself.³³⁶ And, just as His name must be called upon with true and firm belief in His identity as God and in His divine power, so too must the invocation of Him by these synonyms be done with an understanding and firm faith that He is true God and true man.

Finally, the invocation of the name of Jesus Christ can be done in two different ways. Even though sacred language is different from daily language,³³⁷ with regards to the invocations at least, it follows a similar structure. Therefore, a person can be invoked directly, for example, "Peter, please come!" or indirectly, "May Peter come?" Even though the invocation of the name of Jesus Christ refers explicitly to a supernatural reality, and therefore to a meta-empirical dimension that transcends the order of the natural,³³⁸ the distinction remains valid and, therefore, two important conclusions must be made.

5.2.1. Imperative Invocations

The direct form of invoking the name of Jesus Christ is called the imperative invocation. Among Pentecostals and Charismatics, this practice is quite common. Catholics are often not familiar with it; in some instances, this practice has even been abandoned. Nevertheless, an imperative usage signifies addressing something or someone directly in the name of Jesus Christ and in His power. This form is often found in the New Testament — for example, in the Acts of the Apostles, when Peter said to the cripple "In the name of Jesus Christ the Nazorean, (rise and)

---

[336] *CCC*, 2665.

[337] Uwe Michael Lang points out three main characteristics "1) Sacred language is stable; it shows tenacity in holding on to archaic linguistic forms"; "2) Foreign elements are introduced in order to associate with ancient religious tradition; a case in point is the Hebrew biblical vocabulary in the Latin use of Christians"; "3) Sacred language uses rhetorical figures that are typical of oral style, such as parallelism and antithesis, rhythmic clausulae, rhyme, and alliteration." Lang, *The Voice of the Church at Prayer. Reflections on Liturgy and Language*, (San Francisco: Ignatius Press, 2012), 47–48.

[338] Cf. Louis Depré, *Symbols of the Sacred*, (Grand Rapids: William B. Eerdmans Publishing Company, 2000), 46.

walk" (Acts 3:6). This form is frequently used during exorcisms, as also described in the Acts of the Apostles: "I command you in the name of Jesus Christ to come out of her" (Acts 16:18).

These examples show that the "I" together with the imperative are the characteristic expressions of this form. Also, certain prayers include this type of invocation. In his Letter to the Romans, Paul wrote of the great trials and difficulties he had experienced: "I urge you, [brothers,] in the name of our Lord Jesus Christ and by the love of the Spirit, to join me in the struggle by your prayers to God on my behalf, that I may be delivered from the disobedient in Judea, and that my ministry for Jerusalem may be acceptable to the holy ones, so that I may come to you with joy by the will of God and be refreshed together with you" (Rom. 15:30–32).

"In the name of Jesus Christ" implies an appeal to His authority, and it usually entails a certain authority on behalf of the minister. At this point, it is helpful to call to mind that the minister must assure — as can. 1168 affirms — that he has been provided with the requisite power. Especially when referring to exorcisms, the imperative form is generally reserved for an ordained minister.[339] The observance of these rules is crucial, since authority must be respected and applied correctly.

Imperative prayer is distinct from imprecatory prayer. Especially in the Old Testament, several forms of the latter can be found. An imprecatory prayer, unlike an imperative prayer, does not necessarily imply a "command," but it does contain curses. They are usually meant to be invoked against the enemies of God and against one's own enemies. This is reflected, for example, in one of the Psalms: "May no one treat him with mercy or pity his fatherless children. May his posterity be destroyed, their name rooted out in the next

---

[339] Cf. Letter to Ordinaries regarding norms on Exorcism, September 29, 1985, in https://www.vatican.va/roman_curia/congregations/cfaith/documents/rc_con_cfaith_doc_19850924_exorcism_en.html [12.2.2023].

generation" (Ps. 109:12–13). To *imprecate* means to "curse or invoke evil upon." King David used this form quite frequently — for example: "Make their way slippery and dark, with the angel of the LORD pursuing them" (Ps. 35:6).[340] Jesus Christ referred to this Psalm in the Gospel of John (cf. John 15:11), but He significantly modified this practice of imprecation when He instructed us to pray for our enemies (Matt. 5:44–48). The new criterion is different: "Do not be conquered by evil but conquer evil with good" (Rom. 12:21).

Imprecatory prayers refer above all to the spiritual battle as described in the Letter to the Ephesians: "For our struggle is not with flesh and blood but with the principalities, with the powers, with the world rulers of this present darkness, with the evil spirits in the heavens" (Eph. 6:12). However, Christ's injunction to pray for our enemies and this reminder from Ephesians about the identity of our chief adversaries notwithstanding, it is remarkable to notice that the imprecatory prayer remains valid within an orthodox context. Additionally, because of the testimony provided in the New Testament, it becomes clear that any deviation from the revealed truth is a grave violation. In this context, such exhortations are still valid because Jesus Christ has revealed Himself as *the* truth (cf. John 14:6). For one example of the right context for imprecatory prayer in the New Testament, a look at Paul's Letter to the Galatians will be helpful: "But even if we or an angel from heaven should preach (to you) a gospel other than the one that we preached to you, let that one be accursed! As we have said before, and now I say again, if anyone preaches to you a gospel other than the one that you received, let that one be accursed! [imprecatory prayer]" (Gal 1:8–9). Because renouncing the truth signifies renouncing Jesus Christ Himself, this is where imprecatory prayers remain valid and still have a place. Outside of Scripture, this same procedure was adopted in the writings of several

---

[340] See also: Ps. 7, 55, 58, 69, 109, and 139.

councils with the so-called *"anathema sit."* Based on the New Testament, it derives from the Greek word *anathema*, which means being accursed, and, therefore, excommunicated. However, though canon law still mentions this in a rudimentary way, [341] the Second Vatican Council and the1983 Code abandoned this tradition.

In summary, then, the imperative form is distinct from the imprecatory prayer. They are different from each other in terms of basic meaning, and the imprecative prayer is a distinct form of invoking the name of Jesus Christ.

5.2.2. Deprecative Invocations

The second form of invoking the name of Jesus Christ is called a deprecative invocation. In this case, something or someone is addressed indirectly in the name of Jesus Christ. In this case, the minister generally doesn't use the "I" nor the imperative form. The Lord is invoked that He might hear the prayer and intervene on behalf of the one(s) praying. This type of prayer includes deprecatory language, emphasizing the weakness, smallness, or other littleness of condition of the one requesting help; the invocation reflects a request directed to God with the hope that He might grant what was requested. This is illustrated in the Psalms, for example: "Have pity on me, LORD, for I am weak; heal me, LORD, for my bones are shuddering" (Ps. 6:3).

Concerning the administration of the sacramentals, this distinction is important since it marks a big difference when making use of exorcisms. Whenever the deprecative form is used, the minister normally does not engage in the spiritual battle directly; rather, he invokes God to act against evil forces and/or to obtain certain graces. It is an intercessory prayer directed to God, often through the intercession of the Blessed Virgin Mary, St. Michael, and other angels and saints.

---

[341] can. 1364.

In a special way, deprecatory prayers reflect the ecclesiological dimension of the sacramentals,[342] for graces are requested through the mediation of members of the Mystical Body of Christ, being members of the Church. No direct commands are given. The prayer appeals to God to intervene, generally through the intercession of the invisible Church. It is also worth noting that, unlike other forms of invocation, the deprecative form is usually not reserved to the ordained minister; it is open to be exercised by every faithful person of goodwill.

These distinctions among the different types of invocations are of significance, especially regarding the different forms of liberation prayers (exorcisms). However, as indicated before, any type of prayer becomes fruitful to the degree in which the personal lifestyle of the one praying corresponds to it; yet again, the importance of the concept and application of devout participation becomes apparent.

5.3. Spiritual Effects Achieved through the Invocation of the Name of Jesus Christ

The Letter of James says that the "fervent prayer of a righteous person is very powerful" (James 5:16). However, there was and is no man more righteous than Jesus Christ. For that reason, it is important to invoke the name of Jesus Christ with the attitude of Martha, the sister of Lazarus, who confessed: "Lord, if you had been here, my brother would not have died. (But) even now I know that whatever you ask of God, God will give you" (John 11:21–22). Something similar is also expressed in the solicitation of the Blessed Virgin Mary for wine when she said to the servers: "Do whatever he tells you" (John 2:5).

The spiritual effects achieved through the invocation of the name of Jesus Christ depend above all on our personal acceptance of Jesus as Savior and Redeemer. The communion with Him makes them become fruitful, for, without Him, we "can do nothing" (John

---

[342] Cf. chap. 2.3.4.

15:5). Conversely, this means that anything can be done with Him. When considering what this means in practice, some of the most important spiritual fruits will be summarized, which were discussed in this chapter, and which can be achieved through the invocation of the name of Jesus Christ:

- ✜ Purification, sanctification, and justification
- ✜ Liberation and protection against demonic actions
- ✜ Healing
- ✜ Salvation

Besides other graces, these spiritual fruits can be obtained by anyone who invokes the name of Jesus Christ with faith. This invocation works at all times and in all places, especially if everything is done in the name of the Lord Jesus Christ. The recommendation of the Letter of James reminds us that the principle *ex opere operantis* always remains valid. Any petition must be presented "in faith, not doubting, for the one who doubts is like a wave of the sea that is driven and tossed about by the wind. For that person must not suppose that he will receive anything from the Lord, since he is a man of two minds, unstable in all his ways" (James 1:6–8).

The authority and spiritual power of the sacred name of Jesus Christ should be rightly understood, since all authority was given to Him (cf. Matt. 28:18). Thus, His name should be invoked with confidence appealing to His *divine* authority. He is the living Word of God. For this reason, this invocation is an integral part of any sacramental. By revealing His name, and by making it accessible, Jesus Christ provided us a type of vehicle (invocation) through which He grants spiritual benefits (grace). He is the primordial sacrament, and the very act of praying "Jesus Christ" effects what it signifies: God saves.

At this point, it becomes understandable that His name is not some sort of a magical formula, as if someone would just need to say it often enough to obtain whatever He desires. His name is a "program" through which we receive purification, liberation, healing, and salvation. To understand more fully what is said, one must contemplate this in the context of the Holy Eucharist, since in the Eucharist the holy name of *Jesus* is invoked so that He Himself becomes present.

SIX

✣ ✣ ✣

The Sign of the Cross

IN ADDITION TO THE invocation of the name of Jesus Christ, the sign of the cross is supposed to be included whenever a sacramental is administered. It is not "merely" a sacred sign similar to others; it is in fact *the* sign of victory over evil, death, and sin. Besides this, it is also an expression of faith.[343] The cross has a profound meaning, and it is even inscribed into the cosmos. As we enter into this discussion, there are two aspects of it to consider that will be useful for our understanding.

Even though it was generally considered the sign of humiliation and unspeakable torture in the ancient world, already as early as the fourth-century BC, Plato introduced a new interpretation that considered crucifixion in the context of righteousness. The Athenian philosopher was aware that it is difficult to find a just man, but even more difficult to prove that someone is just. Thus, accepting the cross voluntarily would reveal the purest love. Grounding his explanations on natural reason, this great philosopher was able to sense what was about to be revealed some four

---

[343] In general see Bert Ghezzi, *Recovering the Power of the Ancient Prayer. The Sign of the Cross*, (Chicago: Loyola Press, 2006). For an Orthodox perspective see Andreas Andreopoulos, *The Sign of the Cross: The Gesture, the Mystery, the History*, (Brewster, Massachusetts: Paraclete Press, 2010). See also Bernhard Vošicky, *Schau auf den Herrn*, 131–141.

centuries later. Joseph Ratzinger brought this into evidence in his bestseller *Introduction to Christianity*. He wrote:

> There is a curious presentiment of this situation in Greek philosophy: Plato's image of the crucified "just man." In the *Republic* the great philosopher asks what is likely to be the position of a completely just man in this world. He comes to the conclusion that a man's righteousness is only complete and guaranteed when he takes on the appearance of unrighteousness, for only then is it clear that he does not follow the opinion of men but pursues justice only for its own sake. So according to Plato the truly just man must be misunderstood and persecuted in this world; indeed, Plato goes so far as to write: "They will say that our just man will be scourged, racked, fettered, will have his eyes burned out, and at last, after all manner of suffering, will be crucified."[344]

This is one of the most profound reflections on righteousness. It shows that a *recta ratio*, that is, a right reason, can comprehend the ultimate truth of life, which leads necessarily to the question of God, who is the ultimate justice. Far ahead of his time, Plato had a certain sense of this mystery that surpasses reason.

There is another important reference that will help to understand the magnitude of the sign of the cross, inscribed as it is in the cosmic nature of the universe. Again, the remarks of Joseph Ratzinger are enlightening. He mentioned that the Greek Fathers discovered in the writings of Plato another significant reality, with an even more profound impact concerning the Cross. The Greek philosophers had come to the idea that the Cross is physically inscribed in the cosmos. Ancient astronomy had led them to observe "the ecliptic (the great circle in the heavens along which the sun appears to run its course) and the orbit of the earth. These two intersect and form together with the

---

[344] Joseph Ratzinger, *Introduction to Christianity*, trans. J. R. Foster, (San Francisco: Ignatius Press, 2004), 292.

Greek letter *Chi*, which is written in the form of a cross (like an X). The sign of the cross is inscribed upon the whole cosmos."[345] Joseph Ratzinger comments on this, affirming that the "Cross of Golgotha is foreshadowed in the structure of the universe itself. The instrument of torment on which the Lord died is written into the structure of the universe. The cosmos speaks to us of the Cross, and the Cross solves for us the enigma of the cosmos. It is the real key to all reality. History and cosmos belong together. When we open our eyes, we can read the message of Christ in the language of the universe, and conversely, Christ grants us understanding of the message of creation."[346]

These two aspects — the ability by pure reason to arrive at the symbolic weight of the Cross and its natural place on the grand scale of the cosmos itself — are important to mention at the beginning of these explanations on the sign of the cross, as they help to broaden the horizon, and allow us to recognize how the whole of creation is directed toward salvation. As, with "only" the help of right reason, such profound reflections were possible, how much more can it be understood with the assistance of revelation! From this grand starting point, some of the most important biblical foundations concerning the sign of the cross will be presented.

6.1. The Biblical Foundation

There is in fact such a strong scriptural foundation for the power of the sign of the cross that the following points of reference will be limited to only the most pertinent passages, rather than providing a comprehensive view. Beginning as early as the Old Testament, some prefigurations can be found that point toward a sacred sign of salvation. The book of Ezekiel, for example, says: "Pass through the city, through the midst of Jerusalem, and mark an X [*Tav*] on the foreheads

---

[345] Joseph Ratzinger, TL, 112.
[346] Ibid., 113.

of those who grieve and lament over all the abominations practiced within it" (Ezek. 9:4). Joseph Ratzinger mentions that the *Tav* is "the last letter of the Hebrew alphabet ... which was written in the form of a cross (T or ✠ or X). The *Tav*, which, as a matter of fact, had the form of a cross, becomes the seal of God's ownership. It corresponds to man's longing for God, his suffering for the sake of God, and so places him under God's special protection."[347]

Also in the Old Testament, salvation is related to sacrifices, through which redemption from sin is granted. There are several signs which prefigured the sign of the cross; in this context, two of them will be mentioned.

The first is related to Abraham and his son Isaac. According to the divine will, he was supposed to "offer him up as a burnt offering on one of the heights" (Gen. 22:2). Every detail of this prefiguration is important. First, Abraham's beloved son had to carry the wood himself. Next, Abraham built an altar and arranged the wood on the top of the altar (cf. Gen. 22:9). Then, even though Abraham did not have to complete the sacrifice of his son, they did still sacrifice the ram in his place. Abraham "went and took the ram and offered it up as a holocaust in place of his son" (Gen 22:13); "God himself will provide the sheep for the holocaust" (Gen 22:8). The very fact that God did indeed provide the sacrifice himself for Moses and Isaac — a sheep, no less — is an essential detail of the prefigurement at play in this episode; it foreshadowed what was about to be fulfilled in Jesus Christ. In Him, sign and sacrifice become one. This becomes even more evident in the second passage, which shows how the prefiguration is fulfilled in Jesus Christ. The book of Exodus describes the Passover of the Lord. In this instance, the sign for salvation becomes an unblemished lamb; after it is sacrificed, its blood is applied "to the two doorposts and the lintel of the houses in which they eat it"

---

[347] Ibid., 111–112.

(Exod. 12:7). The blood of the lamb saves and protects the people who are inside the houses from the angel of death. This prefiguration is fulfilled in the sublime sacrifice of the "Lamb of God, who takes away the sin of the world" (John 1:29). This is particularly meaningful because Jesus Christ was sentenced to death at the hour at which, in the Temple, the priests began to slaughter the Passover lambs. Keeping in mind the incarnational principle, it becomes clear how the sign of salvation and the sacrifice became one in Jesus Christ. With this understood by means of these prefigurements from the Old Testament, the attention can turn to the New Testament, which follows the same principle.

Already, before His death on the Cross, Jesus Christ affirmed on several occasions the importance of accepting the Cross for eternal salvation. For example: "Jesus said to his disciples, 'Whoever wishes to come after me must deny himself, take up his cross, and follow me'" (Matt. 16:24). From this passage, it becomes understandable already that both cross and sacrifice have a redemptive value in the life of the believer. However, the full meaning of this truth is only revealed through the Cross of Jesus Christ.

He had foreseen His own Crucifixion. Even more, He had accepted it willingly for the salvation of many (cf. Luke 22:22). He is the good shepherd, who "lays down his life for the sheep" (John 10:11). This act of self-giving and self-surrender to the will of the Father is the act of greatest and purest love, as already foreseen by the philosopher Plato. It is clearly described by John, who came to the most profound understanding of this mystery since he was the apostle "whom he [Jesus] loved" (John 19:26). He wrote: "No one has greater love than this, to lay down one's life for one's friends. You are my friends if you do what I command you" (John 15:13–14). Salvation was granted through the self-giving love of the Son of Man on the Cross. Therefore, it became the sign of victory, hope, and salvation. "And just as Moses lifted up the serpent in the desert, so must the Son of Man be lifted up, so that everyone who believes in him may have eternal life. For God so loved the world that he gave his only Son, so that everyone who believes in him might not perish but might have eternal life" (John 3:14–16). It was by the Cross that this essential moment in the history of salvation was accomplished — this same Cross which is intrinsically related to His sacrifice. Both the Cross itself and His sacrifice are reflected in the sign of the cross.

The Letter to the Philippians affirms: "Rather, he emptied himself, taking the form of a slave, coming in human likeness; and found in human appearance, he humbled himself, becoming obedient to death, even death on a cross" (Phil. 2:7–8). St. Paul understood that this sign, which is linked to the divine mystery of salvation, is the source of all grace. He wrote to the Galatians: "But may I never boast except in the cross of our Lord Jesus Christ, through which the world has been crucified to me, and I to the world" (Gal 6:14). The cross, sign of shame and contempt, has taken on a whole new meaning through Jesus Christ. The cross is the sign of salvation, even though the "message of the cross is foolishness to those who are perishing, but to us who are being saved it is the power of God" (1 Cor. 1:18). Continuously, Sacred Scripture affirms: "For in him all the fullness was pleased to dwell, and through him to reconcile all things for him, making peace by the blood of his cross (through him), whether those on earth or those in heaven" (Col. 1:19–20). The First Letter of Peter, in similar words, says: "He himself bore our sins in his body upon the cross, so that, free from sin, we might live for righteousness. By his wounds you have been healed" (1 Pet. 2:24).

This clear biblical foundation underlines the importance of the sign of the cross, emphasizing that its devout use will help to receive spiritual benefits. This was expressed in the formula *per crucem ad lucem* — through the Cross, the light of grace comes to us. It is to this light that every person should turn, and "the light shines in the darkness, and the darkness has not overcome it" (John 1:5). From the very beginning of Christianity, the sign of the cross was of special importance within the Church. This is, for example, reflected in an exhortation from John Chrysostom (d. 407), the Patriarch of Constantinople: "Never leave your house without making the sign of the cross. It will be to you a staff, a weapon, an impregnable fortress. Neither man nor demon will dare to attack you, seeing you covered with such powerful armor. Let this sign teach you that you are a soldier, ready to combat against the demons, and ready to fight for the crown of justice. Are you ignorant of what the cross has done? It has vanquished death, destroyed sin, emptied hell, dethroned Satan, and restored the universe. Would you then doubt its power?"[348]

The Fathers of the Church were the first Christians to interpret Sacred Scripture. They were convinced of the great spiritual benefits, which can be obtained through the sign of the cross—benefits which will be addressed later in this same chapter.

6.2. Some Theological Considerations

A basic knowledge of the gesture of the sign of the cross is necessary for a fruitful administration of the sacramentals. This becomes even more essential when calling to mind how heavily creation is affected by the reality of sin.[349] Original sin in particular, and sin in general, are overcome through the salvation of Jesus Christ obtained on the Cross. Through the Cross, Jesus Christ re-established and elevated the wounded order of creation, making possible a new and reconciled relationship between God and man. He took upon himself the sins of the world (cf. John 1:29), and this is of lasting validity, even in our time. All of the sacraments and all of the sacramentals are related to this salvific event. In connection to this point, Pope Leo the Great said in a homily about the Passion of our Lord:

---

[348] So quoted in Bert Ghezzi, *Recovering the Power*, 6.
[349] Cf. chap. 2.3.1.

Now there is a more distinguished order of Levites, a greater dignity for the rank of elders, a more sacred anointing for the priesthood, because your cross is the source of all blessings, the cause of all graces. Through the cross the faithful receive strength from weakness, glory from dishonor, life from death. The different sacrifices of animals are no more: the one offering of your body and blood is the fulfillment of all the different sacrificial offerings, for you are the true Lamb of God: you take away the sins of the world. In yourself you bring to perfection all mysteries, so that, as there is one sacrifice in place of all other sacrificial offerings, there is also one kingdom gathered from all peoples.[350]

This quotation reveals the theological meaning of the mystery of the Cross, which is a powerful instrument, "capable of communicating grace and efficacy to people and objects, and as the seal that brings protection and leads to eternal life."[351] As pointed out by Daniel Cardò, the close connection between the sign of the cross and sacramentals can also be seen since the sign of the cross, as a liturgical action, signifies "God's protection and possession";[352] it is a holy seal. It is through the Cross that sacramental efficacy is granted; therefore, the "sign of the Cross is necessary in every sacramental action."[353]

Jesus Christ died for our sins (cf. Rom. 4:25) to free us and to redeem us. This was realized through the Passion and death of Christ, and, in this sacrifice, he established the new and eternal covenant. The exterior sign for the new and eternal covenant is the Cross. For this

---

[350] Leo the Great, *Sermo 8 de passione Domini*, 6–8; PL 54, 340–342, trans. in https://www.crossroadsinitiative.com/media/articles/power-of-the-cross-st-leo-the-great/ [9.5.2023].

[351] Daniel Cardó, *The Cross and the Eucharist in Early Christianity: A Theological and Liturgical Investigation*, (Cambridge: Cambridge University Press, 2019), 99.

[352] Cf. ibid., 100.

[353] Geoffrey W.H. Lampe, *The Seal of the Spirit: A Study in the Doctrine of Baptism and Confirmation in the New Testament and the Fathers*, 2nd ed., (London: SPCK, 1967), 266.

reason, among the many others already enumerated, it should always be included in any type of sacramental; even though it might not be indicated in the ritual, it still should be made. There is no Christian way of blessing but through the holy sign of the cross.[354]

Bernhard Vošicky rightly calls the sign of the cross the ultimate symbol of Christian faith because, besides its salvific dimension, it addresses the Most Holy Trinity, revealed through Jesus Christ. The full meaning of what has been said is revealed in his reflection. Salvation is a work of the Holy Trinity, as expressed in the Letter to the Hebrews: "For if the blood of goats and bulls and the sprinkling of a heifer's ashes can sanctify those who are defiled so that their flesh is cleansed, how much more will the blood of Christ, who through the eternal spirit offered himself unblemished to God, cleanse our consciences from dead works to worship the living God" (Heb. 9:13–14). Pope John Paul II provided a profound explanation of this in his encyclical *Dominum et Vivificantem*, affirming that salvation is the work of the Holy Trinity:

> The Holy Spirit as Love and Gift comes down, in a certain sense, into the very heart of the sacrifice which is offered on the Cross. Referring here to the biblical tradition, we can say: He consumes this sacrifice with the fire of the love which unites the Son with the Father in the Trinitarian communion. And since the sacrifice of the Cross is an act proper to Christ, also in this sacrifice he "receives" the Holy Spirit. He receives the Holy Spirit in such a way that afterwards — and he alone with God the Father — can "give him" to the Apostles, to the Church, to humanity.[355]

[354] Cf. Bernhard Vošicky, *Schau auf den Herrn!*, 133.
[355] John Paul II, Encyclical Letter *Dominum et Vivificantem*, May 18, 1986, 41, in http://www.vatican.va/content/john-paul-ii/en/encyclicals/documents/hf_jp-ii_enc_18051986_dominum-et-vivificantem.html [12.5.2023].

In this sense, the sign of the cross is not only the sign of salvation but also the ultimate symbol for the belief in the triune God.

Since the sacramentals are liturgical actions, and every liturgical action becomes effective through divine grace accompanied by living faith, it must be emphasized that the Christian liturgy is on the way; it is a "liturgy of pilgrimage toward the transfiguration of the world, which will only take place when God is 'all in all.'"[356] Therefore, in the liturgy, the horizontal and vertical dimensions that were previously described come together. This becomes comprehensible through the incarnational principle, pointing once again to the cross.[357]

And now, all of this can be related to the sign of the cross. As seen before, the exterior sign must not be separated from the interior attitude and lifestyle, which makes the sign effective. The blessing, and with it divine grace, comes from God (vertical dimension) and fills the world (horizontal dimension), whenever properly invoked. Therefore, the sign of the cross is not any ritual gesture; it is no mere ornament. Rather, it is a call to participate in Jesus Christ's sacrifice. St. Paul wrote:

> Now I rejoice in my sufferings for your sake, and in my flesh I am filling up what is lacking in the afflictions of Christ on behalf of his body, which is the church, of which I am a minister in accordance with God's stewardship given to me to bring to completion for you the word of God, the mystery hidden from ages and from generations past. But now it has been manifested to his holy ones, to whom God chose to make known the riches of the glory of this mystery among the Gentiles; it is Christ in you, the hope for glory. (Col. 1:24–27)

Pope John Paul II wrote in his apostolic letter on human suffering: "The Cross of Christ has become a source from which flow rivers of living

---

[356] Joseph Ratzinger, TL, 30.
[357] Cf. chap. 2.3.3.

water."[358] In other words, many spiritual effects are related to the sign of the cross and, for that reason, the cross is marked upon persons, objects, and places, "as the gesture that seals and communicates Christ's grace. The Cross becomes a necessary sign of sacramental efficacy, introducing those who are sealed into the new covenant of the Cross."[359] To conclude, it is helpful to remember that the cross is not only related to Jesus Christ's self-offering, but also to the Most Holy Trinity.

6.3. Some Practical Considerations

As the sign of the cross is the ultimate symbol of the Christian faith, there are different traditions related to its practical application. Since the sign becomes effective through devout participation,[360] they need to be understood and used correctly.

According to the Latin tradition, the sign of the cross is done from the forehead to the chest, from the mind to the heart; then from the left to the right. According to one allegorical explanation, this signifies our passing from misery (left) to the future glory (right). The left is usually related to misery and curse. For that reason, the sheep are on the right, while the goats remain on the left side (cf. Matt. 26:33), and the severe judgment of the Lord refers to the ones being on the left side: "Then he will say to those on his left, 'Depart from me, you accursed, into the eternal fire prepared for the devil and his angels'" (Matt. 25:41). The Latin tradition brings to evidence that the sign of the cross is related to our participation in Christ's redemption.

The Greek tradition is different. The sign of the cross starts by the head, moves down to the chest, and then it moves from the right

---

[358] John Paul II, Apostolic Letter *Salvifici Doloris*, February 11, 1984, 18, in http://www.vatican.va/content/john-paul-ii/en/apost_letters/1984/documents/hf_jp-ii_apl_11021984_salvifici-doloris.html [9.5.2023].

[359] Daniel Cardó, *The Cross and the Eucharist*, 104.

[360] Cf. chap. 3.2.–3.3.

to the left. The allegorical explanation emphasizes that Christ descended from Heaven to earth, and from the Jews to the pagans. Both explanations are fine, as long as both forms are done with the right understanding and reverence.

Additionally, within the Latin tradition, there are two common ways of holding the fingers on the right hand while using it to make the sign of the cross. The first can be called the "one-finger sign of the cross." Most frequently, the first Christians used the thumb alone or the single forefinger to make the sign of the cross. This one-finger sign of the cross is known from very early baptismal practice, and it is still used today. When a small child is baptized, the priest, parents, and godparents mark the infant with this one-fingered sign of the cross. It is also used when the Gospel is read. The one-finger symbolizes that in Christianity we understand that there is only one God. Both at Baptisms and at the Gospel reading, this sign is made on the forehead, on the lips, and on the heart — and each of these also has a profound meaning. The forehead denotes the human faculties of reason and will. Reason ought to be enlightened by the light of faith, and the will ought to be guided toward the good, which is God. The lips signify that faith needs to be publicly confessed; but public confession through the lips is not enough on its own. Above all, faith needs to be accepted with the heart.[361] Our Lord complained that "this people honors me with their lips, but their hearts are far from me; in vain do they worship me, teaching as doctrines human precepts" (Matt. 15:8–9). Rather than living with inconsistencies such as these, every Christian ought instead to align himself to the injunction of Jesus Christ when He reaffirms that "You shall love the Lord, your God, with all your heart, with all your being, with all your strength, and with all your mind, and your neighbor as yourself"

---

[361] Bernhard Vošicky, *Schau auf den Herrn!*, 134–137.

(Luke 10:27). This is what is expressed by the one-finger sign of the cross, which every faithful person is allowed to make.

The two-finger sign of the cross is made to emphasize the two natures of Jesus Christ; it does not need to be explained beyond that in this context. But the most common sign of the cross is the so-called five-finger sign of the cross. It spread through the Franciscan movement in the thirteenth century, for St. Francis bore the stigmata of Jesus Christ; this is significant, because the Franciscans soon became aware that the five wounds had special importance, and a general awareness among the faithful grew through their emphasis on them. They started to use the five fingers to make the sign of the cross, reflecting that, through the sign of the cross, God becomes present in the whole person (from our hands to our hearts to our feet) — this is supposed to glorify the living God.[362] All of this is expressed by moving the hands from the foreheads — on which each Christian bears the name of Jesus Christ through Baptism — to the hearts, in which He should dwell. The blessing of persons, objects, and places by the five-finger sign of the cross is reserved to the ordained minister.

The three-finger sign of the cross, symbolizing the Most Holy Trinity, was originally in common use in the West and East. However, after the Great Schism in 1054, the Orthodox started to use this sign as a way to mark their distinction from the West. They signed themselves from the right to the left, as explained above. The thumb, index, and middle finger are brought together; meanwhile, the other two fingers symbolize the two natures of Jesus Christ. According to the tradition of the Eastern Rite Churches, the sign of the cross is made frequently — when entering or leaving a church, when ending or starting a prayer, when venerating an icon or relics, and so on. However, if an Eastern Rite priest or a bishop blesses, he does it in such a way that his fingers form the Greek abbreviation for Jesus Christ (IX XC). The

---

[362] Ibid., 140–141.

index finger marks the "I" and is extended, the middle finger symbolizes the "C"; the lowered finger touches the thumb signifying the "X" and the little finger signifies the "C." Eastern Rite Churches emphasize the mystery of the Incarnation, and for that reason, when making the holy sign of the cross, they bow down: "the Word became flesh" (John 1:14). Furthermore, through the sign of the cross, the Father is venerated as the Creator of all things, the Son as the Redeemer, and the Holy Spirit as the one who brings everything to fulfillment through love.[363]

Concerning the effectiveness of the sign of the cross, it is of utmost importance to avoid any type of thoughtless routine. Romano Guardini wrote: "It is the holiest of all signs. Make a large cross, taking time, thinking what you are doing. Let it take in your whole being, — body, soul, mind, will, thoughts, feelings, your doing and not-doing, — and by signing it with the cross strengthen and consecrate the whole in the strength of Christ, in the name of the triune God."[364] Whenever the sign of the cross is done with living faith and love, divine grace will be obtained. These divine graces and effects will be addressed in the following chapter.

6.4. Spiritual Effects and the Sign of the Cross

Several spiritual effects can be obtained by making the sign of the cross. However, from a systematic perspective, two main effects emerge, which are supposed to be present in every blessing: first, purification and liberation, and second, sanctification. The cross is the sign of salvation; it brings purification and liberates the world from evil, and, consequently, it also brings sanctification. For this reason, it should never be omitted, especially when administering sacramentals. Priests in particular should be aware of the importance of this holy sign, never neglecting or denying a blessing when the faithful, who are properly disposed, ask for it.

---

[363] Cf. ibid., 139.
[364] Romano Guardini, *Sacred Signs*, 14.

To obtain the desired effects, the gesture should be made consciously and devoutly, for the sign of the cross is the sign of our salvation and is a confession of the Most Holy Trinity. It is *the* symbol of God's love — a love that is stronger than death and promises everlasting life. Additionally, the sign of the cross should be accompanied by certain invocations. The Tradition of the Church recommends the well-known, common formula: "In the name of the Father, and of the Son, and of the Holy Spirit. Amen." It also recommends the less frequent: "Our help is in the name of the Lord." The tradition that is common in the Orthodox churches may also serve as a valid option: "Holy God, Holy Mighty One, Holy Immortal One, have mercy on us." This prayer is called the *Trisagion* (Thrice holy), and it is also chanted during the veneration of the Cross in the Western Liturgy of Good Friday.

6.4.1. Fruits of Purification and Liberation

Through the Cross, the evil one, sin, and its destructive consequences are overcome. The Church participates in the salvific mission of Jesus Christ. Following this line of thought, St. Paul wrote in the Letter to the Romans: "If God is for us, who can be against us?" (Rom. 8:31). If someone is under God's protection, he does not need to fear.

The cross is the symbol of the crucified Christ, the Son of God, who, through His Cross, broke the power of the devil. Therefore, this holy sign is a spiritual weapon, against "the world rulers of this present darkness" (Eph. 6:12). Thus, the sign of the cross also has an indwelling power to expel the devil, to free people from the influence and work of the evil one, and to reverse curses. In itself, it can be considered a minor exorcism; through it, persons, objects, or places can be purified from evil influences and are sealed by divine grace.

Furthermore, the sign of the cross serves as a protection against temptations and attacks from the evil one. It is said that St. John Vianney had affirmed that a genuinely made sign of the cross "makes all hell tremble." For that reason, it is a powerful protection against temptations and other evil influences. The Church Fathers recommended that if someone were angry, full of lust, fearful, and so forth, he should make the sign of the cross to dispel these temptations.[365] Thus, it serves as a protection against temptations, against dangers of soul and body, and even against sickness.

One of these effects of the sign of the cross is illustrated in a fresco at the Benedictine monastery in Subiaco. One day, St. Benedict was asked to govern a monastery in which religious discipline was badly observed. For a long time, he resisted the invitation of the monks to become their superior, but, finally, he was persuaded to undertake the charge. They had heard that he was living a saintly life, recognized by many, and they saw the need to improve their own lifestyle. St. Benedict did his best to introduce religious discipline and devotion, but initially he only succeeded in exciting against himself the hatred of certain monks. In their wickedness, they formed a plot to poison him. Gregory the Great describes the episode:

> Taking counsel together, they agreed to poison his wine: which being done, and the glass wherein that wine was, according to the custom, offered to the Abbot to bless, he, putting forth his hand, made the sign of the cross, and straightway the glass, that was held far off, broke in pieces, as though the sign of the cross had been a stone thrown against it: on which accident the man of God by and by perceived that the glass had in it the drink of death, which could not endure the sign of life.[366]

Additionally, by making the sign of the cross, even the forgiveness of sins may be obtained. The *Apostolic Penitentiary* grants a partial indulgence to the faithful, who "devoutly sign themselves with the sign of the cross, using the customary words: In the name of the Father and

---

[365] Cf. Bert Ghezzi, *Recovering the Power*, 107–108.
[366] Gregory the Great, Book Two of the Dialogues: The Life of Saint Benedict, in https://www.osb.org/gen/greg/dia-05.html [25.2.2023].

of the Son and of the Holy Spirit. Amen."[367] As seen above, all of these spiritual effects depend primarily on the interior disposition of the recipient; if he or she is properly disposed, the sign of the cross may lead to the forgiveness of venial sins.

In light of this, the conclusion of the *Confiteor* — the prayer said near the beginning of Mass (and, in the Extraordinary Form, it is repeated again just before the distribution and reception of Holy Communion) in which the faithful confess their own sins — is accompanied by the sign of the cross. Also, at the examination of conscience at the end of Compline (the last hour of prayer in the daily Divine Office), the following prayer is said and accompanied by the sign of the cross: "May almighty God have mercy upon us, ✠ forgive us our sins, and bring us to everlasting life." If the sign of the cross is done with the right interior dispositions, venial sins might be forgiven here as well. This was done until the liturgical reform after each *Confiteor*, including the one at the beginning of each Holy Eucharist. It was an essential expression from both priest and faithful, asking for purification and liberation before approaching the altar. Today, it is usually omitted because its meaning simply and most unfortunately got lost. However, it would be a logical consequence to recover the sign of the cross at this moment and to teach the faithful accordingly. Since the sign of the cross has an indwelling power, it should be repeated during the day or in other circumstances.

The purifying character of the sign of the cross becomes most evident in the sacrament of Penance. The absolution of sins is intrinsically linked to the sign of the cross made over the penitent when all sins are correctly confessed; this is clear when the priest says: "I absolve you from your sins, in the name of the Father, ✠ and of the Son, and of the Holy Spirit."

---

[367] Apostolic Penitentiary, *Manual of Indulgences. Norms and Grants*, trans. United States Conference of Catholic Bishops, 4th ed., (Washington, D.C.: USCCB, 1999), 28 §2.

6.4.2. Fruits of Sanctification

There are also various fruits of sanctification that can be obtained by making the sign of the cross. Fr. Cassian Folsom explains that the sign of the cross "consecrates and sanctifies us. It does so because it is the sign of the universe and the sign of our redemption. On the cross, Christ redeemed mankind."[368] Since the cross is inseparably linked to our Lord's salvific mission, rich fruits of sanctification may be obtained through it.

Thus, it is an ancient tradition to start and to end the day with the sign of the cross, dedicating it to the Lord and asking for His sanctification. When a Christian gets up in the morning, the first thing he should do is to kneel and to make the sign of the cross, invoking the holy name of Jesus Christ. This can be repeated throughout the day. The holy Curé d'Ars recommended to his faithful to do this frequently and to consecrate every hour to God. The sign of the cross marks the beginning and the end of prayer; in this and in all other circumstances, it is a powerful means to obtain fruits of sanctification.

Fruits of healing may also be obtained through the sign of the cross. Even sicknesses, diseases, or sufferings can be overcome through the sign of the cross. Christ healed our fallen nature through his Cross, reconciling humanity with God. "By his wounds we were healed" (Isa. 53:5); therefore, the cross has a protective and healing dimension — it is spiritual medicine.

The sign of the cross is the mark of the disciple since the baptized person is incorporated into Christ. Invisibly, this mark is inscribed on the soul of the baptized. The *Catechism* states: "Baptism seals the Christian with the indelible spiritual mark (*character*) of his belonging to Christ. No sin can erase this mark, even if sin prevents

---

[368] Cassian Folsom, Sacred Signs and Active Participation at Mass, Adoremus Conference held in Los Angeles on November 22, 1997, 2, in http://www.ewtn.com/library/liturgy/SIGNS.HTM [29.6.2021].

Baptism from bearing the fruits of salvation."[369] St. Paul came to a profound understanding of this new reality, relating it to his own life. As he wrote in the Letter to the Galatians: "I have been crucified with Christ, yet I live, no longer I, but Christ lives in me; insofar as I now live in the flesh, I live by faith in the Son of God who has loved me and given himself up for me" (Gal 2:19–20). Therefore, through the sign of the cross, fruits of justification can be obtained. The cross is the cause of our justification because Jesus Christ offered Himself on the Cross "as a living victim, holy and pleasing to God, and whose blood has become the instrument of atonement for the sins of all men."[370] Justification becomes effective through Baptism and, therefore, the sign of the cross reminds every baptized person of his or her adherence to Christ, through whom we are saved. The adherence to Jesus Christ is the foundation from which to obtain fruits of sanctification, for the baptized person is incorporated into Christ.

Many other spiritual fruits are related to the sign of the cross, such as strength and consolation in suffering and in the moment of death. John Paul II wrote in his Apostolic Letter *Salvifici Doloris*, on human suffering: "Those who share in Christ's sufferings have before their eyes the Paschal Mystery of the Cross and Resurrection, in which Christ descends, in a first phase, to the ultimate limits of human weakness and impotence: indeed, he dies nailed to the Cross. But if at the same time in this *weakness* there is accomplished his *lifting up*, confirmed by the power of the Resurrection, then this means that the weaknesses of all human sufferings are capable of being infused with the same power of God manifested in Christ's Cross."[371]

Whoever submits himself under the cross in moments of suffering is more willing to embrace difficult situations because he or she

---

[369] CCC, 1272.
[370] CCC, 1992.
[371] John Paul II, Apostolic Letter *Salvifici Doloris*, 23.

shares in Christ's salvific sufferings. As Jesus Christ was obedient to the will of the Father, the faithful person is obedient to divine law. He makes the Lord's words his own: "Not my will but yours be done" (Luke 22:42). Such an inner attitude helps the person of faith to participate in Christ's suffering, which grants suffering a new meaning, because suffering and the relatively small crosses we bear are always linked to the risen Christ, who grants a share in His Resurrection. Making the sign of the cross makes true what is said in the Letter to the Ephesians: "Finally, draw your strength from the Lord and from his mighty power. Put on the armor of God so that you may be able to stand firm against the tactics of the devil" (Eph. 6:10–11).

SEVEN
✠ ✠ ✠
Exorcisms and Their Anti-Demonic Character

7.1. Introduction

THERE IS AN OLD saying: Whenever faith diminishes, superstitious and esoteric practices will flourish. The truth of this is evident in our time; many people are involved in occultism and spiritualism, seeking help from mediums, witches, sorcerers, and even Satanists. Many people, consciously or unconsciously, are exposed to the power of evil, with sometimes dramatic consequences, as will be shown. At the same time, more than a few priests, religious, and sometimes even bishops are not aware of the consequences resulting from such experiences.[372] Often, they underestimate them as stupidity or as a type of play-acting, without any relevance to real life.

To understand what is at stake, it must be affirmed that the first commandment is at the center of all commandments. Therefore, all practices of magic, yoga, sorcery, and anything related to occult powers are a grave violation of the first commandment: "You shall not have other gods beside me" (Exod. 20:3). For modern man, this sounds very hard, because he has become accustomed to making many compromises. And yet compromises are not possible if someone seeks to

---

[372] Cf. Gabriele Amorth, *An Exorcist Tells His Story*, trans. Nicoletta V. MacKenzie, (San Francisco: Ignatius Press, 1999).

establish and maintain a sound spiritual life. Whoever neglects or transgresses the first commandment will have to be responsible for the consequences, as Psalm 16 says: "They multiply their sorrows who court other gods" (Ps. 16:4). For this reason, the first Christians made no concessions to the gods, even refusing to incense the image of Caesar.

The reasons that people today become engaged in esoteric practices can vary greatly. As the *Catechism of the Catholic Church* affirms, it is frequently curiosity that misleads people. The *Catechism* therefore encourages the faithful to trust in divine Providence, "giving up all unhealthy curiosity."[373] Young people especially are fascinated by the mysterious, which they often do not find any more at church. The Internet and some in-person groups offer plenty of options to get in touch with the "other world." Some people want to get in contact with deceased ancestors, others hope for a glimpse into the future, and still others are simply looking for an experience of the mysterious.

This type of curiosity becomes even more dangerous when it is accompanied by a loss of faith. "Right faith orients reason to open itself to the light which comes from God."[374] Without this light, man remains in the darkness, and he is more easily tempted by the occult. The *Catechism of the Catholic Church* acknowledges that the Church will experience a time of persecution "in the form of a religious deception offering men an apparent solution to their problems at the price of apostasy from the truth. The supreme religious deception is that of the Antichrist, a pseudo-messianism by which man glorifies himself in place of God and of his Messiah come in the flesh."[375] In other words, faith enlightens reason, providing orientation and guidance. Whenever the light of faith diminishes, people tend to become increasingly vulnerable to what is contrary to God. They no longer even realize how serious the resulting consequences can be.

---

[373] *CCC*, 2115.
[374] Francis, LF, 36.
[375] *CCC*, 675.

Besides esoteric practices, idolatry is of course opposed to God and is another gateway for the devil. "Idolatry consists in divinizing what is not God. Man commits idolatry whenever he honors and reveres a creature in place of God, whether this [real or imagined creature or construct] be gods or demons (for example, Satanism), power, pleasure, race, ancestors, the state, money, etc. Jesus says, 'You cannot serve God and mammon.'"[376] In this connection, the *Catechism* enumerates a raft of practices associated with idolatry, such as consulting "horoscopes, astrology, palm reading, interpretation of omens and lots, the phenomena of clairvoyance, and recourse to mediums."[377] All these practices are contrary to the first commandment.

Exorcisms are closely linked to the first commandment, re-directing persons, objects, or places toward God, giving Him primacy. For this same reason, as mentioned before, all sacramentals should include an anti-demonic element as an indispensable part of their formulas, through which deliverance from evil influences is granted. This inclusion of anti-demonic elements is clearly described in several passages of the Old and New Testament, above all in the Lord's Prayer, which includes the petition "deliver us from evil." Contrary to the common understanding of the text, the devil/Satan is meant and not evil in general.[378] Deliverance and liberation from evil is the necessary condition "that God may be all in all" (1 Cor. 15:28); it is the acknowledgment of the first commandment, and it necessarily excludes other gods.

From this perspective, it becomes understandable why a direct violation of the first commandment is a grave sin: it is not only an insult to God, but, even more, it signifies dancing around the golden calf (cf. Exod. 32:1–6), and it provokes the wrath of God (cf. Exod.

---

[376] Ibid., 2113.
[377] Ibid., 2116.
[378] Cf. ibid., 2851.

32:10). Furthermore, it is taking a pathway that leads astray. There is a tendency today to trivialize such transgressions, not taking them seriously; in reality, a violation of the first commandment is among the most serious offenses of the divine law. Esoteric practices and demoniac interactions must be judged from this perspective. Consequently, the *Catechism of the Catholic Church* calls all practices related to occult powers, such as magic and sorcery, even if done with a "good intention," "gravely contrary to the virtue of religion."[379] Therefore, such practices are grave matters that, when engaged in consciously and freely, constitute grave and mortal sin.

Besides the sacraments, then, the sacramentals, too, are supposed to have an anti-demonic character. They are meant to free people from the power of evil. Such liberations are generally called exorcisms. Unfortunately, due to much confusion, ignorance, lack of faith, and the pressure of public opinion, exorcism is a difficult topic today. To get a better understanding of the situation, it is worthwhile to describe what *exorcism* actually means. First of all, it is a "prayer that the Church uses against the power of the devil,"[380] referring to persons, places, and objects. Once again, it must be emphasized that not only persons but also objects and places can be affected by the devil and may need liberation. Thus, exorcism aims toward the liberation from one or more demoniac presence(s) "through the spiritual authority which Jesus entrusted to the Church."[381] When exorcism is spoken of, people usually refer to the great exorcisms, those that are accompanied by extraordinary phenomena. However, exorcisms — as a prayer against the power of the devil — exist in different ways. They have always been part of the Church's tradition and

---

[379] Ibid., 2117.
[380] USCCB, Art. "Exorcism," in https://www.usccb.org/prayer-and-worship/sacraments-and-sacramentals/sacramentals-blessings/exorcism [10.5.2023].
[381] CCC, 1673.

practice, since the devil is the "ruler of this world" (cf. John 12:31–32). The ministry of deliverance from evil is explicitly entrusted to the Church and administered especially through sacramentals that "God may be all in all" (1 Cor. 15:28).

Today, a growing number of people are affected by diabolic activity, not only due to the increase of some of the esoterical practices mentioned above, but also due to the consumption of drugs, pornographic addiction, "pagan activities," and the general collapse of moral life. In Italy, for example, a "green number" (hotline) has been set up which people can call if they are in need of liberation, offering professional help. This is in response to demoniac cases in that country being on the rise.[382] There, as in any such event, discernment on the part of the priests who are called to help is crucial, for people who are truly affected suffer tremendously; meanwhile, people who pretend to be possessed may cause damage to the priest (exorcist) and the Church.

7.2. Some Necessary Premises

The First Letter of John says: "We know that we belong to God, and the whole world is under the power of the evil one" (1 John 5:19). This is not a pessimistic view of the created world; it corresponds to a sound realism that acknowledges the reality of Original Sin and its consequences.[383] Sin separates from God and causes chaos, confusion, and death. God's commandments are guideposts; they are not a limitation of freedom but, on the contrary, lead to true freedom, for only truth sets us free (cf. John 8:32). Accordingly, obedience to God's commandments is the necessary condition to remain in communion with God. Leaving the path of God, who is the supreme good, opens the door toward evil. For this reason, the Letter to the Ephesians admonishes: "You were dead in your transgressions and sins in which

---

[382] See Aldo Buonaiuto, *Le mani occulte viaggio nel mondo del satanismo*, (Rome: Città Nuova, 2005), 133–145.

[383] See chap. 2.3.1.

you once lived following the age of this world, following the ruler of the power of the air, the spirit that is now at work in the disobedient" (Eph. 2:1–2). Thus, evil and sin are overcome by grace, leading to conversion and a change of life: "The kingdom of God is at hand. Repent, and believe in the gospel" (Mark 1:15). In our time, the consciousness that sin and evil are intrinsically related is widely lost. In spite of this, the fact remains that whoever wants to overcome evil must first overcome sin. The First Letter of John affirms: "Whoever sins belongs to the devil, because the devil has sinned from the beginning. Indeed, the Son of God was revealed to destroy the works of the devil" (1 John 3:8). It would be very good for all people if a new awareness of sin and its fatal consequences would arise. To begin with, this would change the way that society at large deals with sin; it would no longer be tolerated so lightly or even allowed to flourish under the protection of the laws, as it currently is in some countries.

The whole mission of Jesus Christ is a battle to free mankind from sin and the demonic forces. The very name of Jesus signifies that "he will save his people from their sins" (Matt. 1:21). Joseph Ratzinger offers a profound explanation of how to understand the relationship between the name and the mission of Jesus Christ, a connection that was discussed at some length already: "His own name, Jesus, brings the mysterious name at the burning bush to its fulfillment; now we can see that God had not said all that he had to say but had interrupted his discourse for a time. This is because the name 'Jesus' in its Hebrew form includes the word 'Yahweh' and adds a further element to it: God 'saves'. 'I am who I am' — thanks to Jesus, this now means: 'I am the one who saves you.' His Being is salvation."[384]

Salvation always means salvation from sin. This implies a battle against the devil, who tempts people as he tempted Jesus Christ (cf.

---

[384] Joseph Ratzinger, *The God of Jesus Christ: Meditations on the Triune God*, trans. Brian McNeil, (San Francisco: Ignatius Press, 2008), 24.

Matt. 4:1–11). The Lord's Prayer can also be quoted in this context, which states: "and lead us not into temptation but deliver us from evil." This reference to the work of the devil must be correctly understood; it must be seen within the context of a reality that surpasses the realm of the natural. It refers to what Christians confess in the Creed as the "invisible world." For the purpose of this book, it is not necessary to provide a detailed explanation of the world of the angels (angelology) and demons (demonology),[385] but some of the most basic elements will be mentioned.

7.2.1. Angels — Spiritual Beings

It is an elemental part of the Catholic Faith to believe in the existence of the invisible world, to which belong not only God Almighty, but also the angels, saints, souls in Purgatory, and the fallen angels, the demons.[386] Sacred Scripture, Tradition, and the Magisterium of the Church all affirm this belief continuously. Who, it might be asked, are these spiritual beings, and why did some of them turn away from God? These basic questions have to be answered in the form of an overview before considering how they relate to the importance of sacramentals and their anti-demonic character.

---

[385] See, for more information, Serge-Thomas Bonino, *Angels and Demons: A Catholic Introduction*, trans. Michael J. Miller, vol. 6, (Washingthon, D.C.: The Catholic University of America Press, 2016). Johannes Heinrich Oswald, *Angelogie. Das ist die Lehre von den guten und den bösen Engeln im Sinne der Katholischen Kirche*, 2nd ed., (Kulmbach: Verlagsbuchhandlung Sabat, 2019). A good overview is also provided by: Francesco Bamonte, *Gli Angeli Ribelli. Il mistero del male nell'esperienza di un esorcista*, (Milan: Paoline Editoriale, 2008). So do the following two books: Giovanni Mongelli, *Gli Angeli Buoni. Ministri di Dio per la salvezza degli uomini*, vol. 1, (Caposele: Edizioni Michael, 2009). Giovanni Mongelli, *Gli Angeli cattivi. Nostri avversari nell'opera della salvezza*, vol. 2, (Caposele: Edizioni Michael, 2009).

[386] See Ralph Weimann, "Die Bedeutung der heiligen Engel in der Heilsgeschichte und Heilsordnung Gottes," in Theologisches 46 9/10 (2016): 409–416.

The angels are creatures of God, created by Him from nothing. They differ from us humans in that they are purely spiritual beings — their nature is not composed of soul and body. In the account of Creation, Sacred Scripture does not expressly mention them, but, since the time of St. Augustine, the words "let there be light" (Gen. 1:3) were interpreted by many of the Fathers of the Church as the moment of the creation of the angels, coinciding with the creation of light.[387]

The Old Testament not only mentions the existence of the angels and their work, but also affirms that they worship God most high. From this, it becomes clear that Angels are creatures with specific tasks directed to the praise and worship of God (cf. Ps. 148:2).[388] Thus, Psalm 103 says: "Bless the LORD, all you his angels, mighty in strength, acting at his behest, obedient to his command" (Ps. 103:20). The number of angels is "countless" (Rev. 5:11), and the book of Daniel affirms: "Thousands upon thousands were ministering to him, and myriads upon myriads stood before him" (Dan. 7:10). Angels also intervene in the history of salvation, even in a "physical" way (cf. Gen. 19:1–29). St. Raphael, for example, becomes a visible companion of Tobit. Sacred Scripture describes that he protects, guides, and cures (cf. Tob. 11:1–15), and he reveals himself as "Raphael, one of the seven angels who stand and serve before the Glory of the Lord" (Tob. 12:15).

In the New Testament, angels take an even more central role. The presence of the angels accompanies the Holy Family and all major events of salvation: An angel appears to Joseph in the dream about his divine destiny (cf. Matt. 1:20), and the angel Gabriel is sent to Mary to transmit the message of salvation: "The Holy Spirit will come upon you, and the power of the Most High will overshadow you. Therefore, the child to be born will be called holy, the Son of

---

[387] Cf. Aurelius Augustinus, *Der Gottesstaat*, 11. Book, 9.1.
[388] Cf. Ralph Weimann, "Die Bedeutung der heiligen Engel," 411.

God" (Luke 1:35). Besides many other appearances and interventions, the message of the Resurrection is proclaimed by angels who roll away the stone from the tomb (cf. Matt. 28:1–8). All of this angelic activity does not diminish after the Ascension of the Lord; rather, it continues in the Church (cf. Acts 5:19; 8:26–28). The book of Revelation gives deep insights into the invisible world; it describes how the angels stand in front of the throne of God and worship Him (cf. Rev. 7:11). These references to the angelic presence in the Sacred Scripture are only a small number of all those that are in the Bible, but they are sufficient for our purpose.[389] However, it will be necessary to look briefly at the fallen angels.

7.2.2. The Fallen Angels

Angels have in common with human beings that they are creatures. They too were free to choose between God and being "like gods" (cf. Gen. 3:5). Even though created as good angels, some were disobedient and fell out of the order of grace, becoming evil.[390] Their choice is irrevocable and definitive due to their spiritual nature. Even though the power of Satan is not infinite, he is still immensely powerful, since he is a pure spirit.[391] His strength goes beyond any natural power because of his angelical nature. Through his sin of pride, he lost the grace of God, on which everything depends; consequently, he fell out of the supernatural order. This has led to the sad reality that one-third of the angels (cf. Rev. 12:4) — this exceptionally large number of spiritual beings — fell into rebellion against God and His commandments. Thus, a dramatic struggle between good and evil started, as described in the book of Revelation: "Then war broke out in heaven; Michael and his

---

[389] Cf. ibid., 409–416. See also the remarks by Jean Daniélou, *The Angels & Their Mission*, trans. David Heimann, (Manchester, New Hampshire: Sophia Institute Press, 2009).
[390] Cf. Lateran Council IV (1215): DH 800.
[391] Cf. CCC, 395.

angels battled against the dragon. The dragon and its angels fought back, but they did not prevail and there was no longer any place for them in heaven. The huge dragon, the ancient serpent, who is called the Devil and Satan, who deceived the whole world, was thrown down to earth, and its angels were thrown down with it" (Rev. 12:7–9). Ever since this clash, the fallen angels have tried to associate human beings with their revolt against God, promising us that we would be like God.[392] Their disastrous influence is witnessed in Scripture, persuading human beings to disobey divine law (cf. Gen. 3:1–7).

Even though Christ has already won the victory against evil, it is a great mystery that divine providence permits diabolical activity, but "we know that all things work for good for those who love God" (Rom. 8:28). God allows the devil to carry out his evil plans, to some extent. St. Thomas provided a profound explanation: "Every evil that God … permits to be done, is directed to some good; yet not always to the good of those in whom the evil is, but sometimes to the good of others, or of the whole universe: thus He directs the sin of tyrants to the good of the martyrs, and the punishment of the lost to the glory of His justice."[393] Nevertheless, there is the hopeful promise that God will not allow us to be tempted beyond our capacity: "No trial has come to you but what is human. God is faithful and will not let you be tried beyond your strength; but with the trial he will also provide a way out, so that you may be able to bear it" (1 Cor. 10:13). God allows all this to draw us closer to Him, as described in the book of Job.

The most common work of demons consists in seducing human beings to evil to separate us from God. Pope John Paul II spoke about this during one of his general audiences:

> According to Sacred Scripture, and especially the New Testament, the dominion and the influence of Satan and of the other evil spirits

---

[392] Cf. Thomas Aquinas, STh, I, q.63, a.7.
[393] Thomas Aquinas, STh I–II, q.79, a.4.

embraces all the world.... The action of Satan consists primarily in tempting men to evil, by influencing their imaginations and higher faculties, to turn them away from the law of God.... It is possible that in certain cases the evil spirit goes so far as to exercise his influence not only on material things, but even on man's body, so that one can speak of "diabolical possession" (cf. Mark 5:2–9). It is not always easy to discern the preternatural factor operative in these cases, and the Church does not lightly support the tendency to attribute many things to the direct action of the devil; but in principle it cannot be denied that Satan can go to this extreme manifestation of his superiority in his will to harm and to lead to evil.[394]

It is indeed the devil who comes and takes away the Word that people might not believe (cf. Luke 8:12). It is the devil who induced Judas to hand Christ over to His executioners (cf. John 13:2). Jesus battles directly against the demons, healing people who are possessed by unclean, deaf, and dumb spirits (cf. Mark 9:25). Sacred Scripture shows clearly that the devil is not part of a fantasy world — he is a disastrous reality. The existence of the devil is something known through revelation; he is not, therefore, a myth. Neither is he a projection nor a symbol; he is all too much a personal and real spiritual being.

Due to their nature, demons operate within a preternatural order that surpasses the natural but is less than the supernatural. The category of the preternatural (deriving from the Latin word *praeter*, meaning *beyond*) indicates a realm that goes beyond the natural possibilities of any human being. However, demons cannot perform miracles, for miracles can only be done through the power of the supernatural. This means that only God can work miracles, either directly or through the mediation of saints and angels. They act as "instruments of divine power," not as a result of some gratuitous or natural power of their

---

[394] John Paul II, General Audience August 13, 1986, trans. Lawrence J. Gesy, in https://www.ewtn.com/library/NEWAGE/JP2DEVIL.htm [26.3.2022].

own.[395] Nevertheless, the work of the demons might appear to be "miraculous" to us, even though in reality it is not. Because demons are spirits, they can be in places, objects, or the bodies of people, and they are capably of physically influencing all of these things; "they are present where they are at work."[396] The Gospel says that it is even possible for several demons to enter the same body simultaneously, for Mary Magdalene was freed from seven demons (cf. Luke 8:2).

The devil is not an abstract figure, but a personal being. "The term Satan derives from the Hebrew 'sàtàn', which means the 'adversary, enemy, persecutor, accuser, calumniator'.... In Greek 'Satan' is called '*diàbolos*' (devil),... meaning 'to separate, to divide', referring to him as one who tries to separate us from God."[397] The very name describes the main task of this fallen angel—he causes division and separation through his opposition to divine truth. The Gospel of St. John calls the devil "a murderer from the beginning" since he seduces people to sin, guiding them toward eternal death. The same Gospel affirms that the devil "does not stand in truth, because there is no truth in him. When he tells a lie, he speaks in character, because he is a liar and the father of lies" (John 8:44). He is the adversary of God, contrary to His works and to His divine truth, even though he is "only" a creature. And he is not alone, for there is a multitude of perverse spirits, all of whom the Letter to the Ephesians calls "rulers of this present darkness" (Eph. 6:13).

In the period after the conclusion of the Second Vatican Council, and under the influence of rationalism, it was increasingly considered "unscientific" to speak about angels and even more unscientific to speak about demons. When Pope John Paul II addressed this topic in six catecheses during his general audiences, it was judged as

---

[395] See: Thomas Aquinas, De Pot., q.6, a.4.
[396] Francesco Bamonte, *Diabolical Possession and Exorcism: How to Recognize the Shrewd Deceiver*, trans. Benedict Ejeh, (Somolu Lagos: Bertie-John (Nig.) Printers, 2008), 33.
[397] Ibid., 26.

"politically incorrect" by some. Nevertheless, he was merely following and explaining the actual teaching of the Church. His predecessor, Pope Paul VI, had also addressed this topic in various audiences, calling the devil the occult enemy.[398] In a striking and memorable phrase, on June 29, 1972, he stated during a homily, given at a Mass for the solemnity of St. Peter and St. Paul, that the "smoke of Satan" had entered the Church. Through this dramatic image with great expressiveness he described the increasing confusion within the Church following the closure of the Second Vatican Council.[399]

The material that was covered in the preceding paragraphs is sufficient for the understanding of the fallen angels in this context. A general outline is presented in the *Catechism of the Catholic Church*, which provides a good overview about the fall of the angels and its consequences for the history of salvation.[400]

7.2.3. People Looking for an Exorcist

In recent decades, the concept of a *militia Christi* (Church Militant) has been largely abandoned or rejected, and, through the increase of the esoteric practices that was mentioned at the beginning of this chapter, many — especially the youth — have been exposed to demoniac activities, often leading them into situations which make them look for an exorcist. Since there is also an increasing number of people who are affected by severe psychological disorders who might also look for an exorcist, discernment is of great importance.

According to Fr. Francesco Bamonte, president of the International Association of Exorcists, it is important to discern between

---

[398] Cf. Paul VI, General Audience, 15 November 1972, in https://www.ewtn.com/library/papaldoc/p6devil.htm [26.6.2022].

[399] Paul VI, Omelia Solemnità dei Santi Apostoli Pietro e Paolo, June 29, 1972, in http://w2.vatican.va/content/paul-vi/it/homilies/1972/documents/hf_p-vi_hom_19720629.html [10.5.2023].

[400] CCC, 391–395.

three different categories of people asking for an exorcist. He writes: "The first consists of those who wrongly believe they are possessed by demons; the second consists of persons who knowingly or unknowingly pretend to be possessed; and finally the third are those who are truly affected by phenomena and disturbances that come from the extraordinary action of the devil."[401]

Prudence and experience are of great importance to avoid confusion, to protect the people involved as well as the exorcist, and to provide deliverance. As seen before, persons who wrongly believe they are possessed or who pretend to be possessed may cause much damage, especially if they are in contact with the media. Given the potential difficulties in such matters, some helpful criteria will be discussed that can assist in approaching the issue prudentially.[402]

7.2.4. Priests and Exorcism

Every priest has a specific personality. Every priest is different, and this has an impact on the way he approaches the topic of exorcism. "The term exorcism is understood … as an action (i.e. a set of words and/or gestures) aimed at expelling, casting out demons, spirits or evil entities, from people, places or things that are believed to be possessed or infested by them, or that are likely to become victims or instruments of their malice."[403] Therefore, some basic distinctions must be made which can be helpful in understanding why some priests struggle when confronted with this topic. Even though simplifications bring the danger of distorting something, they are still helpful to get an overview.

The former chief exorcist of Rome, Fr. Gabriele Amorth (d. 2016), complained often about the lack of exorcists in many parts of the world. He had helped possessed people from France, Austria, Germany, Switzerland, Spain, England, and other countries, providing deliverance and

---

[401] Francesco Bamonte, *Diabolical Possession*, 19.
[402] Cf. chap. 7.3.2.1.–7.3.2.4.
[403] IAE, 155.

support. People in need would come to Rome because of their desperate situation, and because no one in their own countries was willing to help them. Although he performed exorcisms almost every day, in the mornings and in the evenings, he said he had a waiting list three months long of people asking for his help. Within the Catholic Church, exorcists are often hindered in providing their service. At best, they are viewed with suspicion. As a result, those persons who believe themselves to be affected and in need of assistance end up looking elsewhere — that is, outside of the Catholic Church — for help; this includes looking to Evangelical communities. Fr. Amorth suspected a lack of faith as the origin of this particular attitude within the Church; this lack of faith also affects the many priests who overemphasize rationalism (reality is reduced to reason alone) and immanentism (reality is reduced to self-consciousness). This difficulty — a lack of faith negatively affecting exorcisms — is even described in the Gospel:

> When they came to the crowd a man approached, knelt down before him, and said, "Lord, have pity on my son, for he is a lunatic and suffers severely; often he falls into fire, and often into water. I brought him to your disciples, but they could not cure him." Jesus said in reply, "O faithless and perverse generation, how long will I be with you? How long will I endure you? Bring him here to me." Jesus rebuked him and the demon came out of him, and from that hour the boy was cured. Then the disciples approached Jesus in private and said, "Why could we not drive it out?" He said to them, "Because of your little faith. Amen, I say to you, if you have faith the size of a mustard seed, you will say to this mountain, 'Move from here to there,' and it will move. Nothing will be impossible for you." (Matt. 17:14–20)

If priests do not believe anymore that the invisible world is real, they will not be able to provide help to those who are greatly suffering from it, nor will they support those priests who are willing to serve as exorcists. Some clerics are even strongly opposed to the practice of exorcism, incorrectly reducing the preternatural phenomenon to natural phenomenon and to mental disorders.[404]

Others are simply ignorant. Since this topic is not usually taught during the preparation for the priesthood, and because angelology or demonology is not usually included in the academic or pastoral formation of priests, many priests have no real foundations from which to approach these issues. Consequently, when such ill-prepared priests are confronted with this topic, they have no idea what to do or how to proceed. I have, for example, known a priest who was named an exorcist after concluding his sabbatical year. He told me that he had no idea whatsoever what he would need to do. Ignorance in this field usually leads to four possible attitudes: 1) The priest rejects the possibility of any type of preternatural activity and looks instead for some kind of psychological explanation, which will not solve the problem but with which he can try to hide his ignorance. 2) The priest holds the mistaken view that the laity themselves can fight the extraordinary diabolic activity, forgetting that Christ is ontologically (by nature) present in priests — including himself. In this way, the priest refuses to help those affected by an extraordinary diabolic activity, increasing the burden upon them. 3) The priest claims that the devil is a "legalist" and so, without having the bishop's permission, they won't make use of the minor exorcism and thus they refuse to help. 4) Finally, there are priests who are either well-prepared, or humble enough, to ask for help from experts, and to learn from experienced men.

There are also priests who, by their character, are not well-suited to perform an exorcism. This reality is difficult to describe, but exorcism is not something that one simply "does." It necessarily requires, besides spiritual qualities and a certain lifestyle, a balanced character and a solid human formation. In other words, a strong character is required, one that will help the priest to cope with this heavy burden. To

---

[404] Cf. Gabriele Amorth, *An Exorcist Tells His Story*, 13–14.

put it simply, if someone has a very sensitive character, the inhibition threshold is high for him to face a direct confrontation with the devil.

Since the way of life is of great importance in determining and maintaining a priest's suitability for such confrontations, any double life or loss of the state of grace in the priest would make his attempts at offering this service not only dangerous but even impossible. Since the sacramentals become effective through the principle of *ex opere operantis Ecclesiae*, exorcisms necessarily require holiness of life.

Finally, there are those priests gifted with a balanced character, deeply rooted in faith, well-formed, and striving to live a holy life. If they are named exorcists, they too often find themselves inundated by requests from persons who seek help. Sadly, they are confronted with a long waiting list, for the reality is that there is a growing number of people requesting exorcisms. There is a real need for their abilities, and the gap is growing between this necessity and the number of trained priests who are able to meet it.

7.3. The Work of the Devil

As established earlier in this chapter, Sacred Scripture affirms that the devil is a personal and real spiritual being, opposed to God and His truth, giving men a difficult time. This is noted as early as the book of Genesis (cf. Gen. 3:1–7), but the personal component of this spiritual being emerges more clearly in the book of Job. All people find themselves in a spiritual battle, having to decide whether to serve the truth of God or the lie of the devil. Therefore, the book of Job calls man's life on earth "a drudgery" (Job 7:1). St. Paul encourages us to practice spiritual warfare against sin, erroneous doctrines, and the "evil spirits" (cf. Eph. 6:12). This becomes more clear when considering the very nature of what it means.

Man consists of a substantial unity of body and soul. Even though everything we do through the body can be perceived by the devil, the human soul is perfectly known only by God. Therefore, evil spirits cannot come to a certain knowledge of our thoughts, but they can deduce our thoughts — in other words, they learn who we are, and they get very good at guessing our thoughts. They can get to know everything exterior, such as our behavior, attitudes, tendencies, likes and dislikes, weak points, defects, sins, and so on. Consequently, they can use all this information against us, influencing our thoughts, sentiments, and choices.

At this point, a basic distinction must be made: there are two different ways that demonic activity functions. One is called ordinary action, which signifies the way demons approach every human person. The second is the extraordinary way, which implies a specific use of preternatural force against specific humans. Some time will be devoted to explaining this distinction because it is of great importance to understanding the essence of an exorcism.

7.3.1. Ordinary Actions of the Devil

The ordinary action of the devil is called temptation. Jesus Christ was tempted, and we too are tempted, for "no slave is greater than his master nor any messenger greater than the one who sent him" (John 13:16). This is another reason why this aspect is also echoed in the Lord's Prayer, which contains the petition "and lead us not into temptation." It is a petition to free us from the devil and his influences within a twofold perspective: on the one hand, through divine grace, and on the other hand, through our collaboration with divine grace.

Our evil inclinations and sins, unless sins are blotted out by Confession, are known to the demons. They have a precise knowledge of these and ordinarily make use of this knowledge through temptations. Being in a state of grace is our best defense system, for the loss of sanctifying grace separates us from God and leaves us vulnerable.[405] Weakened as a consequence of Original Sin (concupiscence) and seduced by

---

[405] Cf. *CCC*, 1861.

temptations, it is not always easy to remain in the state of grace; it requires a spiritual and militant attitude. Pope Paul VI, commenting during a general audience on the Lord's Prayer and the meaning of the petition of liberation from evil, said: "The Christian must be militant; he must be vigilant and strong (1 Pet. 5:8); he must at times make use of special ascetical practices to escape from certain diabolical attacks; Jesus teaches us this by pointing to 'prayer and fasting' (Mark 9:29) as a remedy. And the Apostle suggests the mainline to follow: 'Do not be conquered by evil but conquer evil with good' (Rom. 12:21; Matt. 13:29)."[406]

In the years after the conclusion of the Second Vatican Council, this idea of the *militia Christi* was mostly abandoned throughout the Church,[407] even though this request and prescription for it is very present in Scripture. The Second Letter to the Corinthians says, for example: "For, although we are in the flesh, we do not battle according to the flesh, for the weapons of our battle are not of flesh but are enormously powerful, capable of destroying fortresses" (2 Cor. 10:3-4). There is an old saying that whoever fights may lose, but whoever does not fight has already lost. This becomes true especially when concerning the ordinary action of the devil. Without a "militant and vigilant spirit," it will be impossible to resist temptations. Any passivity in spiritual warfare makes people fall into temptation. And temptations — if given into — lead to sin and death, as affirmed in the Letter of James: "Rather, each person is tempted when he is lured and enticed by his own desire. Then desire conceives and brings forth sin, and when sin reaches maturity it gives birth to death" (James 1:14-15). However, the distinction must be drawn between being tempted by sin and actually consenting to that temptation, actually falling into sin.[408] Temptation becomes sin only if it is

---

[406] Paul VI, General Audience, November 15, 1972.
[407] Cf. Johann Auer, "*Militia Christi*. Zur Geschichte eines christlichen Gottesbildes," in Geist und Leben, vol. 32 (1959): 340-351.
[408] Cf. CCC, 2847.

freely and consciously consented to. Temptations are a real challenge for all people, no matter their faith or lack thereof; therefore, every Christian is urged to be vigilant (cf. Matt. 26:41), to pray without ceasing (cf. 1 Thess. 5:17), to persevere in the state of grace (cf. John 15:15), and to live a virtuous life aiming toward final perseverance (cf. 2 Tim. 4:7).[409] Temptation is *not* a sin in itself, but it *becomes* a sin when consented to.

Furthermore, there is a difference between trials and temptations. A trial is a difficulty one must face—it does not necessarily lead to sin. Sickness can be a trial, and it can in fact lead to a growth in spiritual life, as in the case of St. Ignatius of Loyola. But it may also be a weighty burden that prompts a man to surrender to temptations such as anger, resentment, self-pity, or despair. A trial is fundamentally different from temptation.

7.3.2. Extraordinary Actions of the Devil

Besides the ordinary action of the devil, to which all people are exposed, there is also the possibility that the devil becomes active in a more specific way. Although this is less common, the possibility and reality of it should not be underestimated or dismissed. For this, the *terminus technicus* (that is, the technical term) "extraordinary action" is used. It can equally affect living beings, objects, and places. The exorcist Fr. Bamonte explains that the goal of such an extraordinary activity of the devil "is that of instilling fear and trepidation into a soul and dragging it into eternal perdition. Bodily harm is used to procure spiritual harm; it is only a means to achieve his objectives."[410] It becomes understandable why sacramentals ought to contain apotropaic elements, and why it is important to exorcise and bless objects and

---

[409] Other helpful remedies are explained by Jean-Nicolas Grou, *Handbüchlein für innerliche Seelen*, trans. Wilhelm Schamoni, (Arensberg: Verlagsdruckerei Josef Kral, 1983), 114–116.

[410] Francesco Bamonte, *Diabolical Possession*, 60.

places as well as people. So, what exactly is an extraordinary action of the devil? How can it be defined?

For this, it is helpful to turn to the International Association of Exorcists, approved in its juridical status by the Holy See in 2014, even though their history began some thirty years earlier.[411] After the promulgation of the new rite of exorcism by the Congregation for Divine Worship and the Discipline of the Sacraments in 1998, the Italian Episcopal Conference asked the International Association of Exorcists to provide more specific explanations regarding the extraordinary action of the devil, explanations that could be helpful for discernment.

A group of well-known and recognized exorcists followed a long-existing tradition to provide the desired classification. They identify four different categories of extraordinary action: infestations, vexations, obsessions, and possessions. This classification was accepted by the Italian Episcopal Conference and used as a point of reference during the official presentation of the rite of exorcism.[412] Even though this distinction is particularly helpful, it must be said that, in practice, boundaries between one form and the other are not always clear; it takes a wealth of experience and knowledge to make this discernment accurately.

As we are going to see, Sacred Scripture describes the extraordinary action of the devil in different ways. The main goal of the extraordinary demonic presence is to enslave people, leading them to despair and to eternal damnation. Therefore, the best defense against the attacks of the evil one is communion with God through a life of grace. Thus, it is important to keep watch over life with moral strictness so as not to be exposed to the influence of the devil, for whoever is not in communion with God is not only susceptible to evil, but virtually exposed to it. The understanding of this has been lost to

---

[411] Cf. International Association of Exorcists (ed.), *Guidelines for the Ministry of Exorcism: In the Light of the Current Ritual*, (Dover: Two Hearts Media Organization, 2022). From now on as: IAE.

[412] Cf. Francesco Bamonte, *Diabolical Possession*, 55.

modern man (including Catholics), and so many are without a (spiritual) defense.

The extraordinary action of the devil usually causes divisions and misfortunes. But not all misfortunes are the result of an extraordinary action of the devil, and not all sins are directly the result of diabolical actions. Thus, while nobody knows for sure what they will face on any given day and in any given trial, it would be well to bear in mind the admonition of the Apostle Peter: "Be sober and vigilant. Your opponent the devil is prowling around like a roaring lion looking for (someone) to devour. Resist him, steadfast in faith" (1 Pet. 5:8–9). With these introductory thoughts forming a foundation for the understanding of the four types of extraordinary diabolical action, it is possible to turn now to a more detailed discussion of each type.

7.3.2.1. Infestation *(Infestatio)*

The first category is called infestation. This form describes demonic powers that can come into possession of inanimate objects, like houses and places, but also animals.[413] The Gospel of Mark describes that Jesus Christ liberated a man of many unclean spirits, called "Legion." These spirits were sent into a herd of swine; the "herd of about two thousand rushed down a steep bank into the sea, where they were drowned" (Mark 5:13). Moreover, places and entire cities may become the dwelling place for demons, as the book of Revelation affirms: "Fallen, fallen is Babylon the great. She has become a haunt for demons. She is a cage for every unclean spirit, a cage for every unclean bird, [a cage for every unclean] and disgusting [beast]" (Rev. 18:2).

Some of these infestations occur occasionally, while others can be permanent, as described in the previous two examples. If an infestation manifests itself permanently, for example, every night, or always in the same place or time, it becomes more

---

[413] Cf. IAE, 070–073.

evident to the people that something inexplicable through the natural world is happening.

The causes for such a demonic presence can vary. Often, they are caused by curses or by cursed objects. Even many Catholics are not aware of what can be at stake with these things. They keep in their homes, often with pride, objects or statues related to other deities from Asia, Africa, or other places, "souvenirs" which they have brought back from various journeys. But even something that is perhaps so seemingly innocuous as this may, by itself, open the door to an infestation. Besides the direct violation against the first commandment, these objects are often cursed since they are related to other gods — which are actually demons. They work the opposite of a blessing. "Instead of grace being attached to an object to make it holy, a demon has been attached to the object to make it associated with evil."[414] Furthermore, certain sins, especially if repeated and persistent, may become the cause for extraordinary diabolic action. This is especially true for "sins that cry to heaven."[415] Another possible cause for infestation could be crimes. The specific places where they were committed may also become the cause for a diabolical infestation. For example, when abortion or suicide was committed, or a satanic or esoteric ritual was celebrated in a house, apartment, or basement, this may cause a diabolic presence.[416] Likewise, the presence of certain magical and superstitious objects, unknown deities or images, symbolizing demons or being linked to esoteric practices, may also cause an infestation. This is a real issue since these kinds of objects are commercialized today. Just to provide one example, on March 25, 2019, it was reported that Walmart was selling products which might cause a diabolic presence. According to the *National Catholic Register*, they were selling satanic products; their online

---

[414] Adam C. Blai, *Hauntings, Possessions, and Exorcisms*, (Steubenville, Ohio: Emmaus Road Publishing, 2017), 45.
[415] Cf. CCC, 1867.
[416] Cf. Francesco Bamonte, *Diabolical Possession*, 63.

catalogue contained 22 pages (around 440 items) of demonic merchandise. To give some idea of what that entailed: "The products include demonic sculptures and figures; satanic pornography that blasphemes Christ's crucifixion; numerous products and jewelry with pentagrams and other demonic images, and books that include the Satanic bible and books of spells. Especially featured is Baphomet, the horned, goat-headed figure trademarked as the Church of Satan symbol."[417] Clearly, one does not need to travel to Africa or to Asia to obtain such items. They are easily available and commercialized in our so-called "liberal" society. Finally, spiritual meetings and esoterical practice, practicing reiki, yoga, frequenting witches or wizards, channeling, invoking the deceased, and so on, and especially the profanation of the Holy Eucharist may also cause demonic infestations.

There are detailed lists of different manifestations caused by infestations, as indicated by experienced exorcists. However, local infestations manifest in different ways, and there is no strict uniformity, for evil spirits are very creative. With the caveat that this list is far from comprehensive, some of the most common manifestations will be mentioned. These may include such occurrences as noises on rooftops, house pavements, walls, doors, windows, "sounds of walking steps of invisible persons"; "mysterious voices or shrieking, laughing, uproars"; "disappearance of objects that are either no longer discovered or are discovered in the most unimaginable part of the house"; "interruption of electric current without electrical faults"; "unexplainable damage of household electronics"; "lamps that come on and off, bells ringing, without anyone operating the switches"; "various apparitions of shadows or persons or monstrous beings"; "water taps from which blood flows instead of water."[418] The intensity of the action may

---

[417] Patti M. Armstrong, "An Exorcist Comments on Walmart's Satanic Products," March 25, 2019, in http://www.ncregister.com/blog/armstrong/an-exorcist-comments-on-walmarts-satanic-products [8.5.2023].

[418] Francesco Bamonte, *Diabolical Possession*, 60–62. See also: IAE, 070–073.

vary according to the degrees of a demonic action. All of these diabolic activities have in common that they make life very difficult for the people around whom they occur, not only causing nightmares and sleepless nights, but even leading people into despair.

To be able to help, and help is urgent, discernment is of particular importance. In particular, the following fundamental rule must be observed: "Anything that surpasses the natural law, if it does not come from God, is from Satan. There is no midway."[419] Once natural causes, as well as auto-suggestions and psychological problems, are excluded, discernment must take place according to the indicated rule. Special attention must be paid to the possible origins that may have caused these infestations. If they are known, it will be easier to banish the demonic influence through the power of God and with the help of sacraments and sacramentals.

It is not always possible to determine with certainty whether particular things or actions have caused infestations, but having an idea of the cause(s) may serve as a valuable orientation concerning the measures to be taken. This is because there is a difference, for example, between the consequences caused by satanic rituals and Transcendental Meditation; there is a difference between the profanation of the Eucharist and some magical souvenirs or objects related to other deities. If such an object is individuated as a possible cause, it must be burned immediately. It is not enough to exorcise and bless it. Nowadays, many Catholics are very ignorant; they "tolerate" all kinds of things they ought not, but they ignore the first commandment. Concerning this, however, there can be no compromises, as has already been clearly shown. It is quite common that Catholics bring back from their journeys talismans, amulets, statues of deities, and so on, or they receive such things as gifts and then want to keep them so as not to offend the giver.

---

[419] Francesco Bamonte, *Diabolical Possession*, 62.

These are by no means harmless, "nice" objects, but a real danger. Their effects might be surprising for some; however, all these practices have in common that they are a grave violation of the first commandment. The psalmist affirms that those "multiply their sorrows who court other gods" (Ps. 16:4). The *Catechism of the Catholic Church* forewarns not to practice idolatry, divinizing what is not God,[420] and it goes on to say: "All practices of *magic* or *sorcery* ... are gravely contrary to the virtue of religion. These practices are even more to be condemned when accompanied by the intention of harming someone, or when they have recourse to the intervention of demons. Wearing charms is also reprehensible. *Spiritism* often implies divination or magical practices; the Church for her part warns the faithful against it. Recourse to so-called traditional cures does not justify either the invocation of evil powers or the exploitation of another's credulity."[421] In short, infestations are increasing more and more because sin is tolerated and practiced, because more and more people make use of curses, because esoteric practices are expanding — and all of this is often dismissed as some kind of harmless game, even by representatives of the Church. As a result, infestations are increasing at an alarming rate.

At this point, one final comment must be made: The preternatural force of the demonic powers is something totally different from parapsychology. It is not about paranormal phenomena, which usually submit the invisible world to materialistic explanation, which is simply not possible if justice is done to the methodology. Infestations are caused by demonic activity based on preternatural force. They affect people directly or indirectly, causing damage, especially to those things that serve for daily life.[422]

---

[420] Cf. CCC, 2113.
[421] CCC, 2117.
[422] Cf. IAE, 070–071.

7.3.2.2. Vexation *(Circumsessio)*

The second category of extraordinary action of the devil is called vexation. This consists of physical aggression against a person. However, the person being attacked does maintain control of his or her intellect and will, which is not the case in a possession.[423] The transgressions against Job and his family were diabolical vexations (cf. Job 1:7–22), as were the trials of Tobit (cf. Tob. 2–3). These forms of ailment appear and disappear suddenly, and without any clinical prevision. Such a form is also described in the Gospel of Mark (cf. Mark 9:17–22); it was healed by casting out the demon.

The causes leading to vexations are similar to the causes of infestations described above. However, such an extraordinary diabolical action may not necessarily be the result of sins, crimes, or esoteric practices. As in the case of Job, people living a just and holy life can be affected. Several saints suffered through diabolical vexation. For example, St. Padre Pio was frequently whipped by a demon, and the Curé d'Ars was thrown out of his bed by Satan. Indeed, his bed was even set on fire by the devil; the remnants of this bed can still be observed in the museum in Ars. Consequently, Francesco Bamonte affirms: "Diabolical vexations can strike individuals, groups (including large groups), parishes, convents, religious institutes, businesses, etc. in various degrees and in different ways."[424]

This extraordinary diabolic action can result in scratches, burns, bruises, and even in broken bones. It can also become manifest in the case of an inexplicable aversion to prayer, sacred things, and to God, which is often "followed by series of misfortunes, failures, chains of physical evils."[425] However, not all forms of vexation imply an aversion to the sacred. Other typical cases of vexation are illnesses without any

---

[423] Cf. ibid., 56.
[424] Francesco Bamonte, *Diabolical Possession*, 67.
[425] Ibid., 67.

apparent cause that affect the internal organs, provoking pain without visible signs. Thus, vexations can affect health. Fr. Gabriele Amorth provided several examples from his daily experience: "It happened to me that in liberating a demoniac, the woman was contemporaneously cured of a terrible tumor. Evidently, in this case, the spell submitted to by the demon had a duplicate effect, spiritual and physical. On the other hand, the Gospel also attests two cases of physical healing that are tied to a spiritual healing from an evil spell. For example, Jesus heals a mute demoniac (see Matt. 9:32–34) and a blind and mute demoniac (Matt. 12:22–24)."[426]

Fr. Amorth had a great experience with the different types of demonic activity, which allowed him to make a precise discernment. He mentioned another aspect of vexations, which is also of relevance within this context. He said: "As I have said, vexations are not always manifested on a physical level. Sometimes they can strike affections: it can happen, for example, that a couple who are married or are engaged to be married can separate, or, to the contrary, two persons can become engaged, even though they are incompatible."[427] This is also a serious problem nowadays, for, as can easily be understood, it all too often leads to the failure of marriages.

These vexations that have an impact on affections and feelings, misleading people, are sometimes quite easy to discern, but in other cases are much more difficult. If there are unexplainable aversions toward the sacred combined with misfortunes, physical evils, and so on, there might be a vexation; however, there could be forms of vexation even without such an aversion. In any case, natural causes, as well as simulations, must be excluded. Even for an exorcist priest with a lot of experience, it is not necessarily easy to discern what

---

[426] Gabriele Amorth, An Exorcist Explains Demonic Possession and Vexation, September 3, 2020, in https://catholicexchange.com/an-exorcist-explains-demonic-possession-and-vexation [12.2.2023].

[427] Ibid.

exactly is going on. Part of this is because of the growing number of people who are tormented by certain symptoms which are caused by natural disturbances rather than any actual demonic activity.

7.3.2.3. Obsession *(Obsessio)*

The third category of extraordinary action of the devil is called obsession. It is an interior torment on the psychic level. The inner senses of the person are affected, such as imagination and sensible memory.[428] This necessarily affects human capacities, such as the intellect and the will. Fr. Francesco Bamonte offers the following description: It is "a demonic aggression in which, without blocking the intellective faculty and the free will of the person during the crisis, the devil succeeds in communicating to the mind (imagination and memory) obsessive thoughts and images, often rationally absurd, which the victim is not able to do away with."[429] As a result, the person is in a state of confusion and not capable of making a decision. Obsessions differ in forms, grades, and intensity. In the worst case, they can dominate the mind of a person completely. It can be compared to extraordinarily strong and prolonged temptations that occupy the mind.

The word "obsessive" already indicates that it is about obsessive ideas, occupying the whole of the attention, bombarding and invading the mind. For example, it may result in obfuscating the senses concerning appetites such as food or sex. For this reason, it can be seen clearly why pornography is so dangerous. At any time, the devil may use these perverted images, which usually remain on the memory of the inner senses, to create obsessions. To put it more bluntly, pornography makes it much easier for the devil to bring about a state of obsession; mere images or persons who are provocatively dressed can be the source of such obsessive reactions. Awareness of this type

---

[428] Cf. IAE, 061.
[429] Francesco Bamonte, *Diabolical Possession*, 69.

of provocation has been almost completely lost, or is dismissed as a natural and understandable practice.

All of this makes it easier for the devil to cause obsessions. Even though these thoughts contradict right reason and are against the will, they nevertheless occupy the inner senses. This may also be accompanied by the conviction that someone is going crazy, becoming desperate by falling into sin again and again, or is even inclined to suicide.[430] Another outcome may be that, given such intense mental frustration, the affected person considers his or her life useless. This may provoke an aversion against the proper choice of life, responsibilities at home or in the family, or duties — or all of the above. It often causes anxiety, doubts, anger, and rebellion. The person finds it difficult to free himself from this mental and emotional torment and is sometimes even incapable of making a decision. St. Paul might have had in mind these diabolical actions when he wrote in his Letter to the Romans:

> The willing is ready at hand, but doing the good is not. For I do not do the good I want, but I do the evil I do not want. Now if (I) do what I do not want, it is no longer I who do it, but sin that dwells in me. So, then, I discover the principle that when I want to do right, evil is at hand. For I take delight in the law of God, in my inner self, but I see in my members another principle at war with the law of my mind, taking me captive to the law of sin that dwells in my members. (Rom. 7:18–23)

Indirectly, a quotation from the Gospel of Mark can also be related to such situations. The Gospel says: "But what comes out of a person, that is what defiles. From within people, from their hearts, come evil thoughts, unchastity, theft, murder, adultery, greed, malice, deceit, licentiousness, envy, blasphemy, arrogance, folly. All these evils come from within and they defile" (Mark 7:20–23).

---

[430] Cf. ibid., 70.

Diabolical obsessions can affect all: unbelievers, ordinary believers, and fervent souls with an intense prayer life. However, discernment is difficult since the described effects may be similar to psychiatric problems, pathological causes, and hysterical and unbalanced characters. However, in the case of an obsession, the demonic activity becomes "invasive, overwhelming and insistent ... thus heavily disturbing the psyche of the person."[431]

It is one of the problems of our time that many people have lost a healthy balance. Thus, for people tending to be scrupulous, it may happen, for example, that they continuously ask whether they have closed the door, if they have switched off the light, and so on. In the case of a demonic action, such an attitude would be related to inner anxiety. Affected people experience suddenly invasive, overwhelming, and heavy disturbances of the psyche. Often, this is accompanied by a total or partial blockage of prayer, or even a perceived hatred toward the sacred. It also happens that obsessions influence dreams at night, turning them into nightmares.

Already at this point, it becomes clear that non-balanced and mentally disturbed people could more readily become victims of a diabolical obsession. In these cases, it becomes difficult even for an expert to discern what is what, for, as seen above, the extraordinary action of the devil affects especially the natural faculties of a person. However, and this may serve as a criterion for discernment, an obsession is usually related to a maleficent origin; it is not always easy to discover, however, if this is the case or, if it is, what that maleficent origin might be. Consequently, it might be necessary to intervene with both medical therapy and exorcism. Fr. Francesco Bamonte provides an example that is helpful in understanding such obsessions:

---

[431] Ibid., 71.

> As a young university student, I was a non-practicing Christian. In a moment of great difficulty with my studies I had serious fears that I would no longer be able to graduate. I discussed this with a friend who suggested that I go with him to a witch. The woman, who claimed to be involved in "white magic" was practicing "coffee witchcraft" (*caffeomanzia*), an art of divination which she claimed to have learned from her dead husband of Egyptian nationality. She prepared Turkish coffee which she asked me to drink. She told me not to consume all of it but to leave a little inside the cup. The woman was reciting a series of complex prayers both when she was preparing the coffee and when I was drinking it. What struck me was the repetition of the name of St. Cyprian at various points during the prayer. I left some of the coffee in the cup as she had directed, she poured this on a little plant. I was watching her very intently. She told me that I would graduate but that I had to sacrifice a lot and renounce many things. Less than two hours after I had returned home, I started having an obsessive thought that had never occurred to me before: "Make a pact with the devil and he will help you to graduate." I felt that thought very intensely within me. It was agonizing, almost overwhelming, to the extent that at some point I had to struggle seriously with all my power not to give in voluntarily to what was being proposed to me. Though rationally I knew that it was against my will, I felt like that crazy thought was within my person, so alarming and dangerous. There ensued a spiritual combat which caused me much suffering over the years. The assistance of three different psychiatrists did not help me but worsened my health due to the grave collateral effects of the medication I had to take. It was at this point that I went to an exorcist who brought me closer to God.[432]

He also relates a second example, an incident in which a priest was given a packet by someone who had brought it to him from a witch.

Out of curiosity the priest wanted to know what was inside the packet. When the person had left, the priest was trying to open the packet when some dust flew out of it and hit his face so that he inhaled it, at least

---

[432] Ibid., 73.

partially. Shortly after, while celebrating the Holy Mass, during consecration, he heard within him the worst kinds of blasphemies: something that had never happened to him before. From that day on, it happened each time that he celebrated the Holy Mass, once it was time for consecration the same phenomenon repeated itself, against his will.[433]

Countless examples could be introduced showing how much the extraordinary action of the devil affects the natural capacities of people. Thus, while discernment is not easy, it becomes evident that these affected people are in urgent need of help.

The question of how this and the other types of extraordinary diabolic activity can be overcome will be answered in the last part of this chapter. For now, it is sufficient to note that deliverance from obsession might take some time; it might be a while before the positive effects of liberation will be notable to the person who has been affected. Much depends on how long-standing an obsession was and on how much a person's natural capacities have already been affected. In the case of the student, the obsessions had tormented him for several years, causing long-term effects on his psyche that weakened his natural capacities. Consequently, as is often the case, the healing process, which can start at that moment of deliverance, took some time.

7.3.2.4. Possession *(Possessio)*

The delicate and extensive topic of possession cannot be covered as fully it should be in this context.[434] Nevertheless, in lieu of the complete

---

[433] Ibid., 74.
[434] There is a great deal of literature on this subject. Thus, we especially recommend the guidelines prepared by the International Association of Exorcists concerning this topic. See IAE, 294–580. Cf. Istituto Sacerdos (ed.), *Esorcismo e preghiera di liberazione. Atti del corso*, 2nd ed., (Monterotondo: Edizioni Art, 2012). Also, cf. Association of International Exorcists (eds.), *Proceedings of the National Congress of Italian Exorcists, 9th–13th September 2013*, trans. IAE English Secretariat, (Rome, Association of International Exorcists, 2013).

volume or even volumes that it warrants, an overview of its most important aspects will be provided, starting with a definition.

Demonic possession is not a mental or psychological disorder or a double personality; it is present when one or many demonic spirits exercise despotic control over a human body while the victim is incapable of resisting, even in cases where he or she maintains consciousness of what is happening.[435] Due to a preternatural diabolic action, it is a "temporary substitution of personality." Even though the comparison is not very precise, you could compare it to the "team viewer" or "shared screen" of a computer, which allows someone else to take over your computer. These moments of possession are also called "moments of crisis."[436] It is in them that the devil manifests himself through the body of the person.

A diabolic possession is a stable condition with a permanent presence, although there might be moments and periods of calmness. The moments of crisis may be of short or long duration, in which the "person's will is blocked" and, therefore, he "is not in any way responsible for whatever action he does at the time."[437] The devil "could manifest his presence through contortions, bouts of uncontrollable anger against the possessed person or against others, excessive physical force, knowledge of unknown languages or things that the person is incapable of knowing, as well as enormous aversion towards sacred things that is manifested through blasphemies, curses and evil, blasphemous and/or obscene words."[438]

There might be periods of calmness, in which the person is able to pray and even to receive the sacraments. However, this will depend on the degree of the demonic possession; some are stronger than others. The affected person will also suffer from physical

---

[435] Cf. IAE, 052–053.
[436] Francesco Bamonte, *Diabolical Possession*, 75.
[437] Ibid.
[438] Ibid.

vexations and obsessions, "but not all who suffer demonic vexations and obsessions are necessarily possessed as well."[439]

As early as the Old Testament, cases are described of what today is called diabolical possession. The first book of Samuel says: "The spirit of the LORD had departed from Saul, and he was tormented by an evil spirit sent by the LORD" (1 Sam. 16:14). In the New Testament, demonic possessions are frequently described. Sometimes the victims are deprived of sight and speech (cf. Matt. 12:22), while in other passages, preternatural effects are described. For example, in the Gospel of Mark, the demoniac presence throws a boy into convulsions; in the end, the boy was brought to Jesus:

> And when he [the boy] saw him, the spirit immediately threw the boy into convulsions. As he fell to the ground, he began to roll around and foam at the mouth. Then he questioned his father, "How long has this been happening to him?" He replied, "Since childhood. It has often thrown him into fire and into water to kill him. But if you can do anything, have compassion on us and help us." Jesus said to him, "'If you can!' Everything is possible to one who has faith." Then the boy's father cried out, "I do believe, help my unbelief!" Jesus, on seeing a crowd rapidly gathering, rebuked the unclean spirit and said to it, "Mute and deaf spirit, I command you: come out of him and never enter him again!" Shouting and throwing the boy into convulsions, it came out. (Mark 9:20–26)

This passage is revealing for several reasons. First, Sacred Scripture shows that even children can be possessed, meaning that they might well be in need of liberation. For this very reason, exorcisms can be used — inexplicably, this is questioned today even by theologians — for children as well as adults. Furthermore, exorcisms are supposed to be part of the baptismal rite and for immediate

---

[439] Ibid., 76.

preparation for Baptism; however, they were regrettably mostly abolished in the new rite of Baptism.[440]

There are cases when even official exorcists deny exorcisms to children because they falsely presuppose that a child cannot be possessed. Instead, these children sometimes may receive, for example, drug treatments assisted by psychiatrists; however, these treatments cannot free them from an extraordinary diabolical action.

At this point, a brief summary and emphasis on five points will be presented. First, following biblical testimony, even small children may be affected severely by demons. Second, the biblical passage quoted above shows that possessed persons are submitted to preternatural power (see also Mark 5:3–4). Third, in that case, it was "only" one diabolic spirit — however, as already seen before, a person can be possessed by several demons. The Gospel of Luke describes the case of the person who was possessed by a "Legion" of demons, affirming that "many demons had entered him" (Luke 8:30). Fourth, many possessed people struggle for a long time before they realize that there is a preternatural force at work. The demon usually blocks the human faculties of intellect and will, taking control over the body. This is normally reflected in the physiology of the possessed person and becomes visible. In moments of crisis, the devil "makes the body's limbs perform the movements he wants; it is he who imposes his countenance upon the person's face, particularly in the eyes and the mouth, the features that

---

[440] The prayer of exorcism is: "Almighty ever-living God, who sent your Son into the world to drive out from us the power of Satan, the spirit of evil, and bring the human race, rescued from darkness, into the marvelous Kingdom of your light: we humbly beseech you to free these children from Original Sin, to make them the temple of your glory, and to grant that your Holy Spirit may dwell in them. Through Christ our Lord." *The Roman Ritual. The Order of Baptism of Children*, 22. As will become clear in the following, this prayer is not an exorcism, but a prayer against the consequences of Original Sin (concupiscence). Furthermore, it is noticeable that not even the sign of the cross is prescribed.

reveal the characteristic traits of his personality and together reveal his 'emotions' that are subject to sudden changes: his anger, his pride, his conceit, his contempt, his will to deceive, to frighten, his rebellion against God, his malice, his fear, showing himself as a hunted animal who is terrified of God and the exorcist."[441] As said before, the affected person may be conscious or unconscious at this very moment. Fifth, it might take years to free someone from a diabolic possession, depending upon the criteria described above.[442]

What causes a diabolical possession might be similar to those aspects mentioned earlier, that is, those aspects that open the door to lesser demonic activity. Alessandro Pennesi indicates the following possible causes, without presenting a complete list: "Active participation in spiritualistic groups"; if "mediums, wizards, or fortune-tellers have been consulted"; if "they have ever used amulets or a talisman"; if "they have brought home objects ... made for local magic"; if they "practice any technique connected to New Age"; or if "they have been part of a sect or association in which they participated in esoteric or satanic rituals."[443]

For the discernment of a diabolical possession, besides many lessons from experts and reliable authors, experience is important. As seen in chapter 7.2.3., there are three categories of persons who look for an exorcist. To recap, the first group is convinced that they are possessed by a demon when they are not; the second group consciously simulates possession; and the third group is made up of those who really suffer from disturbances due to an extraordinary action of the devil. How can we tell the difference? How can we discern the truth?

---

[441] Cf. IAE, 055.
[442] Cf. chap. 3.
[443] Alessandro Pennesi, "Some Criteria for the Discernment of Some of the Reasons Why People Wish to Meet an Exorcist," in Association of International Exorcists (eds.) *Proceedings of the National Congress of Italian Exorcists, 9th–13th September 2013*, trans. IAE English Secretariat, (Rome, Association of International Exorcists, 2013), 51–58; here 53.

Before answering this question, another basic consideration is necessary. By now, it is clear that bishops, priests, or religious who do not believe in the existence of the devil will not be of any help to people who suffer from diabolic possession. Fr. Gabriele Amorth said that this unbelief needed to be considered as a "mortal sin of omission," doing tremendous damage to the people and denying them necessary help. People who are possessed suffer badly — theirs is an unimaginable suffering. At the same time, God has given to His priests powerful means to overcome these sufferings. If this is not done, or if attempts at requesting it to be done are even outright rejected, it is consequently a grave sin of omission. Simultaneously, these faulty bishops, priests, and religious, who in fact are living a double life and are therefore deprived of the state of grace, cannot be of any help whatsoever. For — as it corresponds to the nature of the sacramentals — they are separated from the grace of God, and so they could only rely on their own human power, a power which is by nature incapable of battling preternatural power. The Gospel of John affirms: "Whoever remains in me and I in him will bear much fruit, because without me you can do nothing" (John 15:5). This attitude and unbelief has led to the sad situation that was already discussed of exorcists who have long waiting lists. Because of the great ignorance of even the most basic concepts in this field among so many priests, all too often it is the few highly trained and specialized exorcists who are left to handle both the most extreme cases (as is right) and the very basic discernments (which should not be necessary). Basic discernments usually could and should be done by any priest facilitating the work of the exorcists.

Regarding the three groups of persons who might approach an exorcist, the first group is inclined to attribute every negative event directly to the devil. If their business is going poorly, if there are family problems, someone is sick, and so on, they blame the devil. These people visit one exorcist after another. For them, it is commonly not even a simulation, but a false conviction; they lack any particular diabolic manifestation. They might be at a "trial" with a "diabolic possession." They continue in their conviction that they are possessed, even though several exorcists have proven and told them the contrary. They must accept the reality that they do not suffer from an extraordinary diabolic action. By way of comparison, this group would, in the medical world, be known as hypochondriacs.

The second group is more dangerous, since it includes those people who simulate possessions. I have seen several cases in person. Once, during Confession, a person started to simulate convulsions, changed their voice, and so on. I arranged a meeting for the next day, inviting another priest and a layperson of confidence to join us. Because I had the impression that the person was simulating, I said that I would pray the exorcism over the person. This is a means of discernment that can be applied if there is any doubt in this direction. Usually, the priest should not say that he would say an exorcism over the person for several reasons, such as not to cause sensation or disturbances. However, in this case, instead of praying the words of the minor exorcism, I started reading the words of the rubrics in a language not known to the person. Were there actually any genuine possession present, these words would not have caused any effects whatsoever. Nonetheless, the person started immediately to "manifest." The result was evident to all; there was no actual possession, but only an imitation of one. Priests need to be aware that there are people who want to deceive, and as touched on before, this becomes even more dangerous when an inexperienced priest is confronted with these issues and when the mass media are involved. Some people do this because they lack affection and, through their behavior, attract attention and compassion. Some have mental problems and psychic or psychological disturbances.[444] Usually, these people need

---

[444] Francesco Bamonte mentions within this context "involuntary simulations" and the "phenomenon of suggestions" that are "never associated with the typical signs of possession." Francesco Bamonte, *Diabolical Possession*, 79.

inner healing, which does not come from exorcism, but from an authentic life of prayer. It is worth noting, too, as there is a need for better preparation in this field in the formation of priests across the board, that a well-prepared priest would soon recognize a pseudo-possession; it is not easy to simulate a real possession.

Now the third group will come into focus: the people who are truly possessed and who suffer tremendously. Careful observation and discernment is the necessary first condition for offering help. When considering this group, one might ask: who can be possessed? The answer, unfortunately, is quite simple: anyone — religious as well as laypeople, Christians and non-Christians, young and old. True possession must be carefully discerned and, in this discernment and eventual prayer and exorcism, special attention must be given to the "moments of crisis" and the diabolical manifestations, especially when applying a diagnostic exorcism. However, two main difficulties have to be mentioned.

First, there are times when true "possession sets in to worsen a subject's previously existing state of psychological weakness or mental or physical illness, in which case one suffers both real psychological, psychic and physical evils and the extraordinary action of the devil at the same time, thereby necessitating the intervention of both a physician and an exorcist."[445] In this case, it becomes clear that the natural capacities have been affected by the preternatural action, which makes the treatment more difficult, since possession affects not only the physical condition but also the psychological and mental state.

Second, when the possession causes a mental or physical ailment, that ailment might be used by the devil to hide his extraordinary action. Since there is a high alteration within the state of consciousness of the possessed person and his mental and physical capacities are affected,[446] discernment becomes difficult. St. Pio of

---

[445] Ibid., 81–82.
[446] Cf. IAE, 056.

Pietrelcina, for example, "was of the opinion that many of the inmates of psychiatric hospitals were not really sick persons but victims of preternatural evil."[447]

The following possible indications of possession, a list that is not exhaustive, will likely not be found in one and the same person. Nonetheless, they are helpful in the process of discernment.[448]

a. Speaking or understanding languages unknown to the person.

b. Awareness of things and facts that the person could never have known. Hidden sins can be revealed, as well as unknown things of the past, hidden facts, objects, and so forth.

c. Abnormal physical force or weight. A possessed person can make use of a physical force disproportionate to his or her normal physical stature, becoming capable of moving heavy objects that ordinarily would be impossible to move, or they themselves become incredibly heavy, and so on.

d. Aversion to the sacred. For example, possessed people find prayer repugnant, even if they were used to praying a lot before; often there is an aversion to the Eucharist, to relics, and to crosses — they elicit a reaction as though the possessed person thinks that touching them would burn them; they also experience strong repugnance toward all blessed things, such as images, rosaries, food, water, and such. When receiving the Holy Eucharist, the mouth of the possessed person might become as if paralyzed.

e. Manifestations during the exorcism. These might include: change of the voice; insulting or assaulting the exorcist;

---

[447] Francesco Bamonte, *Diabolical Possession*, 83.
[448] Concerning the following explanation, see: ibid., 84–105.

changes to the eyes, such as becoming wide open or fierce, and the pupils maybe turning inside out; changes in the bodily structure; vomiting objects such as rings, chains, stones, needles, ropes, and the like; imitating animals; "walking backward on the wall or even with the feet on the ceiling and the head downwards."[449]

f. Other indicative signs. It frequently happens that whenever the day of meeting the exorcist approaches, the person becomes sick, nervous or disturbed in some way. This might include stomach problems, strong headaches, ineffective medicine, and the like. There might be a strong resistance to attend the meeting, or the devil pretends to indicate that he has already left the body, trying to convince the person that there is no need to go. There might be total mental confusion, even to the point of losing consciousness, experiencing feelings of suffocation, suffering nightmares, or having an uncontrollable need to laugh, and such like.

Since, as stated at the beginning of this section, this is only an overview of possessions, and yet the troubles related are so profound, it should be clear that possessions are a real challenge, one that might even become a threat to a person's life. People affected by possession — and the people surrounding them — suffer greatly. Given all of this information, it

[449] Ibid., 97. Fr. Bamonte reports from his experience: "I remember that one day the Parish Priest sent me to bless a house. The family had an eleven year old boy who had been brought severally to the exorcist. As I was blessing the water, the boy, who had been sitting very quietly on the sofa, suddenly began to scream, then shortly he fell into a sort of sleep, until he silently glided towards the pavement. Without touching the floor, he was levitated to about 3 to 4 centimeters from the floor in front of his astonished parents and grandparents who had never seen a thing of the kind before. He began to hiss and to move around the room, imitating the motion of a snake." Ibid., 98.

becomes even more comprehensible why Fr. Gabriele Amorth called the denial of help in these cases a "mortal sin of omission."

In the face of such difficulties, it must be asked: what can be done? How can a simple priest, or even a layperson — neither of them being an exorcist — help to discern? Are there differences when resolving an infestation, a vexation, an obsession, or a possession? When addressing this complex topic, the most important magisterial interventions must be kept in mind since they offer orientation, namely, the solid ground necessary to approach such a delicate topic.

7.4. Overcoming Extraordinary Actions of the Devil

At this point, there will be a shift from explanations of the devil's various forms of actions to focus on possible solutions offering remedies and help to those who suffer from extraordinary demonic actions. Criteria will be provided that should enable priests and laypeople to make a discernment, starting with infestations and ending with diabolical possessions. The general procedure may be similar across the four types of extraordinary action, especially the first steps, concerning deliverance.

7.4.1. Liberation from Infestations

For the reasons explained above, demonic forces can gain power over inanimate objects, animals and places. If this is the case, they usually remain in control unless they are expelled by the power of God. The extraordinary diabolic action generally causes tremendous suffering and hardship, meaning that people need help. The question of how to remedy the situation depends on various circumstances, especially on the degree of an infestation. There are certain infestations which will disappear almost immediately after certain blessings and prayers, and others after a minor exorcism; but there are others that need a more powerful commitment. With this in mind, the various steps in the order they should be taken to properly combat such situations will be mentioned.

A first step should consist in guiding people who live in infested places to be constantly in the state of grace. They should be encouraged to participate — if possible — every day in the Holy Eucharist and to receive Holy Communion. They should frequently go to Confession and intensify their prayer life, as protection and support. Special devotion to the Blessed Virgin Mary and the saints is recommended, as well as a virtuous life. The consecration to Our Lady has proven to be particularly helpful.[450] At the same time, it is of great value to offer Masses with the intention of deliverance. It is recommended to offer a novena of Masses (nine Masses) or — in special cases of a more powerful diabolical presence — even a Gregorian Mass (thirty Masses). These measures will grant people who are affected by an extraordinary diabolic activity a certain calmness and spiritual aid. This is *the* foundation for deliverance and should not be underestimated. Deliverance is not a magical act, according to which the priest solves the problems through certain prayers; the spiritual impact depends on the participation in the prayer. Therefore, the life of the individual must correspond to the grace transmitted through the Church. This becomes apparent in the Gospel of Luke, stating: "When an unclean spirit goes out of someone, it roams through arid regions searching for rest but, finding none, it says, 'I shall return to my home from which I came.' But upon returning, it finds it swept clean and put in order. Then it goes and brings back seven other spirits more wicked than itself who move in and dwell there, and the last condition of that person is worse than the first" (Luke 11:24–26). This basic principle must be respected. Consequently, it would be of no use to remove an infestation that was caused by grave sin when people continue to live in grave sin.

In a second step, the following structure has proved to be particularly effective, starting with invoking the Most Holy Trinity and

---

[450] Cf. chap. 8.4.1.2.

making the sign of the cross — that is, the sign of salvation, protection, and deliverance. Thus, a threefold invocation may follow:

> a) Invoking the Most Precious Blood of Jesus Christ. Today, many Catholics consider this invocation "kitschy," unaware as they are of its meaning, even though this devotion was quite popular at the beginning of the last century.[451] But the prophet Isaiah had said that "by his wounds we were healed" (Isa. 53:5) and, through His wounds, the Precious Blood was shed for our salvation. There is a liberating and sanctifying power related to the invocation of His precious blood. Because of this, whenever deliverance is needed, His Precious Blood should be invoked, for "Jesus also suffered outside the gate, to consecrate the people by his own blood" (Heb. 13:12). The First Letter of John affirms: "If we walk in the light as he is in the light, then we have fellowship with one another, and the blood of his Son Jesus cleanses us from all sin" (1 John 1:7). Jesus Christ is the Lamb of God, who redeemed mankind through his blood, granting purification, healing, and sanctification. It is through His Precious Blood that the sacraments and the sacramentals receive their spiritual effect. The book of Revelation points out that the chosen ones are wearing white robes, and it affirms: "These are the ones who have survived the time of great distress; they have washed their robes and made them white in the blood of the Lamb" (Rev. 7:14). When the Church spreads and promotes the devotion to the Precious Blood,[452] she indicates the path of purification and sanctification. Hence, various invocations of the Precious Blood can be used, such as chaplets, litanies, supplications, and the like.

---

[451] Cf. Hermann Reifenberg, "Art. Blut Christi III. Liturgisch u. frömmigkeitsgeschichtlich," in LThK, vol. 2, 3rd ed., (Freiburg im Breisgau: Herder, 1994), 537.

[452] The latest document of the Magisterium in this regard was published by Pope John in 1960. John XXIII, Apostolic Letter *Inde a Primis*, June 30, 1960, in https://www.vatican.va/content/john-xxiii/la/apost_letters/1960/documents/hf_j-xxiii_apl_19600630_indeaprimis.html [9.5.2023].

b) Invoking the presence of the Immaculate Conception. At the same time, the invocation of the Immaculate Virgin proves to be powerful since the Blessed Virgin Mary — as Pope Pius IX declared *ex cathedra* in the bull *Ineffabilis Deus* — was preserved free from all stain of Original Sin.[453] The Blessed Virgin Mary is the Mother of God and is rightly praised as "full of grace" (Luke 1:28).[454] She is the great sign who "appeared in the sky, a woman clothed with the sun" (Rev. 12:1). To invoke her name signifies invoking her presence, which will have a strong impact and may cause deliverance from the evil one. Since she is the queen of the angels, every satanic power is submitted to her. Thus, several prayers, litanies, and invocations of the Immaculate Conception have proved to be of great spiritual value in the service of deliverance.

c) Invoking St. Michael the Archangel. The Hebrew word *Michael* means *Who is like God*. Angels are "purely spiritual creatures … surpassing in perfection all visible creatures, as the splendor of their glory bears witness."[455] St. Michael is of particular importance in the fight against the devil. The book of Daniel calls him "the great prince, guardian of your people" (Dan. 12:1). He is the one who will fight the dragon and its angels, as the book of Revelation affirms (Rev. 12:7). Special power is given to him, as recognized by Scripture and Tradition. He fights with the power of God and will defeat Satan and his demons, since he defends the rights of God. In 1884, Pope Leo XIII was granted a vision that is relevant to this point. One day, after celebrating Mass, he sank to the floor. Physicians hastened to his side fearing the worst. After a short while, "the Holy Father opening his eyes, exclaimed with great emotion: 'Oh what a horrible picture I was permitted to see!' He had been shown in spirit the tremendous activities of the evil spirits and their ravings against the Church. But in the midst of this vision of horror he had also beheld consoling visions of the glorious Archangel Michael, who had appeared and cast Satan and

---

[453] Pius IX, Bull *Ineffabilis Deus*, December 8, 1854, in *DH*, 2800–2804, here 2801.
[454] Translation, see 2.3.3.
[455] *CCC*, 330.

his legions back into the abyss of hell."[456] Soon afterward he composed the well-known prayer:

St. Michael the Archangel, defend us in battle. Be our defense against the wickedness and snares of the devil. May God rebuke him, we humbly pray, and do thou, O Prince of the heavenly hosts, by the power of God, thrust into hell Satan, and all the evil spirits, who prowl about the world seeking the ruin of souls. Amen.

Until 1964, this prayer was obligatory for every priest after Low Mass; afterward, it was suppressed during the liturgical reform. This might have been due to the fact that, in times of rationalism, it was simply difficult to believe in angels. Nevertheless, since its institution, the popes have always pointed out the importance of this prayer. For example, Pope John Paul II affirmed that Satan infests the world with his disorder and evil actions, and he recommended invoking St. Michael.[457] Pope Francis also recommended invoking his protection, and he consecrated the Vatican to St. Michael in 2013 and again in 2018.[458]

---

[456] So quoted in Lawrence Lovasik, "St. Michael, Strength of God," in http://www.catholictradition.org/saint-michael4.htm [9.5.2023].

[457] See John Paul II, Discorso alla Popolazione di Monte Sant'Angelo, May 25, 1987, in http://w2.vatican.va/content/john-paul-ii/it/speeches/1987/may/documents/hf_jp-ii_spe_19870524_montesant-angelo.html [9.5.2023]. Friedrowicz offers a good overview of the devotion to St. Michael and its spiritual fruits. Cf. Michael Friedrowicz, "Saint Michael, Defender of the Church Militant," Gregorius Magnus vol. 10 (2020): 20–24.

[458] For example, at the blessing of the statue of St. Michael in the Vatican Gardens, consecrating the Vatican to St. Michael. Cf. Francis, Blessing of the New Statue of St. Michael the Archangel, July 5, 2013, in https://www.vatican.va/content/francesco/en/speeches/2013/july/documents/papa-francesco_20130705_statua-san-michele.html [9.5.2023]. Pope Francis has encouraged us to say this prayer at the end of the Rosary. He explicitly mentions the fight against the devil: "The Holy Father has decided to invite all the faithful, from all over the world, to pray the Holy Rosary every day during the entire Marian month of October; and thus to unite in communion and penance, as the people of God, in asking the Holy

With all of this in mind, various litanies, prayers, and other approved devotions by the Church invoking St. Michael also ought to be used to combat extraordinary action.

Of course, it is also recommended to invoke other saints, especially those who are particularly venerated in the place, community, or family, such as St. Benedict, the patron saint of the exorcists, St. Padre Pio, St. John Paul II, and so on. Before moving on to the third step that may be taken to combat extraordinary action, it is helpful to consider the following caveats regarding these avenues of prayer and invocation recommended above. The International Association of Exorcists recommends observing the following criteria when the faithful use private prayers in spiritual combat:

> a) it is not even licit that the faithful use the formula of exorcism against Satan and the fallen angels, extracted from the one published by order of the Supreme Pontiff Leo XIII, and even less that they use the integral text of this exorcism; b) the lay faithful must absolutely avoid speaking on possible curses, possessions, obsessions or diabolic infestations of any kind; c) the lay faithful may not bless objects or persons except within the limits and within the terms provided by the dispositions of the Church; d) the lay faithful, in particular, may not lay hands or make gestures normally reserved for sacred ministers.[459]

These norms provide valuable guidance. If these prayers should cause special reactions, they are to be stopped immediately; it is not allowed for the faithful to use them directly against Satan. Prudence and humility regarding the right procedure are of great importance since the angels, as spiritual beings, are superior to us.

Mother of God and St. Michael the Archangel to protect the Church from the devil, who always aims to divide us from God and from each other." Own translation from Comunicato della Sala Stampa della Santa Sede, September 29, 2018, in https://press.vatican.va/content/salastampa/it/bollettino/pubblico/2018/09/29/0707/01504.html [12.5.2023].

[459] IAE, 175.

Now, moving on: The third step is called specific deliverance. A prayer of deliverance always and necessarily includes apotropaic elements and is, therefore, an exorcism. As already said above,[460] an exorcism is a sacramental, which is defined by the *Catechism of the Catholic Church*:

> When the Church asks publicly and authoritatively in the name of Jesus Christ that a person or object be protected against the power of the Evil One and withdrawn from his dominion, it is called exorcism. Jesus performed exorcisms and from him the Church has received the power and office of exorcizing. In a simple form, exorcism is performed at the celebration of Baptism. The solemn exorcism, called "a major exorcism," can be performed only by a priest and with the permission of the bishop. The priest must proceed with prudence, strictly observing the rules established by the Church. Exorcism is directed at the expulsion of demons or to the liberation from demonic possession through the spiritual authority which Jesus entrusted to his Church. Illness, especially psychological illness, is a very different matter; treating this is the concern of medical science. Therefore, before an exorcism is performed, it is important to ascertain that one is dealing with the presence of the Evil One, and not an illness.[461]

This description is helpful since it shows that exorcisms are always done in the name of Jesus Christ and with the authority of the Church. They are a prayer against the power of the evil one. The definition underlines that the power of the devil may also have an impact on objects, which would lead to infestations.

Moving forward from this step, things become more complicated. And so, at this point, attention must be paid to a clarification concerning the minor exorcism.

---

[460] Cf. chap. 2.2.3.
[461] CCC, 1673.

7.4.1.1. The Minor Exorcism of Pope Leo XIII

Since many priests no longer believe in the existence of the devil and consequently are not willing to help, laypeople have often taken the initiative in performing exorcisms. Especially for charismatics, it is quite common to pray exorcisms as if they were "normal" prayers. Even though this approach might be understandable, it is problematic and may cause even further damage because, as was already said, it is an unequal struggle. To better understand these problems, a look at the recent past is helpful.

In 1985, the Congregation for the Doctrine of the Faith (CDF) issued a document called *Inde ab Aliquot Annis* ("Recent years have seen"), a letter to the ordinaries regarding norms on exorcism.[462] Under the guidance of Joseph Cardinal Ratzinger, the Congregation explained canon 1172 of the *Code of Canon Law*, stating that no one "can perform exorcisms legitimately upon the possessed unless he has obtained special and express permission from the local Ordinary."[463] In the following paragraph, the document states: "From these prescriptions it follows that it is not even licit that the faithful use the formula of exorcism against Satan and the fallen angels, extracted from the one published by order of the Supreme Pontiff Leo XIII, and even less that they use the integral text of this exorcism. Bishops should take care to warn the faithful, if necessary, of this."[464] Even though this note is very clear and precise concerning laypeople and the exorcism in use for those being possessed, it had nevertheless caused some confusion. This is due to the fact that it wasn't made clear whether the "exorcism" referred to was the "major" or "minor" exorcism, and it did not make reference to infested places as such, but only to persons. Furthermore, while it is clear that the faithful cannot licitly use the "formula of

---

[462] Cf. CDF, *Letter to Ordinaries regarding the norms of Exorcism*.
[463] CIC, can. 1172 §1.
[464] Ibid., 2.

exorcism," what about priests? After the publication of this letter, some exorcists argued that the note was exclusively talking about the major exorcism; others believed that it also applied to the minor. Only thirty years later, in 2015, was further clarification provided; this will be explained below, but first we need to highlight two important aspects of this 1985 direction.

First, it is clear that laypeople are not allowed to pray this prayer of exorcism; and second, the exorcist has to be provided with special authority through the bishop to undertake the major exorcism, the *"De Exorcismis et Supplicationibus Quibusdam."*[465] However, in the case of infestations, the minor exorcism alone may be sufficient to solve most of the problems.

But how does the minor exorcism work? And, are priests allowed to use it licitly without a specific episcopal mandate? If so, on what basis and under what circumstances? In 2007, Pope Benedict XVI published *Summorum Pontificum*, affirming that the old Roman Missal was never abrogated. Consequently, he called this the Extraordinary Form of the Church's Roman liturgy. As already seen, in his Motu Proprio *Traditionis Custodes*, Pope Francis limited the faculty to celebrate the Extraordinary Form of the liturgy. As sacramentals are not mentioned in this motu proprio, it may be assumed that, with regard to them, the norms enacted by Pope Benedict are still in force. This affects especially the administration of sacramentals. In other words, any priest can use them.

Why is all of this mentioned here? Because the former ritual includes a minor exorcism that has special importance concerning infestations and which no longer exists in the new form. It is called *Exorcism against Satan and his Apostate Angels* (*Exorcismus in Satanam et Angelos Apostaticos*).[466] This prayer is part of the Church's living tradition and

---

[465] *Rituale Romanum, ex decreto sacrosancti oecumenici Concilii Vaticani II instauratum auctoritate Ioannis Pauli II promulgatum, De exorcismis et supplicationibus quibusdam*, Typis Polyglottis Vaticanis, MMIV, 71–77.
[466] RR, 602–605.

was probably developed along the lines of baptismal exorcisms. After the CDF published the document *Inde ab aliquot annis* in 1985, the question arose whether priests may use this prayer or whether they needed special authorization from the bishop, except when it is used directly on possessed persons. The CDF and its Pontifical Commission, *Ecclesia Dei*—established by Pope John Paul II in 1988, and abolished by Pope Francis in 2019—provided an answer only on June 26, 2015, as a response to a *dubium* (doubt). The so-called *dubia* are a standard procedure within the Church, consisting in the submission of one doubt (*dubium*) or several doubts (*dubia*) concerning faith and morals to the Magisterium for final clarification. The answer is significant, since it provides an authoritative interpretation of can. 1172 §1 of the *Code of Canon Law*, helping to understand what it means that no one "can perform exorcisms legitimately upon the possessed unless he has obtained special and express permission from the local ordinary."[467] The question of whether any priest may use it, in the case of an infestation, was presented to the Holy See by the Superior General of the Priestly Fraternity of St. Peter. The answer given by the commission was helpful.

First of all, an important distinction was made between the public and private use of the exorcism of Leo XIII, presented below, and also called the minor exorcism. Regarding the public use of this exorcism, that is, when it is used "in the name and with the authority of the Church," the previous norms are clearly upheld. "In situations other than over persons, such as over places, objects, or in other circumstances, this is also subject to the authorization of the ordinary."[468] The document confirms once more that laypersons are not allowed to use it. Then it says: "As regards the private use of the Exorcism of Leo XIII by priests, i.e. outside of any pastoral context and/or requested by the

---

[467] CIC, can. 1172 §1.
[468] CDF, Pontificia Commissio "Ecclesia Dei", Prot. N. 153/2009, 26 June 2015.

faithful, and simply as a *pia oratio*, this Dicastery sees no grounds for which to deny this to priests on the basis of the discipline currently in force."[469] In other words, for the private use of this exorcism, there is no need for authorization of the bishop. In this way, the Congregation follows a long-established tradition. It is a matter of fact that, historically, this exorcism was used for the consecration of water on the feast of the Epiphany, consequently, it was recited by any priest.[470] Moreover, it bears a resemblance to the baptismal exorcisms that were in use in the Catholic Church until the liturgical reform.

According to proven practice, such prayers were not said in public for various reasons. Their public use would only confuse the faithful, making the priest appear to be an exorcist, even though he was not. It could endanger his mission and could lead people suffering from psychological pathologies to react unreasonably. Therefore, the CDF underlines a private use of the exorcism only by priests and with prudence and caution. The United States Conference of Catholic Bishops defines minor exorcisms as follows: they "are prayers used to break the influence of evil and sin in a person's life, whether as a catechumen preparing for Baptism or as one of the Baptized faithful striving to overcome the influence of evil and sin in his or her life."[471] Now, it will be helpful to take a look at the text of this minor exorcism.

7.4.1.2. Commentary on the Prayer

The prayer of the minor exorcism is in Appendix 1 at the back of this book. If this powerful prayer is used with living faith and devotion, even

---

[469] Ibid. The International Association of Exorcists argues in the same direction. A public exorcism can be determined by the following three criteria: "1. in the name and by the authority of the Church; 2. by ministers appointed by the Church; 3. in the form determined by the [Church] itself, otherwise it is called *private*." IAE, 160a.

[470] Cf. RR, 427–428. The minor exorcism is part of the consecration of holy water on Epiphany, which every priest is authorized to do.

[471] USCCB, Art. "Exorcism."

though in "private," most infestations will be removed. It should go without saying that the priest who uses this prayer does not need to shout, nor does he need to make any theatrical gestures; he serves as an instrument of divine grace which does not need or benefit from dramatic gestures. Like the faithful, the priest must also be in a state of grace when performing these prayers. Even more, he should prepare himself through prayer, fasting, and sacrifices, but, above all, he should go to Confession himself beforehand to gain the indulgence attached to that. This aspect is very important since such an indulgence and our participation in the sacrament of Confession are expressions of our participation in divine grace.

Now the question arises, where in the infested house should this prayer be said? The recommendation is to do it in whatever part of the house where the most disturbances have been observed. This might be the bedroom, the kitchen, a closet, or any other room.

Who should participate in the prayer? It is recommended that the faithful accompany the priest with their prayers. They are not allowed to pray the minor exorcism; nevertheless, they ought to participate in reciting the rosary or other prayers, supporting the priest in his mission of deliverance. However, like the priest, these people who participate must also be in a state of grace. If not, they should first go to Confession, or they should not participate. If any people involved, especially children, are particularly sensitive, they should not be present. There is no shame and in fact a great deal of prudence in being realistic about the limitations of what individual characters can confront and witness.

It is also recommended that the priest wears his cassock during this minor exorcism. Failing that, he ought in any case to wear his purple stole. This is no mere decorative attachment; it is a powerful protection and an expression of his indwelling power.[472] Furthermore,

---

[472] For a detailed explanation of the significance of the stole and some notes on the cassock, see chap. 8.4.

it is recommended that the priest says the prayer in a language unknown to the people who participate in this prayer. On the one hand, so that the priest does not appear as an exorcist; on the other hand, so as not to cause any kind of sensation. Also for that reason, the Latin language is of great importance, since it is part of the living tradition of the Church. Although a priest *should* know Latin, he ought not to pray in it in this instance if he does not understand it; he should use a language he understands. This is because the sacramentals work *ex opere operantis*; therefore, they presuppose the living faith of the priest, which means he must understand what he is saying in order for it to be effective. If he does not know Latin or another language foreign to the assembly, he should recite the prayer in silence; the other participants may, meanwhile, accompany the priest with their prayers. This all has to do with the fact that the priest must avoid appearing to be an exorcist, both for his own protection and for that of the people around him. Humility and prudence are fundamental; they protect the priest and make his work of deliverance fruitful.

After the prayers are said, the priest concludes the minor exorcism by using holy water to bless the whole place. This water also must have been exorcised before its use in this context in order for it to have sufficient spiritual impact.[473] In other words, the blessing of the water needs to include apotropaic elements; they are necessary for deliverance. Care should be taken to bless the whole house, that is, every single room. If it happens that only one single room is not blessed, the devil's extraordinary activity can be concentrated there after the rest of the house is cleared of the infestation.

No one should take photos or videos during the prayer or the blessing of the house, as this can only do harm and cause confusion. Clarification is helpful for this: there is a difference between the public exorcism given during Baptism and the exorcism concerning

---

[473] Cf. chap. 8.4.2.1.

an extraordinary action of the devil. The difference is "not only in species, but also in genre, although they are all indicated with the same generic term of 'exorcism.' "[474] Whenever it is about an extraordinary diabolic activity, the utmost prudence and discretion are needed. Taking pictures or videos during an exorcism would be a violation of the virtue of prudence. Then, the minor exorcism would appear to be a public and solemn exorcism, negating the priest's authority to perform it. This aspect is of great importance and must be rigorously observed.

If the minor exorcism does not bring deliverance, a fourth step is recommended: the celebration of the Holy Eucharist or the celebration of several Masses at the place of infestation. This is another delicate topic and must be given the proper explanation. In 2004, the Congregation of Divine Worship and the Discipline of the Sacraments issued an instruction called *Redemptionis Sacramentum*, which says: "The celebration of the Eucharist is to be carried out in a sacred place, unless in a particular case necessity requires otherwise. In this case the celebration must be in a decent place. The diocesan Bishop shall be the judge for his diocese concerning this necessity, on a case-by-case basis."[475] This could be understood in a twofold way. Does the bishop need to judge in each case — as it was done until the Second Vatican Council — or is it sufficient that, through discernment, a priest sees that there is a real need for it? Outside of exorcisms, it is common, for example, to celebrate Masses for youth camps in the open air in the countryside, and normally a priest does not request permission for such circumstances anymore. Although the Instruction *Liturgicae Instaurationes* from 1970 indicates that the

---

[474] IAE, 167.
[475] Congregation of Divine Worship and the Discipline of the Sacrament, Instruction *Redemptionis Sacramentum*, 108.

bishop must grant permission,[476] the *Code of Canon Law* has changed this stipulation.[477] Canon lawyer John M. Huels states: "Particular cases are not only single occasions but also situations in which an individual priest must regularly celebrate outside a sacred place by reason of necessity. Cases of need could include sickness, old age, distance from a church, and, in general, whenever there is some pastoral advantage to celebrating outside a sacred place."[478] Deliverance is a "particular necessity." For that reason, priests involved in deliverance do not need to explicitly request this permission.

The instruction provided by the Congregation (in 1970) indicates that the place chosen must be a worthy place in the house. Therefore, the dining room, or a dining-room table, is to be excluded.[479] As an altar, an object should be used which is not available for everyday use, and it should be used in a place which afterward — if possible — can be used as a place of prayer. Before the celebration of the Eucharist, this place should be blessed. The celebration of the Eucharist must comply with the liturgical norms and should correspond to the dignity of the celebration. Therefore, the priest has to wear the chasuble (not just a stole),

---

[476] Cf. Congregation for Divine Worship, Instruction *Liturgicae Instaurationes*, n. 9, in AAS 62 (1970): 701.

[477] Regarding the preference of the CIC see can. 34 §2, which says: "The ordinances of instructions do not derogate from laws. If these ordinances cannot be reconciled with the prescripts of laws, they lack all force."

[478] John M. Huels, "The Most Holy Eucharist," in John P. Beal, et a[(eds.), *New Commentary on the Code of Canon Law*, (New York: Paulist Press, 2000), 1095–1137, here 1121. An official request for the celebration of the Eucharist in a house has been answered by the Congregations as follows: "In merito alla Sua richiesta di proroga della facoltà di dire Messa in casa, Le comunico che, a norma del nuovo Codice di Diritto Canonico (can. 932 §1), potrà regolarsi secondo la Sua propria responsabilità." Congregation for Divine Worship and the Discipline of the Sacraments, Letter from 13 April 1985, Prot. N. 481/85, in Leges Ecclesiae VI, n. 5122, 9135.

[479] CIC, can. 932 §2 says: "The Eucharistic sacrifice must be carried out on a dedicated or blessed altar; outside a sacred place a suitable table can be used, always with a cloth and a corporal."

candles have to be on the altar, flowers might be provided, people need to kneel during the Consecration, and so forth.

The place or house should be exorcised both before and after the celebration of the holy mysteries, in the power and grace of the sacrament, as described above. It is also recommended to have blessed objects in the house, such as crosses, sacred images, and exorcised medals of St. Benedict or the Miraculous Medal.[480] The priest might also consecrate or bless these items after the Holy Mass.

At this point, one final thought is worth mentioning. Similar to the necessarily private form of the minor exorcism, the Masses celebrated in such places should not have a public character. Strict care should be taken that only the family or a few faithful, who are discrete, are present. Furthermore, as mentioned above, no one should take any pictures or videos. They would give rise to misunderstandings and other problems.

If even this celebration of Holy Mass in the affected place does not remedy the situation of infestation, a fifth step may be taken: calling an official exorcist. Provided with the authority of the bishop, he may recite the major exorcism. If he cannot solve the problem right away, additional sessions may be needed. However, this occurs only in very rare cases when there is a massive demonic presence. At this point, it is helpful to remember that following the four prior steps before calling in the actual exorcist might well relieve that exorcist of unnecessary work, in consideration of the many demands on his time and abilities. Most problems can be solved through the indicated first four steps; in addition to relieving the burden of work for the exorcist, such a resolution would, above all, be an act of mercy in helping the affected people who live in or near the infested place.

People often ask how a priest should act when non-Catholics or even non-Christians approach him, asking for deliverance from

---

[480] Cf. chap. 8.4.2.2.

infestations or even possessions. What should be done in such cases? The five steps indicated above follow an internal logic that is actually found and so is rooted in the Gospel (cf. Luke 11:24–26). Because it is not enough to "purify" the house, because it also must be kept "clean," a state of grace is, therefore, generally a crucial condition for success. Nevertheless, Fr. Francesco Bamonte reminds us that Jesus Christ Himself performed exorcisms on people who were not Jews. With this fact in mind, it can be affirmed that any deliverance from the demonic presence is realized through Jesus Christ. Concerning non-Catholics or non-Christians, Bamonte writes: "The exorcism becomes then a moment of first evangelization, an annunciation of the faith that can bring the believer of a different religion to experience the power of salvation of Jesus Christ as the only Savior and therefore to follow him."[481] In any case, it would be advisable to lead the affected persons to the fullness of truth, that is, to the Catholic Church. In this context, it must not be forgotten that the sacraments are more powerful than the sacramentals; they offer the most powerful spiritual help.

7.4.2. Liberation from Vexations and Obsessions

The remedy for vexations and obsessions is similar; thus, both will be discussed at once. Generally speaking, it is possible to follow what has been said before. Accordingly, the first two steps remain the same. And, as with infestations, a preliminary step is making sure that the affected person is in a state of grace before beginning the prayers. In addition, the three invocations previously mentioned (the Precious Blood, the Immaculate Conception, and St. Michael) can also be prayed over these people with great spiritual benefit.

---

[481] Francesco Bamonte, "The Evangelical Fundaments of The Signs of Diabolical Possession Mentioned in the Ritual of Exorcism," in Association of International Exorcists (eds.) *Proceedings of the National Congress of Italian Exorcists, 9th–13th September 2013*, trans. AIE English Secretariat, (Rome, Association of International Exorcists, 2013), 59–93, here 60.

However, if this were to cause a "moment of crisis" (a type of manifestation), everything should be stopped immediately and, in full prudence, an official exorcist should be contacted. If, however, everything proceeds normally, would the priest be able to pray the minor exorcism over a person who is suspected of suffering from vexation or obsession? Fr. Francesco Bamonte provides advice on the subject with the following helpful example.

> I remember that a priest once sent me a woman from his parish who, for about twenty years continued to suffer regularly from very serious headache every Saturday and Sunday, even after consulting many doctors and taking various medications. The woman was going daily to the Holy Mass and the sacraments. The only suspicion I had of a possible extraordinary diabolic action was when she told me that a sister of hers was practicing magic and what she told me made me suspect an evil repercussion on the woman who actually showed no hatred towards her sister but kept praying for her to stop practicing magic. I believed that there were necessary conditions to proceed with a diagnostic exorcism. The woman remained calm all through the duration of the exorcism and did not manifest any unusual signs. I greeted her and asked her to let me know of any developments regarding her situation. Shortly after about one month the woman phoned informing me very gladly that for the first time after many years, she had been able to spend Saturdays and Sundays without the slightest headache. Five years have passed since then and the woman continues to be well.[482]

At this point, the question arises, what is a "diagnostic exorcism"? To answer this, these things must be looked at in a larger context.

The norms provided in the document *Inde ab aliquot annis*,[483] offer some orientation regarding the use of the exorcism of Leo XIII, also called: "minor exorcism." The document affirms that

---

[482] Francesco Bamonte, *Diabolical Possession*, 68.
[483] Cf. CDF, *Letter to Ordinaries regarding the norms of Exorcism*.

unless a priest has specific permission (he must have an official mandate from his ordinary), he cannot say this prayer over those who are possessed. However, the question remains whether priests may use it over persons who are suspected to be suffering from vexation or obsession.

In the tradition of the Church, exorcisms that include the imperative form were continuously practiced. This becomes clear in the rite of Baptism. Baptismal exorcisms — there were several of them — included imperative forms, as the following example illustrates. The priest would pray over the one who is about to be baptized:

Latin	English
Exorcízo te, immúnde spíritus, in nómine Pa ✠ ris, et Fi ✠ lii, et Spíritus ✠ Sancti, ut éxeas, et recédas ab hoc fámulo Dei N. Ipse enim tibi ímperat, maledícte damnáte, qui pedibus super mare ambulávit, et Petro mergénti déxteram porréxit.[484]	I exorcise you, unclean spirit, in the name of the Father ✠ and of the Son, ✠ and of the Holy ✠ Spirit, that you goest out and depart from this servant of God, N. For He commands you, accursed one, He who walked upon the sea, and stretched out His right hand to Peter as he was about to sink.

It can be assumed, therefore, that if any priest was obliged to pray these prayers for centuries, a priest today may also use them in the ministry of deliverance, even though they include imperative forms.[485] Their use is powerful. However, the question remains, is a priest allowed to pray such an exorcism in a case of vexation and obsession?

Point 1 of the document *Inde ab aliquot annis* speaks of the fact that "no one can legitimately perform exorcisms over the possessed [*obsessos*] unless he has obtained special and express permission

---

[484] RR, 34.
[485] At this point there is no need to take up the whole debate about *Summorum Pontificum* and *Traditiones Custodes*; here we are talking about a common assumption.

from the local Ordinary."[486] Thus, a priest who is not an exorcist may not legitimately use the exorcism on anyone who is possessed; this would also include the minor exorcism. This is a general prohibition concerning possessed persons. In other words, if a priest obtains clarity that a person is possessed, he has no authority whatsoever to make use of such a prayer in the presence of the possessed. These norms of the Church reflect great wisdom, for whoever enters this spiritual battle without the authority of the Church can only lose. This prohibition serves to protect the priest and the faithful.

It has already been pointed out that every priest may consecrate holy water on the day of Epiphany using the old ritual that contains the minor exorcism. If there is no certainty whether a person is possessed (no manifestation of a "moment of crisis"), then this prayer can be used over persons to serve as a diagnostic exorcism. This assumption is also supported by the letter issued in 2015 by the CDF.[487] In any case, it should be used only as a private prayer, respecting the indicated rules. Even though some of the following rules were already mentioned before, it will be beneficial to repeat them in this context once again.

Whenever a priest who is not an exorcist prays the minor exorcism, he should be very careful not to appear as an exorcist in the eyes of the faithful. He should not even say that he is praying the minor exorcism. It is recommended to pray in silence and/or in a language unknown to the persons involved. Under no circumstances should the prayer be said in public or be recorded. Discretion is of paramount importance. The faithful should be invited to accompany the priest in prayer — but their prayers must not, of course, be the prayers of exorcism that the priest is praying. Their ability to accompany him with their own private prayer will help to avoid any anxiety among them and — at the same time — it will serve as a protection and help for the

---

[486] Cf. CDF, *Letter to Ordinaries regarding the norms of Exorcism*, 1.
[487] Cf. CDF, Pontificia Commissio "Ecclesia Dei," Prot. N. 153/2009.

priest. The minor exorcism can be used as a "diagnostic exorcism," which helps to discern. Since there are different types of people looking for an exorcist,[488] maximum prudence is needed.

According to the Dominican Father and exorcist François-Marie Dermine, in some cases, when there is a suspicion that the person is psychologically sick but looking for an exorcist, it is helpful not to start directly with the minor exorcism. He recommends reciting in a loud voice, but in a language unknown to the affected person, some parts of a poem, rubrics, or something else — something that is not related to the exorcism.[489] If the person in this very moment should start to show any "moment of crisis," he/she would belong to the second group of people, namely, the ones feigning possession. In this case, there would be a psychological problem, and exorcism would not be required. However, if the person in question is truly possessed and starts to manifest when the priest starts to recite the prayer, the priest must stop immediately. From there, as explained before, only an authorized exorcist can help, for the indicated norms must be observed. The question remains: what about the minor exorcism in the case of vexation or obsession?

Similarly, as in the case of infestations, many vexations and obsessions may be resolved in this way, depending on the power of the diabolic presence on the one side and the power of grace on the other (cf. *ex opere operantis*) and in strict conformity to what has been outlined above. It is very helpful if deliverance is accompanied by the sacraments. An affected person should frequently receive the Holy Eucharist, the sacrament of Penance, and the Anointing of the Sick. It has also been proven to be very helpful if Holy Masses are celebrated with the intention of deliverance. Such Masses would increase grace so that liberation and healing can occur.

---

[488] Cf. chap. 7.2.3.
[489] Cf. François-Marie Dermine, *Carismatici, sensitivi e medium. I confini della mentalità magica*, (Bologna: Edizioni Studio Domenicano, 2010).

If this should not lead to solving the problem, then the fourth step must be taken: contacting an authorized exorcist. As mentioned before, given the demands on exorcists' time, it is right and charitable to do prudently what can be done of these first four steps with the help of a priest to resolve the issue before contacting an exorcist.

7.4.3. The Major Exorcism

As already seen, exorcisms are frequently described in Sacred Scripture. For example, Jesus Christ fought against Satan, casting out demons with the power of His Word (cf. Matt. 17:18). However, Jesus did not only cast out demons; He also gave that same power to His apostles (cf. Mark 3:14–15). The Church conserves this power by exercising it in the name of Jesus Christ (cf. Acts 8:7; 19:12). Jesus Christ entrusted His spiritual authority to the Church; this authority becomes manifest in a special way during the major or solemn exorcism. Francesco Bamonte presents a good overview of its development. He writes that at the beginning of the history of the Church, especially in the Eastern Church, exorcisms were done, not after receiving holy orders, but based on a personal vocation, good will, spiritual fortitude and grace. Among the great exorcist figures remembered by the Church, we cannot forget St. Martin of Tours and then the monks, like St. Anthony the Abbot, Pacomius, Hilarion. Gradually, however, in the Western Church, the strong tendency to regulate everything, partly due to the influence of Roman law, led to the institutionalization of the order of "exorcists" already in the second century, even though all could form part of it.[490]

The Church began to regulate the practice very early. The "office of exorcist could be said to have been definitively instituted beginning with the year 416 when Pope Innocent I established that exorcisms could be done by priests but only with the permission of the

---

[490] Francesco Bamonte, *Diabolical Possession and Exorcism*, 121–122.

bishop."[491] The *Code of Canon Law* follows this line, indicating a clear regulation: "No one can perform exorcisms legitimately upon the possessed unless he has obtained special and express permission from the local ordinary."[492] The document *Inde ab aliquot annis* reaffirmed this norm, emphasizing the strict prohibition that not everyone is authorized to perform an exorcism.[493] If the priest (based on the results of the diagnostic exorcism) or the exorcist (based on his experience), using the criteria described above,[494] concludes that there is a case of possession, *only* the major exorcism will help, and *only* the authorized exorcist may use it.

The process and timeline of deliverance will depend on many factors. The following factors have a significant influence: the "seriousness of the case; the person's commitment to prayer as well as the commitment of his loved ones and all those offering their help," "the plans of God for the person in allowing such a suffering," and "grave sins that have never been confessed or sufficiently repaired."[495] This is an incomplete list, but it does show that deliverance is a complex issue and that many different factors have to be taken into consideration. Given its complexity, it is not surprising that successful exorcisms can sometimes take quite some time; indeed, Fr. Bamonte acutely shows that cases of possession can last for several years.[496]

As outlined by the International Association of Exorcists, in the case of true possession, a "public exorcism" (also called a major or a solemn exorcism) is necessary. However, the adjective "public" must be understood correctly. "Public" does not mean that it is performed in front of running cameras; on the contrary, it refers to the public

---

[491] Ibid., 122.
[492] CIC, can. 1172 §1.
[493] CDF, *Letter to Ordinaries regarding the norms of Exorcism*.
[494] Cf. chap. 7.3.2.4.
[495] Francesco Bamonte, *Diabolical Possession and Exorcism*, 106.
[496] Cf. ibid.

mandate provided by the Church, in whose authority the authorized priest performs the exorcism.[497] In doing so, the exorcist should meet the following criteria: a) be a qualified minister; b) carry out the exorcism according to the rites approved by the Church; and c) act with the intention of doing what the Church does.[498] For these reasons, a priest can only perform the major exorcism if he is accordingly authorized. Even though, following an inner logic, this norm is of utmost importance, it proves to be difficult in practice. There are not a few bishops who are not willing to appoint an exorcist. Thus, many affected persons do not receive help; as already mentioned before, this circumstance is something that Fr. Gabriele Amorth called rightly a grave sin of omission for the clerics who allow the situation to continue unresolved.

One last general aspect of major exorcisms must be mentioned before concluding this subject. The extraordinary action of the devil is often closely linked to sicknesses; this is, for example, described in Sacred Scripture in two places: "As they were going out, a demoniac who could not speak was brought to him, and when the demon was driven out the mute person spoke" (Matt. 9:32–33). Another episode says that "Jesus rebuked him and the demon came out of him, and from that hour the boy was cured" (Matt. 17:18). Additionally, Francesco Bamonte distinguishes three categories of persons who are afflicted by the extraordinary action of the devil: "truly sick people healed by Jesus; victims of vexations and possession whom Jesus delivered by casting out the devil; those who were afflicted by both sickness and vexation or possession whom Jesus healed by casting out the devil."[499] Even though exorcisms and healing are frequently presented in one context, it must be understood that they are actually distinct from each

---

[497] Cf. IAE, 163.
[498] Cf. ibid.
[499] Francesco Bamonte, *Diabolical Possession and Exorcism*, 109.

other. Healing refers to a natural capacity that can be affected by an extraordinary diabolic activity. Exorcism, however, is done with the power of the supernatural to overcome the preternatural, which can also have a healing effect on the natural level.

Jesus Christ came "to destroy the works of the devil" (1 John 3:8). As a part of this, He gave His disciples the power to cast out demons. However, any type of deliverance has to be integrated into a "Catholic lifestyle" that is receptive to grace, in order that that grace may abound. "Deliverance is part of ongoing conversion."[500] Therefore, deliverance and exorcisms should never be considered as a reality separated from the sacraments. The sacraments are more powerful than the sacramentals, and therefore, everyone involved in deliverance should be led to a more profound and conscious sacramental life. Deliverance is usually realized in the context of the three sacraments (Reconciliation, Eucharist, and the Anointing of the Sick), presupposing that the persons involved are baptized.

At this point, it is not necessary to go further into detail on the general circumstances surrounding major exorcisms. The precise procedures and criteria are known to experienced exorcists and can be found in specialized literature for anyone who needs to receive further education on the subject.

7.4.4. Healing and Deliverance

At this point, a more detailed look at one aspect that was so far only mentioned in passing is necessary. Today, it is fashionable to offer so-called "services of healing," which are often attended by large crowds. Even if the participants have little to do with the Church and the sacraments, as soon as the subject of "healing" is mentioned, interest and attendance spike. This shows, on the one hand, that many people are

---

[500] Cf. Neal Lozano, *Resisting the Devil. A Catholic Perspective on Deliverance*, (Huntington, Indiana: Our Sunday Visitor, 2010), 117.

looking for healing and deliverance; on the other hand, these "events" are often linked to a magical understanding of healing. Therefore, it is important to point out a few basic aspects of what healing actually is.

The liturgical reform of the Roman Rite includes the possibility of many "optional elements," as clearly indicated in the rubrics. However, until the liturgical reform, this was unthinkable. The priest who acts *in persona Christi capitis* (in the person of Christ the head) does not stand for himself, but in the person of Christ. This is expressed in the axiom of the principle *ex opera operato*.[501] In other words, it is not the priest who decides, chooses, and changes things according to his own ideas; rather, he is responsible simply for handing on what he himself has received (cf. 1 Cor. 11:23). Introducing optional elements — for the sacraments and sacramentals — was a novelty, and it has led to the erroneous attitude of administering them according to the desires and wishes of the people. Even more, the basic rule not to mix sacraments was abandoned. For example, Baptism, Matrimony, or the Anointing of the Sick were not celebrated in the Mass, but apart from it (e.g., the sacrament of Matrimony used to be celebrated immediately before the celebration of Mass rather than in the middle of it). Likewise, blessings and consecrations were not performed during Mass, but either before or after. This change has created the impression that the sacraments and sacramentals can be charismatically designed at will.

Charismatic groups, in particular, started to create new forms. Thus, "Masses of healing and/or deliverance" were offered that included sacramentals such as exorcisms, as well as other elements. The classical form of deliverance was widely abandoned, and these new "forms" started to sprawl. The most famous case was the charismatic archbishop and apostate, Emmanuel Milingo (b. 1930); he had been an exorcist, but he ended up becoming a member of the

---

[501] Cf. chap. 3.1.

Unification Church (the cult led by Sun Myung Moon), and he was ultimately reduced to the lay state. He had offered services of healing and deliverance, mixing up different elements as he chose. His circumstances give us an excellent example of what to avoid and, if necessary, what to correct.

With the proliferation of "inventive forms," the Magisterium of the Catholic Church had to intervene. Thus, the Congregation of the Doctrine of Faith issued the "Instruction on Prayers for Healing" in 2000.[502] Due to multiple undesirable developments, this document was urgently needed; it aimed to correct those developments.

It contains two parts: I. Doctrinal Aspects and II. Disciplinary Norms. In this context, it will be sufficient to focus on the disciplinary norms, since most of the doctrinal aspects have already been explained in the first part of this book. Concerning exorcism and the use of the *Rituale Romanum*, the document calls to mind that the "ministry of exorcism must be exercised in strict dependence on the Diocesan Bishop."[503] Then it adds two important norms: "Art. 8 §2. The prayers of exorcism contained in the *Rituale Romanum* must remain separate from healing services, whether liturgical or non-liturgical."

The instruction provides a basic distinction between liturgical and non-liturgical prayers. If the prayers are contained in the liturgical books and were approved by the Church's competent authority, they are considered "liturgical prayers"; otherwise, "they are non-liturgical."[504] When a liturgical prayer is said, the ordained minister must use proper sacred vestments.[505] These exterior signs are important because they underline the ecclesiastical character of the

---

[502] CDF, Instruction on Prayers for Healing, September 14, 2000, in https://www.vatican.va/roman_curia/congregations/cfaith/documents/rc_con_cfaith_doc_20001123_istruzione_en.html [6.5.2023].
[503] Ibid., Art. 8 §1.
[504] Ibid., Art. 2.
[505] Cf. ibid., Art. 3.

celebration. The instruction also affirms that the prayer of exorcism must remain separate from healing services. Even though the document does not distinguish between minor and major exorcisms, it is reasonable to assume (and in fact must be assumed) that this also applies to minor exorcisms. In other words, prayers of deliverance cannot be included in the celebration of the sacraments: "Art. 8 §3. It is absolutely forbidden to insert such prayers of exorcism into the celebration of the Holy Mass, the sacraments, or the Liturgy of the Hours." Some people suggest doing the exorcism (referring to the minor exorcism) within the sacrament of the Eucharist or Confession since integrating them into the sacraments would make them become even more powerful. However, the instruction makes it clear that this is not possible, thus affirming the "basic rule." The instruction mentions several norms, which can serve as guidelines for all types of deliverance.

1. "Art. 9 – Those who direct healing services, whether liturgical or non-liturgical, are to maintain a climate of peaceful devotion in the assembly and to exercise the necessary prudence." This is an essential requirement; healing services are something serious; they are not an opportunity for showy exhibitionism. This includes touching the person or persons who are being delivered excessively or unprudently. The healing service should be limited to those gestures described in Sacred Scriptures, such as the laying on of hands (cf. Mark 10:16); or anointing with holy oil (cf. James 5:14), it proves particularly helpful to anoint the six parts — eyes, ears, nose, mouth, hands and feet — as was customary in the tradition of the Church.

2. The use of means of communication, especially social media, the Internet, and television, with prayers of deliverance, falls

under the vigilance of the diocesan bishop.[506] In such cases, the prayer would be made public, and its transmission by secular means would necessarily provoke misunderstandings and other problems. For this reason, it is recommended that all social media or other public outlets be avoided when performing prayers of deliverance.

3. Any type of "hysteria, artificiality, theatricality or sensationalism, above all on the part of those who are in charge of such gatherings, must not take place."[507] No one should cause the impression of being an exorcist or of having special charismas of healing. Everything should be done in a calm and seemly manner, *ad maiorem Dei gloriam* (for the greater glory of God).

4. "Confusion between such free non-liturgical prayer meetings and liturgical celebrations properly so-called is to be carefully avoided."[508] The liturgy must not be changed to integrate elements of exorcism or other sacramentals.[509]

7.5. Concluding Remarks

Before concluding this chapter, which, though lengthy, has merely pointed out the broad lines concerning a complex topic that requires not only knowledge but also experience, one last aspect of exorcisms will be mentioned. It can be said that exorcisms are the test case for the sacramentals. They bring to light, most compellingly, the meaning of the principle of *ex opere operantis*. At the same time, the limitations of the new ritual stand out, since basic elements are neglected, omitted, and ignored. This becomes most evident in the omission of the

---

[506] Cf. ibid., Art. 6.
[507] Ibid., Art. 5 §3.
[508] Ibid., Art. 5 §2.
[509] A helpful commentary on this topic can be found in IAE, 176.

apotropaic elements that are closely related to the preternatural reality of extraordinary demonic action. This has entailed the reduction or even omission of the sign of the cross and other sacred signs that are rooted in the rich experience and Tradition of the Church.

On October 1, 1998, the new rite of exorcism was published with the title *De exorcismis et supplicationibus quibusdam*, reprinted in 2004.[510] On the one hand, the rite remains faithful to the "logic" of the renewed ritual. On the other hand, and not surprisingly, this is precisely the cause of its weakness and limitation. The possibility of optional elements is constantly given — in the end, the impression arises that each exorcist can decide for himself how to do the prayer. Of course, the prayers always have to be applied according to the circumstances and needs of the affected person and the degree of possession. And yet the many optional elements of the rite are irritating to its effectiveness, for, without compromise, the exorcist ought always to pray in the name of Jesus Christ, following those prayers approved by the Church, and with the authority of the Church.

A brief look at the new rite helps to illustrate the problem. In its appendix, an indicative exorcism can be found called *Supplicatio et Exorcismus qui adhiberi possunt in pecularibus adiunctis Ecclesiae* (A Supplication and Exorcism which may be used in special circumstances of the Church).[511] This exorcism corresponds to the one already listed,[512] except that the plural first person ("we exorcize") is replaced by the singular first person ("I exorcize"). This prayer is to be used not only for those people who suffer from vexations, but also

---

[510] *Rituale Romanum, De exorcismis et supplicationibus quibusdam*, Editio typica, (Vatican City: Librariae Editricis Vaticanae, 2004).

[511] Ibid., 71–77. With regard to a theological analysis of the genesis of the new *Rituale Romanum*, see Manfred Hauke, "The Theological Battle over the Rite of Exorcism, 'Cinderella' of the New *Rituale Romanum*," in Antiphon 10.1 (2006): 32–69.

[512] Cf. chap. 7.4.1.2.

against infestations. Because the singular first person is used, the prayer is reserved in the new ritual explicitly for the authorized exorcist. It starts with a liturgical greeting (*In nomine Patris ... Dominus vobiscum* ...), followed by optional elements. Readings can be inserted, as well as a brief homily — in short, unnecessary elements. Then litanies may be prayed and the universal prayer may be added — so many options. Finally, the priest begins reciting the exorcism itself, in which all but one of the original signs of the cross are omitted. This represents clear impoverishment and weakness.

As mentioned above,[513] the renewed form was probably the work of "experts" who had never participated in an exorcism themselves. Therefore, the new rite is often based on theories that do not do justice to the actual preternatural reality that affects practical circumstances. Fr. Francesco Bamonte addressed this difficulty in several of his publications that provide orientation and information on the subject. Especially when it comes to exorcisms, most exorcists use the old ritual from the *Rituale Romanum*. Indeed, in 1999, the former prefect of the Congregation for Divine Worship and the Discipline of the Sacraments, Cardinal Jorge Medina, issued a note that granted to all exorcists the faculty to continue using the former ritual, with the permission of the bishop.[514] This access to the former rite was further facilitated by Pope Benedict in his publication of *Summorum Pontificum*.[515]

At the end of the day, the most important aspect concerning the extraordinary demonic activity is spiritual combat.[516] Such an attitude, however, has become foreign even to many Catholics. Nevertheless, it

---

[513] Cf. chap. 3,4. See also Gabriel Amorth, Interview with Father Amorth.
[514] See Congregatio de Cultu Divino et Disciplina Sacramentorum, *Notificatio de ritu Exorcismi*, Prot. 1280/98/L, in *Notitiae* 35.3–4 (1999): 156.
[515] As stated before, this permission (concerning sacramentals) was not limited by the Motu Proprio *Traditiones Custodes*.
[516] In this context, the following classic may be mentioned: Lorenzo Scupoli, *The Spiritual Combat*, trans. William Lester and Robert Paul Mohan, (London: Catholic Way Publishing, 2013).

must be remembered that an exorcism is not a magical formula; it requires a virtuous life — a life of prayer, a life in the presence of God and based on the intercession of the saints and angels, as well as frequent participation in the sacraments — in short, a life that trains, prepares, arms, and protects a person for spiritual combat. Such combat does not permit a mediocre lifestyle (cf. Luke 16:13), since no one can serve two masters. The "house" must be kept clean (cf. Matt. 12:44), and all doors must be closed toward the devil, sin, the spirit of the world, and the concupiscence of the flesh. In his devotion to our Lord, the Christian must maintain a focus on resisting "the tactics of the devil" (Eph. 6:11). Friar Benigno Palilla, an Italian exorcist, affirms that the extraordinary action of the devil cannot be overcome without spiritual combat, which can only be won when fighting with the weapons of the Spirit. He enumerates two strategies to make this possible: one of defense, and the other of attack. Concerning the first, he says:

> We defend ourselves from the devil in order to avoid being struck by those sicknesses that come from possession or oppression, or infestation by avoiding opening up windows. Such windows are: becoming a member of satanic sects, participating in a satanic ritual, particularly "black masses"; consecrating oneself to Satan; making pacts with him, participating in séances; the use of wizards, chiromancy, sorcerers, fortune tellers …; listening to satanic rock CDs with messages that invite the listener to the cult of Satan, or to violence, necrophilia or suicide; the use of amulets and talismans.[517]

Every person must have a strategy of defense against these negative factors, all of which must be avoided and/or removed. However, regarding the strategy of attack, positive factors must also be established.

---

[517] Benigno Palilla, "Solemn Exorcism in the Context of Spiritual Warfare," in Association of International Exorcists (eds.) *Proceedings of the National Congress of Italian Exorcists, 9th – 13th September 2013*, trans. IAE English Secretariat, (Rome: Association of International Exorcists, 2013), 137–164, here 158.

These are factors which make the person grow in the grace of God, and serve not only as protection but also as powerful means against the evil one. Among them, Palilla counts "constantly living in the state of grace" as an expression of a "deep friendship with God,"[518] which includes a life of prayer and sacraments. This includes a continuous struggle to overcome sin, supported by apostolates, and the surrender of ourselves to God, especially in moments of suffering and difficulty. In this spiritual combat, special attention may be paid to: promoting the family; practicing "charity towards others"; "doing our job, even our apostolic work, with competence"; and "living the Gospel."[519] In other words, this "strategy of attack" is achieved through living a truly Christian life, every moment of our lives. Palilla concludes that the final combat in life is against the power of death, and "we succeed in offering our death to the Father with love, in union with the death of His beloved Son for the salvation of the world, and that can be the last and greatest victory over the devil that we will score."[520]

---

[518] Ibid.
[519] Ibid., 160.
[520] Ibid. Presented in even greater detail in Fra Benigno, *Il diavolo esiste io lo'ho incontrato*, (Milan: Paoline Editoriale Libri, 2008), 259–280.

EIGHT
✠ ✠ ✠
Blessings of the Church

Since this subject is very broad, only an overview will be offered, pointing out the most important principles and criteria. Everything that will be discussed in this chapter builds on what has been explained in previous chapters; earlier chapters provide the theological foundation for understanding these blessings.[521] Consequently, the distinction between constitutive and invocative blessings must be kept in mind,[522] as well as the fact that certain blessings are reserved for administration by deacons, priests, and bishops. At the beginning, some basic considerations are going to be presented before discussing some practical elements.

8.1. God, the Source of All Blessings

The general introduction to the *Book of Blessings* points out that God is the "source from whom every good gift comes."[523] The human person is always in need of receiving blessings, for man is weakened by sin in both his mental and physical faculties. He strives — or he should strive — for healing, protection, and salvation. Through Jesus Christ, the ancient curse (Original Sin) was transformed into a blessing. In

---

[521] See also Stephan J. Rossetti, *The Priestly Blessing*.
[522] See especially chap. 2.2.1 and 2.2.2.
[523] BoB, General Introduction, 21–31, here 21.

other words, Jesus Christ is the supreme blessing sent by the Father in the power of the Holy Spirit. He blessed (cf. Mark 10:16) and made His disciples participate in His mission (cf. Mark 6:6–12; Luke 10:1–2). Before He ascended into Heaven, He "raised his hands, and blessed them" (Luke 24:50). The most supreme blessing is done over the species of bread and wine in the Most Holy Eucharist (cf. Matt. 26:26–29; Mark 14:22–25; Luke 22:19; 1 Cor. 11:24).

Thus, every blessing comes from God. It is God who blesses the people, either directly or through His ministers who act in His name and with His authority.[524] Whoever blesses in God's name invokes divine grace upon individuals, assembled people, material objects, and/or places. The general introduction to the *Book of Blessings* states: "Blessings therefore refer first and foremost to God, whose majesty and goodness they extol, and, since they indicate the communication of God's favor, they also involve human beings, whom he governs and in his providence protects. Further, blessings apply to other created things through which, in their abundance and variety, God blesses human beings."[525] The minister of blessings should be aware that he is acting in the name of God and as an instrument of God. It is not the human person who, by his own efforts or performance, gains favors and transmits graces; rather, it is God Himself working through His ministers.

Influenced by the so-called "anthropocentric shift," many priests and bishops stopped blessing people. They claim that they do not want to offend anyone, and so they falsely call this rejection of blessing people or things a sort of "tolerance"; but what they are actually rejecting is a false and secular idea of a blessing as some sort of magic. The main problem underlying this interpretation is that it rejects or neglects the sacramental view, which, as already explained, was reaffirmed by the Second Vatican Council. This is what leads to situations where the minister does

---

[524] Ibid., 22.
[525] Ibid.

not consider himself as the instrument of divine grace that he is, but merely as a sort of functionary. For these and similar reasons, priests prefer facing the people during the celebration of the Eucharist instead of turning toward the Lord.[526] Ultimately, this attitude reflects a form of clericalism (to recall: acting against the divine commandment and teaching accordingly); such a "minister" sees only himself, rather than God, in whose service he is supposed to be. Thus, he is no longer a "minister" (of God) but "a hired man, who is not a shepherd" (John 10:12). Sacred Scripture is very strong when affirming that "he works for pay and has no concern for the sheep" (John 10:13). Thus, any functional understanding of the minister will lead to clericalism and arbitrariness.

In contrast to such an erroneous understanding, it has to be kept in mind that, during the priestly ordination, the bishop anoints and blesses the hands of the priest so that he might sanctify the people. The prayer said at this moment becomes even brighter in the old form of the Roman Rite:

New Form	Old Form
The Father anointed our Lord Jesus Christ through the power of the Holy Spirit. May Jesus preserve you to sanctify the Christian people and to offer sacrifice to God.[527]	May it please you, O Lord, to consecrate and sanctify these hands by this anointing and our blessing ✠ Amen. That whatever they bless may be blessed, and whatever they consecrate may be consecrated in the name of our Lord Jesus Christ.[528]

[526] In this context, Uwe Michael Lang's book is highly recommended. Uwe Michael Lang, *Turning Towards the Lord. Orientation in Liturgical Prayer*, (San Francisco: Ignatius Press, 2009).

[527] Congregation for Divine Worship and Discipline of the Sacraments, *The Rites of Ordination in the Roman Ritual and Pontifical*, renewed by Decree of the Most Holy Second Ecumenical Council of the Vatican, (Vatican City: Libreria Editrice Vaticana, 2012), 133, 80.

[528] In Latin "Consecráre et sanctificáre dignéris, Dómine, manus istas per istam unctiónem et nostrum bene ✠ dictiónem. Amen. Ut quaecúmque

This profound prayer, together with the emblematic gesture of consecrating the hands of the newly ordained priest, makes it clear that God is the source of all blessings. The minister is the instrumental cause, a channel of divine grace. Romano Guardini wrote in his book, *Sacred Signs*: "He alone can bless that has the power. He alone is able to bless who is able to create."[529] Guardini adds: "It fails wholly if we assume it of ourselves. By nature, we are petitioners, blessers only by God's grace, — just as we have the virtue of authority, of effectual command, only by God's grace."[530]

8.2. Efficiency and Symbolism

These considerations lead us directly to our next topic. As shown before, sacramentals are sacred signs that have been, for the most part, instituted by the Church; some of them have their origin in Jesus Christ Himself.[531] Their efficacy is closely linked to the principle of the *ex opere operantis Ecclesiae*,[532] i.e., their spiritual effects depend upon the holiness of the minister, the devout disposition of the recipient, and the intercessory power of the Church, which finds its echo in the formula used during the rite. The Church, as the mystical body of Christ, is the dispenser of the sacramentals. She is a "sign and instrument" that makes divine grace accessible to us.[533] The blessings become fruitful if received with living faith — and every person is in need of receiving the divine grace which they offer. Not only every person, but also all of creation is in need of grace. Sacred Scripture

---

benedíxerint, benedicántur, et quaecúmque consecráverint, consecréntur, et sanctificéntur, in nómine Dómini nostri Iesu Christi." *Pontificale Romanum*, Editio Typica 1961–1962, Edizione anastatica e Introduzione (eds.) Manlio Sodi and Alessandro Toniolo, (Vatican City: Libreria Editrice Vaticana, 2008), 54.

[529] Romano Guardini, *Sacred Signs*, 81.
[530] Ibid., 82.
[531] Cf. CCC, 1667.
[532] See chap. 4.1.
[533] Cf. LG, 1.

affirms that the whole of creation is supposed to be "set free from slavery to corruption and share in the glorious freedom of the children of God" (Rom. 8:21).

Modern man finds it difficult to deal with symbolism, not least because it is supposed to be a link to the invisible world. Raising the hands to God, for example, is no longer understood as a gesture of prayer. However ignorant one might be of it, it is in fact a reference to the moment in the Old Testament when Israel was fighting against Amalek: "As long as Moses kept his hands raised up, Israel had the better of the fight, but when he let his hands rest, Amalek had the better of the fight" (Exod. 17:11). The hands raised to God indicate the prayer rising to God. Romano Guardini provides a profound explanation: "There is greatness and beauty in this language of the hands. The Church tells us that God has given us our hands in order that we may 'carry our souls' in them. The Church is fully in earnest in the use she makes of the language of gesture. She speaks through it her inmost mind, and God gives ear to this mode of speaking."[534] This explanation provides a key to understanding: signs become *sacred* signs when they are associated with *the* sacred. Thus, through sacramentality, the sign acquires a new, spiritual value.

In 2020, the International Theological Commission provided a helpful explanation of this invisible reality of the divine within sacramentality. They raised the following question: "How can the sacramental signs or sacred words of Scripture be more than mere human creations and contain the presence of *God himself*?" Their answer: "In order for there to be true communication, it is not enough to send out a message; reception is needed. If God the Father had spoken to us in Jesus Christ and no one had listened to his message (faith), communication between God and humanity would not have taken place. However, according to the New Testament testimony,

---

[534] Romano Guardini, *Sacred Signs*, 18.

whoever enters into relationship with the man Jesus relates to *God himself*, to the Word incarnate."[535]

Sacred signs are "participated signs." The scene of Moses overlooking the battle exemplifies this. He raised his hands to God and accompanied this gesture with a spiritual attitude. He prayed for the victory of his people, and thus, through his participation, the external sign received a spiritual value.[536] From this, it becomes apparent that symbolic understanding is significant for the Church. On this point, Joseph Ratzinger commented that the "theology of the liturgy is in a special way 'symbolic theology,' a theology of symbols, which connects us to what is present but hidden."[537] He underlines that we need these sacred signs because it is through them that "we learn to see the openness of heaven. We need them to give us the capacity to know the mystery of God."[538] This mystery is expressed through symbolism, and for that reason, Romano Guardini wrote: "The people who really live by the liturgy will come to learn that bodily movements, the actions, and the material objects which it employs are all of the highest significance.... It is emancipating in its action, and capable of presenting a truth far more strongly and convincingly than can the mere word of mouth."[539] Blessings are sacred signs; through them, the openness of Heaven becomes real and divine grace becomes present. For this reason, many elements of life can and should be blessed, for they are a powerful means of sanctification.

Some blessings have a "universal" tradition where others might be "local." The universal tradition corresponds to a practice that is in force throughout the universal Church. Local traditions, however,

---

[535] International Theological Commission, "The Reciprocity," 17.
[536] Cf. chap. 3.6.
[537] Joseph Ratzinger, TL, 36.
[538] Ibid.
[539] Romano Guardini, *The Spirit of the Liturgy*, trans. Joanne M. Pierce, (New York: The Crossroad Publishing Company, 1998), 60.

are limited to a local church. Both types of blessings share the following three criteria: a) they correspond to the Faith of the Church; b) they are administered in the name of the Church; and c) they are approved by the Church (universal or local Church).

8.3. What Can and Cannot Be Blessed

Today, one of the lively topics of discussion among concerned parties in the Church is what can actually be blessed. Can everything be blessed in principle, for example, divorced and remarried couples? May amulets be blessed, or places where yoga is practiced regularly?

The previous discussion about the theological nature of the sacramentals can help to answer these questions. To review, blessings, as all sacramentals do, aim to achieve positive spiritual effects that depend on the moral condition of both the person receiving and the person administering grace.[540] The effectiveness of a blessing depends especially on the "work of the doer,"[541] which is where they differ from the sacraments. Moreover, their grace of sanctification will only be effective if the one who receives the blessing is open to that grace. In this context, it is helpful to recall the image of a vessel used before: The vessel needs to be "open" to receive divine grace.[542] In other words, sin — in particular mortal sin — would close the vessel and turn a blessing into a farce, especially if done in public. Ultimately, because blessings ought to impart sanctifying grace, they presuppose that the intended recipient is open to receive that grace, namely, that he or she be in a state of grace.[543]

This can be seen in the Old Testament, when Samuel invites the elders of the city: "Purify yourselves and celebrate with me today" (1

---

[540] Cf. chap. 2.3.
[541] Cf. chap. 3.1.
[542] See. chap. 4.2.
[543] Cf. Ralph Weimann, "Die Sakramentalien – Stiefkind der Theologie," 405–406.

Sam. 16:5). With this, Samuel refers to the law of holiness that was described in the book of Leviticus: "Be careful to observe my commandments. I am the LORD. Do not profane my holy name, that in the midst of the Israelites I may be hallowed. I, the LORD, make you holy, who led you out of the land of Egypt to be your God. I am the LORD" (Lev. 22:31–33). The New Testament aims in the same direction, powerfully expressed in Matthew: "Be perfect, just as your heavenly Father is perfect" (Matt. 5:48). Of course, not all Christians are instantly saints, even though this is the intended goal. The Second Vatican Council had affirmed: "everyone whether belonging to the hierarchy, or being cared for by it, is called to holiness."[544] All Christians must have an openness toward holiness, something that cannot happen in a person who knowingly and willingly lives in grave sin. With these premises in mind, a few conclusions can be drawn for the practical application of determining what can and cannot be blessed.

The basic principle to follow is that everything that is directly opposed to God's law of holiness cannot be blessed — this includes places, objects, and persons. For example, in Mexico, a priest was invited to bless a seedy establishment that bore the name "The Temptation" (*La Tentación*). Even if the owner were Catholic and asked for it, such a place would not be allowed to be blessed. Temptation is the ordinary action of the devil,[545] which must be overcome. To bless such an establishment would be a contradiction in terms.

Some people ask blessings for amulets, believing that such items bring success and protection against misfortune. However, amulets are linked to magic and idolatry, which means that they are in direct opposition to the first commandment. As early as the Old Testament, their use is condemned: "On that day the LORD will do away with the finery of the anklets, sunbursts, and crescents; the pendants,

---

[544] LG, 39.
[545] Cf. chap. 7.3.1.

bracelets, and veils; the headdresses, bangles, cinctures, perfume boxes, and amulets" (Isa. 3:18–21). This is frequently affirmed in Sacred Scripture. When Judas Maccabeus went to war, only those of his soldiers who wore amulets died. Because amulets are linked to idols and thus to sin (cf. 2 Macc. 12:40–42), they are not to be blessed, but should be burnt.

The same logic must be applied regarding persons; that is to say, anyone who is living consciously and willingly in grave sin, and therefore in opposition to God's law, should not ask for a blessing. There is a distinction to be made, for all are sinners, but there is a difference between mortal and venial sin. It would be absolutely incoherent and contradictory if a person who decides to be separated from God — remember that a mortal sin always means that the sinner knows what he or she is doing and is choosing to do it — would ask for God's blessing. Unless he or she actually converts and turns back to the Lord through the sacrament of Penance, asking for and receiving a blessing would only increase personal guilt. The Gospel affirms: "Much will be required of the person entrusted with much, and still more will be demanded of the person entrusted with more" (Luke 12:48). Blessings are a gift of God, which should never be instrumentalized. Thus, when applied to persons, they must follow the logic of the law of holiness, just as when they are applied to places and objects. Jesus Christ was very severe when exhorting the Pharisees; His description of their moral corruption is a stark reminder of what it means to be closed off from the grace of God: "You are like whitewashed tombs, which appear beautiful on the outside, but inside are full of dead men's bones and every kind of filth" (Matt. 23:27). Unfortunately, in many respects, blessings have now become a political issue. This indicates a completely and fundamentally wrong understanding of the sacramentals, as if their efficacy and purpose were completely detached from one's own life. Through this grave misconception, a "magical" or even atheistic misunderstanding of them spreads, as though they are cure-alls that instantly improve whatever they are applied to, no matter the circumstances. But, at the end of the day, the fact of the matter is that no one can ask for grace from God who is knowingly and willingly rejecting the commandments of God.

Care must be taken not to bless items that are either ambiguous or things or persons that could cause scandal. Remember that Jesus Christ did not bless the public sinner; rather, He invited her to convert, to leave behind her sinful life: "Go, (and) from now on do not sin any more" (John 8:11). However, there are also "neutral objects," such as cell phones and computers, that may be blessed. Food and water can also be blessed. In summary, then, the basic principle to follow is that everything that is opposed to faith and thus to God's law is not suitable to be blessed, but other things may be blessed.

8.4. Some Basic Elements Concerning Blessings in Practice

When a priest blesses an object, a place, or even a person, he is supposed to wear a stole (liturgical vestment). It is obligatory for a priest to wear a stole whenever he administers the sacraments; it is also recommended when he administers sacramentals.

According to an allegorical interpretation, the stole has a profound meaning. It reminds the priest of the cords with which Jesus Christ was tied on the Cross. It connotes the yoke, which only becomes light and easy through Jesus Christ (Matt. 11:28–30). The stole signifies that the priest is bound to Christ and receives his sacramental power through Him. It is thus a sign of the priest's heavy responsibility and authority, for the priest is bound to Christ as Christ was bound to the Cross. The Office for the Liturgical Celebrations of the Supreme Pontiff affirms: "The stole is the distinctive element of the raiment of the ordained minister and it is always worn in the celebration of the sacraments and sacramentals."[546] When putting on the stole, the priest is invited to recite the following prayer:

Latin	English
Redde mihi, Domine, stolam immortalitatis, quam perdidi in praevaricatione primi parentis; et, quamvis indignus accedo ad tuum sacrum mysterium, merear tamen gaudium sempiternum.[547]	Lord, restore the stole of immortality, which I lost through the collusion of our first parents, and, unworthy as I am to approach Thy sacred mysteries, may I yet gain eternal joy.

A stole is supposed to have three crosses sewn into it, symbolizing the three nails of Christ's Crucifixion. Before putting it on, the priest kisses the cross at the center. Through this gesture, he unites himself with the redeeming work of Jesus Christ, in whose name and authority he is going to act. Furthermore, the stole used for blessings has two colors, one on each side: white and purple. The purple color is associated with penance, purification, and healing. It is, for example, used in all types of exorcisms, as well as for Confession. The white color symbolizes purity and sanctification. It is used for the blessing of objects, places, and persons.

The stole is the visible sign of the invisible and indwelling authority in which the priest participates through his priestly ordination. Thus, the priest *must* wear a stole when administering certain sacramentals, such as exorcisms and consecrations. As seen, it is also highly recommended that he wear it for all other sacramentals. Whenever the blessing includes apotropaic elements, a purple-colored stole is supposed to be used; when it is instead a simple blessing, the white color should be used.

[546] Office for the Liturgical Celebrations of the Supreme Pontiff, Liturgical Vestments and the Vesting Prayers, in http://www.vatican.va/news_services/liturgy/details/ns_lit_doc_20100216_vestizione_en.html [6.5.2023].

[547] So quoted in ibid.

It is also recommended that the priest wear a cassock or at least a distinctive garb that identifies him as ordained clergy. The priestly vestment is more than symbolism; it is an expression of one's consecration to God. The black color symbolizes dying to oneself to rise with the Lord and in His power. For this reason, the CIC says: "Clerics are to wear suitable ecclesiastical garb according to the norms issued by the conference of bishops and according to legitimate local customs."[548] Except in situations of persecution, the priest should be recognizable as a priest. In this way, he outwardly expresses that he is not a private person, but stands for Christ. In fact, people will only be able to ask a priest for blessings, consecrations, or the sacraments if they can recognize him as such. If the blessing is held in a church — the most appropriate and ordinary place for them — it is recommended that the priest wears the cassock, surplice, and stole in the requisite color. But blessings can be given elsewhere, according to various needs and circumstances. Because of this, a priest should always have his stole and holy water with him.

Moving on from how a priest ought to vest himself to administer a blessing, the focus will be on the fundamental structure of a blessing. Assuming the priest does not have the ritual at hand and is asked to bless something, how should he begin? The following structure has proven to be effective, and it corresponds to the Tradition of the Church.[549]

℣. Our help ✠ is in the name of the Lord.

℟. Who made heaven and earth.

℣. The Lord be with you.

℟. And also with your Spirit.

---

[548] CIC, can. 284.

[549] RR, 368. This blessing is called "Benedictio ad omnia" (General blessing for things).

Then the priest says the proper prayer and includes (✠) the sign of the cross over the person, object, or place. Finally, he sprinkles whatever is to be blessed with holy water, if it is available. This structure is easy to remember and has proved to be efficient. Even when the *Book of Blessings* is used, this structure can be applied, as the new ritual leaves space for optional elements.

A priest blesses with his right hand; this has a profound meaning, since Sacred Scripture often uses the image of a hand as a symbolic gesture. The Egyptian plagues occur after Moses has stretched out his hands (cf. Exod. 8–10). Hands are lifted up in prayer that God answers (cf. Exod. 17:11; Ps. 134:2). The prophet Ezekiel beholds the hand of God (cf. Ezek. 2:9); Daniel interprets to the king Belshazzar the writing hand that appeared on the wall as the hand of God (cf. Dan. 5:24–28). The "hands of the Lord" receive their full meaning with the coming of Jesus Christ. With his hands, he heals the sick, breaks the bread, blesses, and so on. The Fathers of the Church interpreted the hand of God as a symbol of the incarnated Logos, that is, the Word made flesh, the second person of the Trinity.[550] Cursory as these explanations are, they nevertheless reveal the importance of the priestly blessing imparted with the right hand. Consequently, it should never be omitted.

8.4.1. Blessing of Persons

The Church provides a number of different blessings over persons. These blessings consist most commonly of invocative, and sometimes also of constitutive, blessings (consecrations). The *Book of Blessings* contains only invocative blessings (to recall: they grant some temporal good).[551] According to the rubrics, certain blessings can be imparted during and outside of Mass. However, the problems and dangers related

---

[550] Cf. Dorothea Forstner, *Die Welt der Symbole*, (Innsbruck: Tyrolia Verlag, 1961), 495.
[551] See BoB, 35–280.

to mixing sacraments and sacramentals was already explained.[552] Ample space is given to various blessings, such as the blessings of families, married couples, children, mothers before and after childbirth, blessings of parents and of an adopted child, birthday blessings, blessings for elderly people, blessings of the sick, missionaries, catechists, students and teachers, of those gathered at a meeting, blessings of pilgrims, travelers, and so on.[553] As already indicated, the ritual does not distinguish between invocative and constitutive blessings, nor between solemn (public) and simple (private) blessings. The word *consecrare*, which was frequently used in the *Rituale Romanum*, receives a new meaning in the *Book of Blessings* and is used exclusively over persons.[554] Thus, the prayer for "Blessing of a Married Couple" says: "Lord, increase and consecrate the love which N. and N. have for one another."[555] This regrettable novelty in phrasing suggests that it is the love between the spouses that is consecrated, not the persons themselves. This new phrasing thus uses this concept in an equivocal way. It is misleading, because it is not love that is consecrated (nor indeed can it be consecrated), but the persons.

As already mentioned, constitutive blessings have almost completely disappeared. The *Roman Pontifical*[556] enumerates a very few, such as the "Consecration of a Virgin,"[557] and the rite of "Consecrating the Chrism."[558] However, if any priest wishes to avail himself and

---

[552] Cf. chap. 7.4.4.
[553] Cf. BoB, 35–280.
[554] Not even the chalice and the paten are anymore consecrated but only blessed. Cf. BoB, 581–591.
[555] BoB, 65.
[556] Congregation for Divine Worship and the Discipline of the Sacraments, *The Roman Pontifical*, Renewed by Decree of the most Holy Second Ecumenical Council of the Vatican, promulgated by authority of Pope Paul VI and revised at the direction of Pope John Paul II, (Vatican City: Libreria Editrice Vaticana, 2012).
[557] Ibid., 291–334.
[558] Ibid., 383–384.

the faithful under his care with the graces available through the tradition of constitutive blessings, he may consult the *Rituale Romanum*. This will be discussed in the following section.

8.4.1.1. Constitutive Blessings

Since only two consecrations remain listed in the *Roman Pontifical*, the following explanations will focus on one of them: the Consecration of Virgins. This ancient rite goes back to apostolic times. Throughout the centuries, it was maintained in use by nuns in monastic orders, especially among the Benedictines, Cistercians, and Carthusians. It was only in the nineteenth century that the idea was introduced to reinstitute this lifestyle into the Church's discipline among laypeople. The Second Vatican Council addressed this possibility in the Constitution *Sacrosanctum Concilium*: "The rite for the consecration of virgins at present found in the *Roman Pontifical* is to be revised. Moreover, a rite of religious profession and renewal of vows shall be drawn up in order to achieve greater unity, sobriety, and dignity. Apart from exceptions in particular law, this rite should be adopted by those who make their profession or renewal of vows within the Mass."[559] This indication, one notes, is somewhat ambiguous since it does not distinguish between consecrations and religious professions.

In 1970 however, the Sacred Congregation for Divine Worship issued a decree announcing a new form of consecration.[560] It was echoed in canon 604: "§1. Similar to these forms of consecrated life [evangelical councils and hermits] is the order of virgins who, expressing the holy resolution of following Christ more closely, are consecrated to God by the diocesan bishop according to the

---

[559] SC, 80.
[560] Sacred Congregation for Divine Worship, Decree, Prot. No. 600/70, 31.5.1970, in ibid. (ed.) *The Roman Pontifical*, Renewed by Decree of the most Holy Second Ecumenical Council of the Vatican, promulgated by authority of Pope Paul VI and revised at the direction of Pope John Paul II, (Vatican City: Libreria Editrice Vaticana, 2012), 291.

approved liturgical rite, are mystically betrothed to Christ, the Son of God, and are dedicated to the service of the Church."[561]

For our purposes, there is no need to explain either the history or the development of this rite.[562] Instead, a brief theological description of it will be provided, since the consecration is a sacramental of the Church.

The *Roman Pontifical* explains the nature and value of consecrations, affirming that, through consecration, the candidate becomes a "sacred person" and "the glory of the heavenly Bride of Christ. In the rite of consecration of virgins, the Church reveals its love of virginity, begs God's grace on those who are consecrated, and prays with fervor for an outpouring of the Holy Spirit."[563] This consecration implies the permanent sanctification and dedication of a person to God. The *Roman Pontifical* also mentions some requirements necessary to receive the consecration, keeping a clear distinction between a nun and a woman living in the world:[564] a consecrated virgin is

---

[561] CIC, can. 604 §1.

[562] A good overview of the historical development is provided by Maria Luisa Öfele (ed.), *Jungfrauenweihe: Altes und neues Charisma*, (Heiligenkreuz: Medien-GmbH Heiligenkreuz, 2017). See also Raymond Leo Burke (ed.), *An Introduction to the Vocation of Consecrated Virginity Lived in the World*, vol. 1, (Lansing: United States Association of Consecrated Virgins, 2012). An explanation that focuses primarily on the practical-theological arguments was published by Therese Ivers, *A Practical Guide to Consecration Planning for Virgins Being Consecrated to a Life of Virginity in the World under the Provisions of Canon 604*, (CreateSpace Independent Publishing Platform, 2013).

[563] Congregation for Divine Worship and the Discipline of the Sacraments, *The Roman Pontifical*, 293.

[564] "In the case of nuns it is required: a) that they have never married or lived in public or open violation of chastity; b) that they have made their perpetual profession, either in the same rite or on an earlier occasion; c) that their religious family uses this rite either by established custom or by new permission of the competent authority." "In the case of women living in the world it is required: a) that they have never married or lived in public or open violation of chastity; that by their age, prudence, and

supposed to live a "life in prayer, penance, service of her brethren, and apostolic activity."[565]

In June 2018, the Congregation for Institutes of Consecrated Life and Societies of Apostolic Life issued an Instruction, *Ecclesiae Sponsae Imago* ("The Image of the Church as the Bride of Christ").[566] This document provides a more detailed explanation of this consecration, focusing on three aspects in particular: "I. The vocation and the witness of the *Ordo virginum*"; "II. The configuration of the *Ordo virginum* in the particular Churches and in the universal Church"; "III. Vocational discernment and formation for the *Ordo virginum*." The instruction frequently uses the word *consecration*, but sometimes in a contradictory way: "If Jesus, the consecrated one par excellence, lives his consecration not in terms of separation from the profane or impure, in fulfillment of legal prescriptions, but by accepting the body that the Father had given him and by giving himself on the cross, his body is the actual place and the effective sign of his consecration to his Father's plan (Heb. 10:5–10). So it will be also for all who set foot on the path of celibacy or virginity: the body becomes a word, announcing their total belonging to the Lord and their joyful service of their brothers and sisters."[567]

This affirmation is, at the very least, ambiguous, and at the worst, downright false. Whenever the difference between profane and sacred,

---

universally approved character they give assurance of perseverance in a life of chastity dedicated to the service of the Church and of their neighbor; c) that they be admitted to this consecration by the Bishop who is the Ordinary of the place." Ibid. Consecrated virginity is reserved only for women, as well as the order of widows. For men — as in the case of St. Joseph — one speaks of chastity and/or a vow of chastity.

[565] CCC, 924.

[566] Congregation for Institutes of Consecrated Life and Societies of Apostolic Life, Instruction *Ecclesiae Sponsae Imago*, June 8, 2018, in http://www.vatican.va/roman_curia/congregations/ccscrlife/documents/rc_con_ccscrlife_doc_20180608_istruzione-ecclesiaesponsaeimago_en.html [8.5.2023].

[567] Ibid., 16.

between pure and impure, is denied, theology will be misdirected and the sacramentals will become incomprehensible. A consecration necessarily implies that someone is set apart, that he or she has become a "sacred person." This does not mean that the person is automatically better and holier, or incapable of sin; rather it means that the person's state in life is elevated by divine grace. This cannot, as in the case of Jesus Christ, be reduced to a simple matter of biology; that is, it does not affect only somebody's body, but rather their entire person. Contrary to what is said above, a consecrated person is, therefore, separated from the profane and from impurity. Also contrary to what is said above, the same was true of Jesus Christ, who was the "anointed one" and who was "without sin" (Heb. 4:15). This separation is *the* characteristic of being consecrated. However, it remains a lifelong challenge to meet this standard, to live up to this identity.

For a better understanding of this confusion, a brief look at the rite will be helpful. It consists of the following parts:

> a) the calling of the candidates; b) the Homily or address, in which the candidates and the people are instructed on the gift of virginity; c) the examination in which the Bishop asks the candidates about their willingness to persevere in their intention and to receive the consecration; d) the Litany, in which prayer is offered to God the Father and the intercession of the Virgin Mary and all the Saints is invoked; e) the renewal of the intention of chastity (or the making of religious profession); f) the Solemn Blessing or consecration, by which the Church asks the heavenly Father to pour out the gifts of the Holy Spirit on the candidates; g) the presentation of the insignia of consecration, to symbolize a spiritual dedication.[568]

Besides a certain ambiguity regarding the precise value of the religious profession and consecration, there is no clarity offered by the *Roman Pontifical*

---

[568] Congregation for Divine Worship and the Discipline of the Sacraments, *The Roman Pontifical*, 294.

about the meaning of the consecration. The "Prayer of Consecration" says: "Lord, protect those who seek your help. They desire to be strengthened by your blessing and consecration."[569] The formula of this prayer is uncertain, corresponding more to an invocative blessing (2.2.2) and deprecative invocation (5.2.2) than to a consecration. The sign of the cross — constitutive for any type of Christian blessing — is omitted throughout this very long prayer. Ultimately, because a consecration signifies the permanent sanctification and dedication of a person for sacred purpose, it must be concluded that the indicated prayer, as it is presented in the *Roman Pontifical*, does not do justice to the nature and value of the consecration.

Regarding the distinction maintained between consecrated life in a religious community and consecrated life as a lay person in the world, mentioned above, the *Code of Canon Law* says that there are different forms of consecrated life. Normally, a consecration is effected through "the profession of the evangelical councils," that is, through vowing poverty, chastity, and obedience;[570] for this reason, consecration is also called a total dedication to God.[571] Canon law affirms that this is done through "vows or other sacred bonds according to the proper laws of the institutes."[572] The code affirms that by "its very nature, the state of consecrated life is neither clerical nor lay."[573] An institute is called "clerical" when this status corresponds to the intended founder or tradition of the institute, when the institute is under the direction of clerics, when they assume the exercise of sacred orders, and when this is recognized by the authority of the Church.[574]

Although, as noted, some of these terms lack clarity, it is possible to conclude this topic by highlighting three characteristics that are

[569] Ibid., 305.
[570] CIC, can. 573 §1.
[571] Cf. ibid.
[572] CIC, can. 573 §2.
[573] CIC, can. 588 §1.
[574] Cf. CIC, can. 588 §2.

fundamental for a consecration: a) a free and personal self-giving; b) a permanent sanctification and consecration or dedication; and c) the public character of the gift of self and the approval by the authority of the Church. In other words, the basic precondition for being consecrated to God is the willingness to belong completely to Him. This can only be the result of one's own decision, since grace presupposes nature. Through the bishop, who usually presides over such a consecration, the celebration acquires a public character, and it is done with the authority of the Church.

With these brief considerations concluded, one fundamental difficulty on the topic will be mentioned that is now often overlooked. As valuable as it was and is to have reintroduced the rite of the consecration of a virgin, it has proven to be a difficult concept to apply practically. These difficulties show that there was good reason that, for centuries, consecrated virginity was practiced only by nuns. Simply put, compared to a life in the world, their lifestyle is better suited to integrating and maintaining such a state.

Today, the fundamental difficulty is twofold. On one side women who are already advanced in age decide to become "consecrated virgins." Since they live usually on their own and not in a community, they often become eccentric or cranky personalities. There are cases of women who — even with much goodwill — develop a lifestyle based on their own criteria and ideas, which are difficult to reconcile with the consecration. Even if these consecrated virgins plan or propose to live together in a type of community, their rather fixed and individualistic lifestyles make community living a practical nightmare. Moreover, people would wonder, why they don't just live in a monastery? On the other side, younger consecrated virgins, living alone, are often exposed to temptations, loneliness, and gossip. I know one such lady who certainly led an exemplary life; as part of her good work, she helped the bishop with many projects. But malicious tongues quickly spread rumors about her, which greatly harmed the bishop as well as herself. These difficulties cannot be easily solved, nor can they be overlooked.[575]

8.4.1.2. Consecration to the Immaculate Heart of Mary

Among the faithful, the consecration to the Immaculate Heart of Mary has been known and practiced for centuries. Most recently, it was brought into focus once again in 2022, when Pope Francis decided to consecrate Russia, Ukraine, and the whole world to the Immaculate Heart of Our Lady on March 25 (this consecration was made in response to war breaking out between Russia and Ukraine in February 2022). The key phrase of the prayer of this consecration is:

> Therefore, Mother of God and our Mother, to your Immaculate Heart we solemnly entrust and consecrate ourselves, the Church and all humanity, especially Russia and Ukraine. Accept this act that we carry out with confidence and love. Grant that war may end and peace spread throughout the world. The "Fiat" that arose from your heart opened the doors of history to the Prince of Peace. We trust that, through your heart, peace will dawn once more. To you we consecrate the future of the whole human family, the needs and expectations of every people, the anxieties and hopes of the world.[576]

---

[575] Another part of the Instruction *Sponsa Christi* has also proved to be highly problematic, because virginity is no longer assumed for consecrated virgins. It says: "In this context it should be kept in mind that the call to give witness to the Church's virginal, spousal and fruitful love for Christ is not reducible to the symbol of physical integrity. Thus to have kept her body in perfect continence or to have practiced the virtue of chastity in an exemplary way, while of great importance with regard to the discernment, are not essential prerequisites in the absence of which admittance to consecration is not possible." Congregation for Institutes of Consecrated Life and Societies of Apostolic Life, Instruction *Ecclesiae Sponsae Imago*, 88.

[576] Francis, Act of Consecration to the Immaculate Heart of Mary, March 25, 2022 in https://www.vatican.va/content/francesco/en/prayers/documents/20220325-atto-consacrazione-cuoredimaria.html [10.5.2023].

At this point, it is not necessary to explain in detail this act of consecration, which is closely linked to the apparition and message of Our Lady of Fatima.[577] Nevertheless, it will be helpful to consider it as a development in a broader perspective before offering a theological explanation of it.

In the eighteenth century, St. Louis-Marie Grignion de Montfort (d. 1716) spread, first in France and soon in the whole world, what he called the "total consecration" to Our Lady.[578] It requires free and personal self-giving, a separation from the world to be *Totus Tuus* ("wholly yours"), that is, to belong entirely to God through Mary. Even though this devotion spread as a "private form," it was soon approved and recommended by the popes, starting with Pope Pius IX and continuing on until Pope John Paul II. Indeed, John Paul II's episcopal motto, *Totus Tuus*, comes directly from this devotion. These types of consecrations increased especially during the last century. Pope Pius XII, for example, accentuated in his encyclical letter *Haurietis Aquas* (On Devotion to the Sacred Heart) the importance of the consecration to the Hearts of Jesus and Mary.[579] Many other documents stressed the importance of these consecrations, such as the Apostolic Letter *Rosarium Virginis Mariae*, published by Pope John Paul II in 2002. It says: "Hence the most perfect of all devotions is undoubtedly that which conforms, unites and consecrates us most perfectly to Jesus Christ. Now, since Mary is of all creatures the one most conformed to Jesus Christ, it follows that among all devotions that which most consecrates and conforms a soul to our Lord is devotion to Mary, his Holy Mother, and that the

---

[577] Cf. CDF, The Message of Fatima, April 19, 2000, in https://www.vatican.va/roman_curia/congregations/cfaith/documents/rc_con_cfaith_doc_20000626_message-fatima_en.html [10.5.2023].

[578] Cf. Louis de Montfort, *True Devotion to Mary with Preparation for Total Consecration*, trans. Frederick W. Faber, (Gastonia: TAN Books, 2010).

[579] Cf. Pius XII, Encyclical Letter *Haurietis Aquas*, May 15, 1956, in http://w2.vatican.va/content/pius-xii/en/encyclicals/documents/hf_p-xii_enc_15051956_haurietis-aquas.html [10.5.2023].

more a soul is consecrated to her the more will it be consecrated to Jesus Christ."[580]

The many Marian apparitions recognized by the Church, such as in Tepeyac, Rue du Bac, La Salette, Lourdes, Fatima, and so on had led not only the faithful but also the Magisterium to a consciousness of the importance of such consecrations. The apparitions of Fatima in particular received special importance and attention. It is not surprising, then, that Pope Francis was not the first pope to perform such a consecration. In 1942, Pope Pius XII consecrated the world, and later the people of Russia specifically, to the Immaculate Heart.[581] Pope John Paul II repeated this act of consecration in 1982 in Fatima,[582] and again on March 25, 1984, in union with the bishops of the whole world, in St. Peter's Square.[583] In 1986, he addressed the participants of the study week of the Pontifical Academy of Sciences with the following words: "The act of

---

[580] John Paul II, Apostolic Letter *Rosarium Virginis Mariae*, October 16, 2002, 15, in https://w2.vatican.va/content/john-paul-ii/en/apost_letters/2002/documents/hf_jp-ii_apl_20021016_rosarium-virginis-mariae.html [10.5.2023].

[581] He said "Nos interea, ut Nostrae vestraeque preces supplicationesque facilius exaudiantur, utque singulari erga vos benevolentiae Nostrae praebeamus documentum, quemadmodum paucis ante annis universum hominum genus Immaculato Deiparae Virginis Cordi consecravimus, ita in praesens cunctos Russiarum populos eidem Immaculato Cordi peculiarissimo modo dedicamus ac consecramus, fore omnino sperantes ut quae Nos, quae vos, quae boni omnes verae pacis, fraternae concordiae debitaeque omnibus, imprimisque Ecclesiae, libertatis vota facimus, ea, potentissimo suffragante Mariae Virginis patrocinio, quam primum feliciter effecta dentur." Pius XII, Apostolic Letter *Carissimis Russiae Populis*, July 7, 1952, in https://w2.vatican.va/content/pius-xii/la/apost_letters/documents/hf_p-xii_apl_19520707_sacro-vergente-anno.html [10.5.2023].

[582] Cf. John Paul II, Preghiera di affidamento e di consacrazione alla Vergine, May 13, 1982, in http://w2.vatican.va/content/john-paul-ii/it/speeches/1982/may/documents/hf_jp-ii_spe_19820513_vergine-fatima.html [10.5.2023].

[583] Cf. John Paul II, L'Atto di Affidamento, March 25, 1984, in https://www.vatican.va/content/john-paul-ii/it/letters/1983/documents/hf_jp-ii_let_19831208_vescovi-immacolata-concezione.html [10.5.2023].

entrusting ourselves to the Heart of Our Lady establishes a relationship of love with her in which we dedicate to her all that we have and are. This consecration is practiced essentially by a life of grace, of purity, of prayer, of penance that is joined to the fulfillment of all the duties of a Christian, and of reparation for our sins and the sins of the world."[584]

At this point, a brief theological reflection on the value and nature of these consecrations is helpful. First, it must be emphasized that the consecrations to the Sacred Heart of Jesus and to the Immaculate Heart of Mary are real consecrations. If done properly, depending upon the minister and the disposition of the receiver, such consecrations imply free and personal self-giving that leads to permanent sanctification (these same implications are attached to the consecration of virgins). Since this devotion is officially approved by the Church's authority, all criteria for consecrations are fulfilled.

Nevertheless, such a consecration also implies a great responsibility to conform one's life to the standards of these consecrations. It is not by chance that the message of Fatima, which explicitly requested this consecration, is linked to the call for conversion and penance. It would be good to remember the words of the Gospel: "Much will be required of the person entrusted with much" (cf. Luke 12:48).

8.4.1.3. Invocative Blessings of Persons

Invocative blessings have increased, one might say, "inflationarily." So many different blessings are described in the *Book of Blessings* that even a priest runs the risk of getting lost.[585] As a remedy, a basic structure that can be applied has already been proposed.[586] For now, the focus will be

---

[584] John Paul II, Address to the participants of the Study Week of the Pontifical Academy of Sciences, September 26, 1986, in https://w2.vatican.va/content/john-paul-ii/en/speeches/1986/september/documents/hf_jp-ii_spe_19860922_simposio-maria-gesu.html [12.5.2023].

[585] Nearly 250 pages of such blessings are cited only over persons. Cf. BoB, 35–280.

[586] Cf. chap. 8.4.1.

on the spiritual effects that can be achieved through these blessings, which in turn are based on those theological foundations that have already been mentioned.[587]

Priests who are aware of the theological foundation and value of blessings will generously make use of them, not in an imposing way, but with the help of explanations based on sacramentality. For example, whenever a priest visits a family or a house, he should not leave without first having said a prayer and imparted his blessing. The awareness of the importance of a blessing has mostly been lost among the faithful, and even among many priests, but it must be rediscovered. There are of course many reasons for this loss of understanding, and no one will ask for something good unless he knows it is something good; with this in mind, priests should take it upon themselves to assist the faithful in coming back to an understanding of the spiritual benefits of this sacramental. The "goods" related to blessings are, in fact, spiritual fruits. Although the following list does not claim to be exhaustive, it does provide an overview of some of these benefits:

1. A blessing can excite pious affections, leading to conversion;

2. Through a blessing, the remission of venial sins may be achieved;

3. A blessing can free people from the power of evil spirits;

4. A blessing can help to preserve and/or restore bodily health; and

5. A blessing can produce other temporal or spiritual benefits.

Although, as is the case with all sacramentals, the spiritual fruits of a blessing depend upon certain factors, such as faith, personal holiness, and so on, the formula of a blessing is also important.[588] It is hardly

---

[587] Cf. chap. 2–4.
[588] Cf. chap. 3.4.

surprising at this point that the old form fulfills the necessary criteria for blessing more fully than the new form, and this is for various reasons. As one example of this, let us consider the blessing of a woman before childbirth, focusing on the central prayer of the blessing:

New Form (*Book of Blessings*)	Old Form
Introduction (suitable words)[589] Readings Invocations	Introduction (prayer) Prayer to the Most Holy Trinity, invoking the protection against any adversity. Prayer to God the Father, asking for protection and guidance, invoking the saints. Sprinkling Holy Water, Ps. 66.
Prayer: Gracious Father, your Word, spoken in love, created the human family and, in the fullness of time, your Son, conceived in love, restored it to your friendship. Hear the prayers of N. and N., who await the birth of their child. Calm their fears when they are anxious. Watch over and support these parents and bring their child into this world safely and in good health, so that as members of your family they may praise you and glorify you through your Son, our Lord Jesus Christ, now and forever. Amen. … And may almighty God bless you all, the Father, and the Son, and the Holy Spirit. R. Amen.[590]	Prayer. Let us pray. Lord, we beg you to visit this dwelling, and to drive away from it and from this servant of yours, N., all the enemy's wiles. Let your holy angels be appointed here to keep her and her offspring in peace; and let your blessing ✠ ever rest upon her. Save them, almighty God, and grant them your everlasting light; through Christ our Lord. R. Amen. May the blessing of almighty God, Father, Son, ✠ and Holy Spirit, come on you and your child, and remain with you forever. R. Amen.[591]

---

[589] BoB, 102.
[590] BoB, 106–107.
[591] RR, 263. English translation Blessing of an Expectant Mother at the approach of confinement, in https://latinmassbaptism.com/blessing-of-expectant-mothers/ [12.5.2023].

As can clearly be seen, the new form omits important parts of any sacramental, such as any type of apotropaic element. Furthermore, it is a prayer focusing mainly on physical health. Even though this is important, everlasting life is much more important. The old form, however, fulfills all of the necessary criteria for a sacramental, particularly for an invocative blessing.[592] The first blessing includes purification and protection against the evil one, and the angels are invoked as invisible aid. The second blessing invokes divine grace and spiritual benefits for the pregnant woman and her child.

8.4.2. Blessing of Objects

St. Paul writes, "For everything created by God is good, and nothing is to be rejected when received with thanksgiving, for it is made holy by the invocation of God in prayer" (1 Tim. 4:4–5). This affirmation helps in understanding the importance of blessing objects and places. Through the mysterious work of the devil and the devastating consequence of Original Sin, the world fell into disorder, and this disorder continues to this day; although the world was created good and in perfect harmony, this harmony was lost through sin.[593] Thus the devil is the ruler of this world (cf. John 16:11), which means he has an impact on inanimate objects as well as on us; they too can be under the influence of evil spirits.[594] St. Paul describes this reality when he states that "creation was made subject to futility," and "is groaning in labor pains even until now" (Rom. 8:20–22).

Recognizing this reality leads to consequences concerning the sacramentals. As a first step, creation must be freed from the influence of evil; this is an essential part of each blessing. Previously, the

---

[592] Especially the following two elements are constitutive for each sacramental: apotropaic elements and elements of sanctification. See chap. 2.3.1.
[593] Cf. chap. 2.3.1.
[594] Cf. chap. 7.3.2.1.

image of a vessel being open or closed was used to help understand the workings of grace; now the focus will be on the image of a cup, to help us comprehend why animate and inanimate objects must be freed from the influence of evil: Nobody pours a fine wine into a dirty glass. In such a circumstance, even the best wine would become undrinkable. This is similar to the blessings of objects and places. As a first step, they must be purified from all influences of evil. The limits, if not the failure, of the renewed ritual becomes abundantly clear at this point. Since apotropaic elements are excluded, the theological foundations that led to the new ritual are in clear opposition to revelation, not to mention the testimony of Scripture and Tradition. This aspect must be recovered, not only so that the sacramentals develop their spiritual effects, but also so that they correspond to reality. In a second step, the object or place should be sanctified through the blessing. To return once again to the image used above, when the glass is cleaned, it is ready to receive precious content. Nature is perfected through grace.

The principal blessings recognized by the Church are contained in the *Roman Ritual* (*Book of Blessings*) and the *Roman Pontifical*. The latter contains blessings that are usually imparted by bishops. The *Ceremonial of Bishops* also includes sacramentals.[595] Because the frame of this book does not allow us to analyze these things in detail, the following explanations will be limited to some of the most common blessings of the new ritual, which is the most used ritual, especially by priests.

Part II of *De benedictionibus* (*Book of Blessings*) is titled "Blessings Related to Buildings and to Various Forms of Human Activity,"[596] numbering 175 pages in full. This is followed by part III, "Blessings of Objects that are Designed or Erected for Use in Churches, Either in

---

[595] Cf. *Ceremonial of Bishops*, 191–305.
[596] BoB, 283–458.

the Liturgy or in Popular Devotions,"[597] another 153 pages. Part IV is entitled "Blessings of Articles Meant to Foster the Devotion of the Christian People,"[598] 29 pages, wherein the most important and most frequently sought blessings among the faithful, such as the blessing of the Miraculous Medal or the St. Benedict Medal are not even mentioned. This is followed by part V, "Blessings Related to Feasts and Seasons,"[599] another 119 pages. Finally, a sixth part is added, titled "Blessings for Various Needs and Occasions,"[600] consisting of 88 pages.

Besides the problems already mentioned above (absence of apotropaic elements, the omission of the sign of the cross, many optional elements, the option to mix sacraments and sacramentals), the ritual is unreasonable and impractical. On the one hand, the blessings contained in it do not do justice to fallen nature, as explained above; on the other hand, they are not at all practical for pastoral application. Suppose someone asks a priest to bless a rosary: How would he need to proceed if he were to follow with fidelity all the indications of the *Book of Blessings*? Let us take a brief look.

The priest would have to start by gathering the community, and, as the celebrant enters, the community would sing a song or suitable hymn. He makes the sign of the cross. Then he would greet the people with "suitable words," words that he can freely invent. This is followed by a long prayer, which has the purpose of preparing the people present for the blessing. In other words, it does not prepare the object to be blessed, but rather the people participating in the blessing. This is followed by the reading of the Word of God. The priest, or another person present, may read a text of the Gospel. According to the circumstances, this is followed by another suitable song, or a Psalm may be read. From there, the rubrics offer the possibility of a brief

---

[597] BoB, 459–612.
[598] BoB, 613–642.
[599] BoB, 643–762.
[600] BoB, 763–851.

explanation of the biblical text so that the people — who were the ones to ask for a blessing in the first place — may understand the meaning of the blessing. The blessing itself is additionally preceded by the intercessions, which may be adapted or applied to the circumstances. Creativity is given room. The assisting minister is supposed to read these intercessions. If circumstances suggest it, all may pray for a moment in silence. Finally, the celebrant prays with outstretched hands the actual prayer of blessing, which does not include the sign of the cross. And it is not even a blessing of the object, but of the person who asked that the rosary be blessed! The prayer reads: "Blessed be our God and Father, who has given us the mysteries of his Son to be pondered with devotion and celebrated with faith. May he grant us, his faithful people, that by praying the rosary we may, with Mary the Mother of Jesus, seek his joys, sorrows and glories in our minds and hearts. We ask this through Christ our Lord. Amen."[601] Of course, even here, the priest may choose between three different prayers. Then, the recitation of the Rosary follows, concluded with the *Salve Regina*, and, finally, at the end, there is a common blessing of the faithful.[602]

Even though an alternative shorter rite is offered to bless a rosary,[603] the ritual of that form also clearly reveals that those who created it were pure theorists who had no regard for the practical situations that pastors find themselves in, nor any respect for the Tradition of the Church.[604] All the other blessings — for example, the

---

[601] BoB, 630–631.
[602] Cf. BoB, 625–632.
[603] Cf. BoB, 632–634.
[604] Daniel G. van Slyke states that there has been a "radical change in the structure of blessings. First, a 'liturgy of the word,' has been added to the prayer of blessing that constituted the fundamental core of most blessings in the previous *Roman Ritual*. Second, holy water is no longer central to the rites of blessing. Accordingly, the Order for Blessing Water, which once occupied the place of honor, now occupies the relative obscurity of chapter 33." Daniel G. van Slyke, "The Order for Blessing," 12–23.

blessing of holy water — follow this same structure.[605] I have never seen a priest perform such a "blessing," which, in the end, is not even a blessing of the object. Rather, if all rubrics and suggestions are observed, it is a blessing of the people who are present, and it would last a good thirty minutes.

Yet again, the difficulty associated with the new ritual becomes evident. Therefore, in the following two sections, we will limit our focus to the Tradition of the Church, which is the *princeps analogatum*, the valid point of reference. In this context, special attention will be paid both to Sacred Scripture and to those references that have found their way into the Tradition of the Church over the centuries. Our examples will be three sacramentals, the use of which is widespread among the faithful.

8.4.2.1. Holy Water

The use of holy water goes back to the earliest period of Christian history, and even predates it.[606] Sacred Scripture continuously mentions its significance. In the Old Testament, holy water is a powerful means of purification (cf. Exod. 29:4). For example, the book of Numbers says: "In an earthen vessel he shall take holy water" (Num. 5:17) that will lead to the remission of sins (cf. Num. 8:7) when it is sprinkled on the people (cf. Ps. 51:9). In the New Testament, water receives the most prominent importance in the context of Baptism, performed with water and by the power of the Holy Spirit (cf. Mark 1:8). When Jesus Christ was baptized, He sanctified the element of water, which is also presented constantly as a sign of purification (cf. John 13:4–10). This double meaning is fully revealed at the moment when the soldier opened Jesus Christ's side with a lance and immediately blood and

---

[605] Cf. BoB, 593–596.
[606] Cf. John F. Sullivan, *The Externals of The Catholic Church, Her Government, Ceremonies, Festivals, Sacramentals, and Devotions*, 5th ed., (New York: Kenedy & Sons, 1942), 157.

water flowed out (cf. John 19:34). Holy water is therefore closely linked to purification from evil, the forgiveness of sins, and the new birth through sanctifying grace (Baptism).

According to William Barry, a priest who published in 1858 the book *Sacramentals of the Holy Catholic Church*, the blessing of water and the admixture of salt was already in use in the second century;[607] this was abolished only by the new ritual. Besides fresh water, the use of salt is important because of its twofold meaning: 1) According to its natural dimension, salt has preservative and antiseptic properties; 2) According to the spiritual dimension, salt can have an indwelling power to preserve from the corruption of sin and evil spirits (cf. 2 Kings 2:20–21). According to the Tradition of the Church, and as said before, everything about to be sanctified needs first to be purified — this is an acknowledgment and a practical confrontation of the real wounding of nature through Original Sin.

Barry enumerates three types of holy water: baptismal water, holy water blessed by a bishop, and common holy water blessed by a priest.[608] The distinction between a common and a more solemn blessing was always part of the Church's Tradition; a similar distinction was made between a common and a Solemn High Mass. Baptismal water was always considered to be of great relevance; it was usually preserved throughout the year since it was considered to be a particularly powerful sacramental, similar to the water blessed by the bishop. These practices spread from the East to the West; it was common that the water was blessed on special feast days, such as during the Easter Vigil or on Epiphany. The common blessing of holy water was already indicated by Pope Leo IV (d. 855). He is remembered by the Church for repairing the walls that protected the city of Rome

---

[607] William J. Barry, *The Sacramentals*, 57.
[608] So quoted in Michael T. Barrett (ed.), Art. "Holy Water," Catholic Encyclopedia, in http://www.newadvent.org/cathen/07432a.htm [12.5.2023].

(known now as the Leonine Wall), which had been damaged by Arab raids. He was also the one who ordered priests to bless water every Sunday. He wrote: "*Omni die Dominico, ante missam, aquam benedictam facite, unde populus et loca fidelium aspergantur* — Every Lord's day, before mass, holy water should be made, in order that the people and the place might be sprinkled."[609]

Even in the first centuries after Christ, there was this threefold distinction. This leads to the question: is the spiritual quality of holy water the same regardless of it being blessed commonly or solemnly? Does the formula of blessing make a difference? What about the salt? Is it necessary, given its correspondence to the Church's early tradition? Before answering most of these questions, let us start at the beginning: Yes, there is a difference between holy water blessed commonly and holy water blessed solemnly. Its spiritual quality, which depends upon many factors,[610] can be compared to the strength of an alcoholic beverage. Even though the following comparison may seem a shade irreverent, it is still helpful. Someone can think of a common blessing of water to produce something analogous to a beer with a low percentage of alcohol, while the product of a solemn blessing could instead be compared to a good whiskey or fine liquor. The spiritual quality can differ because the sacramentals work *ex opera operantis*; as should be clear from our earlier explanations, the difference depends upon the faith and holiness of the minister and recipient, but also upon the formula used. This will become more evident when looking at the rite for the blessing of holy water.

The basic structure of blessing holy water according to the new ritual was already explained above; here, the focus will be on the old form, especially since it serves as *the* point of reference and includes

---

[609] So quoted in ibid.
[610] Cf. chap. 2–4.

the twofold dimension of purification and sanctification. The priest, usually dressed with a cassock, surplice, and stole, begins the blessing.

The common forms of blessing holy water follow the structure referenced below.[611] The blessing starts with the sign of the cross, using the formula "Our help is in the name of the Lord," followed by "Who made heaven and earth." Then the priest:

- ✛ exorcises the salt, then blesses it;
- ✛ exorcises the water, then blesses it;
- ✛ mixes together the salt and water and blesses them with final prayers.[612]

There are no optional elements in this common form, and the structure of the prayer corresponds to the meaning and purpose of holy water. In prudence, it is usually recommended that the priest pray the exorcisms in Latin, so as to avoid any confusion among the faithful.

There is also a solemn form of blessing holy water, which belongs to the Vigil of the Epiphany. This is the most solemn blessing, and it produces numerous spiritual fruits. The prayer for it contains a rich spiritual heritage, including elements from the East. Today, many priests are not even aware of the existence of this blessing, which, in its most solemn form, is done by the bishop. Without going into too much detail, a look at the general structure of it will be helpful:

1. The Litany of All Saints is sung, during which all kneel;

2. The Lord's Prayer is recited;

3. Psalms 28, 45, and 146 are sung;

---

[611] Cf. *The Roman Ritual: The Blessings*, vol. III, trans. and ed. by Philip T. Weller, 2nd ed., (Hawthorne, CA: Caritas Publishing, 2008). Cf. Appendix 2, The Blessing of Holy Water.

[612] Cf. Frederick R. McManus (ed.), *Parish Ritual*, (New York: Benzinger Brothers, 1962), 265–268.

4. Exorcisms against Satan and the apostate angels are performed;

5. An antiphon and the Benedictus or the *Magnificat* (depending on the time of day) are recited;

6. The exorcism of salt and its blessing are administered, followed by the exorcism of water and its blessing;

7. The final prayer of blessing is prayed;

8. The *Asperges* (rite of sprinkling holy water) is sung or recited while the priest sprinkles the people with the blessed water;

9. The "Te Deum" (an ancient hymn to the glory of God) is sung.[613]

When looking at this rite, it becomes clear why the formula has special significance. The solemn form of blessing water increases its indwelling spiritual power. This allows us to point out some of the most important spiritual effects that can be achieved using this sacramental, always presupposing what was said before concerning the use and effects of the sacramentals.[614] Whenever holy water is used with proper intention and disposition, it may cause:

1. Protection and liberation from evil;

2. Defense and strengthening against temptations;

3. Weakening of extraordinary diabolic action;

4. Remission of venial sins;

5. Protection of bodily health against temporal evils;

---

[613] Cf. *The Roman Ritual*, 42–64.
[614] Cf. chap. 3.

6. Increase of actual graces (growth in virtues and sanctification);

7. Gain of partial indulgences;

8. Healing of illnesses; and

9. Help for the souls in Purgatory (use in cemeteries).

Precisely because many graces can be obtained through the pious use of holy water, priests and faithful should make abundant use of it. It is highly recommended for Catholics to have blessed water in the house. There are also many local traditions related to the use of holy water. For example, parents may bless their children with holy water before they leave the house, or when going to bed. In times of illness, the body can be sprinkled with holy water, and it can also be drunk. The water from Lourdes has also demonstrated the healing power that holy water may unfold. Exorcisms always include the use of holy water, as does the administration of the Anointing of the Sick. In *all* blessings performed by a priest, holy water should be used.

8.4.2.2. The St. Benedict Medal and the Miraculous Medal

Among the faithful, there are two particular medals that are most frequently used as sacramentals: the St. Benedict Medal and the Miraculous Medal. The Church used to bless them with proper blessings, blessings which corresponded to the specific nature of these medals. However, both blessings were simply ignored by the liturgical reform. Even though the *Book of Blessings* dedicates hundreds of pages to various forms of blessings, these two have been omitted for inexplicable reasons. The *Book of Blessings* contains only a general "Order for the Blessing of Religious Articles,"[615] but does not include any specific blessing of these medals.

---

[615] BoB, 617ff.

Therefore, in order to arrive at an understanding of these sacramentals, it will be necessary to look at the old form and its organic development, first for the St. Benedict Medal and then for the Miraculous Medal. These two specific objects will be in focus because blessings for them are frequently requested by the faithful.

a) The St. Benedict Medal

Even though the St. Benedict Medal has been adapted over the centuries, it has always enjoyed great veneration, especially when used with faith and love, trusting in the merits and intercession of St. Benedict. It is popular among the faithful mainly because the medal is meant to protect against the forces of evil, which is closely related to its history as well as to the life of St. Benedict.

Many episodes from St. Benedict's life were reported by Gregory the Great. One of the most prominent episodes, which was already described in 6.4.1, concerns his fight against the powers of evil, which is narrated in the second book of the *Dialogues*. St. Benedict was given a glass of poisoned wine to drink; however, before drinking it, he made the sign of the cross over it. At this blessing, the glass broke, and his life was spared.[616] With the power of God, St. Benedict overcame the evil one and his works on this occasion and on others. He is rightly the patron saint of exorcists. The sign of the cross is, therefore, embossed on the St. Benedict Medal, for it is the sign of salvation through which all evil is overcome. Prosper Guéranger writes in his detailed explanation of the medal: "The cross is an object of terror to the evil spirits; they ever crouch in terror before it; they no sooner see it than they let go their prey and take to flight."[617] Over its history, this medal has proved to be

---

[616] Cf. Gregory the Great, *Dialogues*, trans. Odo John Zimmerman, (Washington, D.C.: The Catholic University of America Press, 2002), 62.

[617] Prosper Guéranger, *The Medal or Cross of St. Benedict. Its Origin, Meaning and Privileges*, trans. Laurence Shepherd, (London: Burns and Oates, 1880), 3.

powerful against spells and superstitious practices, and it has found wide distribution as a sign of protection granted from Heaven.[618]

The medal was officially approved after a careful examination by the Holy See in 1742. Pope Benedict XIV (d. 1758) had authorized the rite of blessing over the medal (see below), as well as a great number of indulgences.[619] Multiple spiritual benefits are attributed to this medal, such as spiritual favors, protection against the devil, preservation in danger, and the like.[620]

The front of the medal shows St. Benedict holding his rule; next to him is the cross that helps to overcome the power of evil. Inscribed on the back are the letters "C S P B," signifying "*Crux Sancti Patris Benedicti* — The Cross of our Holy Father Benedict," and they "explain the nature of the medal."[621] In the form of a cross, the following letters are added vertically "C S S M L," signifying "*Crux Sacra sit mihi Lux* — May the Holy Cross be my Light." On the horizontal bar of the cross are the letters "N D S M D," signifying "*Non draco sit mihi dux* — Let not the dragon be my guide." Guéranger comments: "These two lines put together form a pentameter verse, containing the Christian's protestation that he confides in the holy cross, and refuses to bear the yoke which the devil would put upon him."[622] This is followed, in a circle around the rim of the medal, by the letters "V R S N S M V," signifying "*Vade retro Satana nunquam suade mihi vana* — Be gone Satan and suggest not to me thy vain things" and "S M Q L I V B," signifying "*Sunt mala quae libas ipse venena bibas* — the cup thou offers me is evil; drink thou thy poison." Prosper Guéranger comments: "These words are supposed to be uttered by St. Benedict; those of the first verse when he was suffering the temptation in his cave, and which he overcame by the sign of the cross; and those of the second verse, at the moment of his

---

[618] Cf. ibid., 15–21.
[619] Cf. ibid., 69–99, here 70.
[620] Cf. ibid., 27–68.
[621] Ibid., 12.
[622] Ibid., 12.

enemies offering him the draught of death, which he discovered by his making over the poisoned cup the sign of life."[623]

Until the Second Vatican Council, this blessing was reserved for Benedictine monks. This restriction was removed so that any priest could perform this blessing. However, since this prayer of blessing is no longer to be found in the ritual, it is worth getting a copy of it. The old rite respects the classical approach, starting with a purification (exorcism) followed by a blessing (sanctification). In the following, only the essential parts of the prayers are shown.

Latin[624]	English[625]
S. Adiutórium nostrum in nómine Dómini.	P. Our help is in the name of the Lord.
Exorcízo vos, numísmata, per Deum ✠ Patrem omnipoténtem, qui fecit caelum et terram, mare et ómnia, quae in eis sunt. Omnis virtus adversárii, omnis exércitus diáboli et omnis incúrsus, omne phantásma sátanae, eradicare et effugare ab his numismátibus: ut fiant ómnibus, qui eis usúri sunt, salus mentis et córporis: in nómine Patris ✠ omnipoténtis, et Iesu ✠ Christi Filii eius, Dómini nostri, et Spiritus ✠ Sancti Parácliti, et in caritáte eiusdem Dómini nostri Iesu Christi, qui ventúrus est iudicare vivos et mórtuos, et saeculum per ignem. R. Amen.	I purge you medals by God ✠ the Father ✠ Almighty, Creator of heaven and earth and of the sea and of all that they contain. O every power of the adversary, every cohort of the devil, every attack and appearance of Satan — get thee out of these medals and fly afar! And may they become for all who will use them a help for body and soul, in the name of the Father ✠ Almighty, in the name of Jesus ✠ Christ, His Son, our Lord, in the name of the Holy ✠ Spirit, the Paraclete, and in the love of the selfsame Lord Jesus Christ, Who shall come to judge the living and the dead and the world by fire. R. Amen.

[623] Ibid., 13.
[624] Quoted according to RR 494,
[625] English translation from *The Roman Ritual: Christian Burial, Exorcisms, Reserved Blessings, Etc.*, vol. II, trans. and ed. Philip T. Weller, (Hawthorne, CA: Caritas Publishing 2017), Blessing of Medals of St. Benedict, 355–358, here 355.

Latin[624]	English[625]
Oratio	Prayer
Orémus: Deus omnipotens, bonórum ómnium largítor, súpplices te rogámus, ut per intercessiónem sancti Benedicti, his sacris numismátibus, lítteris ac charactéribus a te designátis, tuam benedictiónem ✠ infúndas: ut omnes, qui ea gestáverint ac bonis opéribus inténti fúerint, sanitátem mentis et córporis, et grátiam sanctificatiónis, atque indulgéntias (nobis) concéssas cónsequi mereantur; omnésque diáboli insídias et fraudes, per auxílium misericórdiae tuae, effúgere váleant, et in cospéctu tuo sancti et immaculáti appáreant. Per Dóminum. R. Amen.	Let us pray: O almighty God, giver of all good things, we humbly beseech Thee that through the intercession of Saint Benedict, Thou wouldst pour forth Thy ✠ blessing upon these Sacred Medals, so that all who shall wear them and earnestly strive to perform good works, may deserve to obtain health of soul and body, the grace of increasing holiness, and the indulgences granted; and that they may strive, by the help of Thy mercy, to escape all the snares and deceits of the devil, and thus be able to appear holy and sinless in Thy sight. Through Christ our Lord. R. Amen.
Oratio	Prayer
Deinde Sacerdos aspergit numismata aqua benedicta.	*The medals are then sprinkled with holy water.*

Prosper Guéranger addresses in detail the spiritual fruits that can be achieved through this medal: "Experience has proved that the medal of St. Benedict, made use of with a proper intention and with prayer, has frequently broken the snares of the devil, procured a visible improvement in cases of sickness, and sometimes even effected a complete cure."[626] It is highly recommended to wear this medal and/or to deposit it in the house or ground, especially if there are any signs of infestation. The faithful may achieve great spiritual benefits if they use these medals with the right intention.

---

[626] Ibid., 26.

b) The Miraculous Medal

Even though the so-called "Miraculous Medal" is still more popular than the St. Benedict Medal, it was not included in the *Book of Blessings*. Pope John Paul II himself officially visited the place of the Marian apparition where the medal was given to us; by his attention to it, he recommended the devotion.[627] Since a proper blessing for this medal is not found in the new ritual, and so its usage is not what it once was, a brief explanation will be provided of the history of it for those who might not be familiar with it.

The Miraculous Medal corresponds to an explicit request from the Blessed Virgin Mary, who appeared to St. Catherine Labouré on November 27, 1830, in the Rue de Bac, Paris.[628] In this vision, the nun saw Our Lady standing on the globe, a snake coiled at her feet, with rays of light streaming from her outstretched hands. This image is depicted not only above the high altar of the chapel where the apparition happened, but also on the front side of the medal, together with the inscription: "O Mary, conceived without sin, pray for us who have recourse to thee." On the reverse of the Medal, the letter "M" is surmounted by a cross, together with the monogram of the Sacred Heart of Jesus, crowned with thorns, and the Immaculate Heart of Mary, pierced with a sword. The first medals were coined in 1832 and then distributed with episcopal permission. In the same year, there was a terrible cholera epidemic in Paris, leading to many deaths. When the medal was distributed, there were instantly many healings and miracles that occurred; this is when people started to call it the "Miraculous Medal." In addition to the miracles, numerous

---

[627] Cf. John Paul II, Discours dans la Chapelle de la Médaille Miraculeuse, May 31, 1980, in https://www.vatican.va/content/john-paul-ii/fr/speeches/1980/may/documents/hf_jp-ii_spe_19800531_medaglia-miracolosa.html [10.5.2023].

[628] Cf. Joseph Dirvin, *Saint Catherine Labouré of the Miraculous Medal*, 2nd ed., (New York: American Book-Stratford Press, 1958), 92–101.

conversions were also brought about. Pope Gregory XVI (d. 1846) started to wear it, Leo XIII (d. 1903) granted a liturgical feast in honor of the Marian apparitions to St. Catherine, and Pope Pius XII (d.1958) gave Miraculous Medals away at audiences.

A special blessing for these medals was approved by the authority of the Church in 1895.[629] The blessing corresponds to the twofold meaning related to the nature of this sacramental: first, a blessing of the medal, and second, an investiture with it for the person who will be wearing it. The blessing starts with the liturgical greeting "Our help is in the Name of the Lord," including the sign of the cross, and the corresponding answer. At this point, only the most important elements of the prayer are going to be presented:

Latin[630]	English[631]
Orémus. Omnípotens et miséricors Deus, qui per multíplices immaculátæ Maríæ Vírginis apparitiónes in terris mirabília iúgiter pro animárum salúte operári dignátus es: super heæc numísmatis signa tuam bene ✠ dictiónem benígnus infúnde; ut pie hoc recoléntes ac devóte gestántes et illíus patrocínium séntiant et tuam misericórdiam consequántur. Per Christum Dóminum nostrum. R. Amen.	Let us pray. Almighty and merciful God, Who by the many appearances on earth of the Immaculate Virgin Mary didst deign to work miracles again and again for the salvation of souls; graciously pour out Thy blessing ✠ on these medals, so that all who devoutly wear them and reverence them may experience the patronage of Mary Immaculate and obtain mercy from Thee; through Christ our Lord. R. Amen

---

[629] Cf. S. Congregatione Rituum, Benedictionis et impositionis S. Numismatis I. M. V., vulgo Medaglia miracolosa, (S. R. C. 19. April. 1895), in ASS 28 (1895–96): 442–443.

[630] Taken from RR, 493–494.

[631] English translation from Blessing and Investiture With the Medal of the Immaculate Conception, in http://www.rosarychurch.net/rituale/miraculous_medal.html [12.5.2023].

Latin[630]	English[631]
Deinde aspergit Numisma aqua benedicta et ipsum postea imponens dicit, si uni tantum imponatur.	*The Priest sprinkles the medal with holy water, and presents it to the person, saying:*
Accipe sanctum Numísma, gesta fidéliter et digna veratióne proséquere: ut piíssima et immaculáta cælórum Dómina te prótegat atque deféndat; et pietátis suæ prodígia rénovans, quæ a Deo supplíciter postuláveris, tibi misericórditer ímpetret, ut vivens a móriens in matérno eius ampléxu felíciter requiéscas. R. Amen.	Take this holy medal; wear it with faith, and handle it with due devotion, so that the holy and immaculate Queen of heaven may protect and defend you. And as she is ever ready to renew her wondrous acts of kindness, may she obtain for you in her mercy whatever you humbly ask of God, so that both in life and in death you may rest happily in her motherly embrace. R. Amen.
Kyrie eléison. Christe eléison. Kyrie eléison. Pater noster …	Lord, have mercy. Christ, have mercy. Lord, have mercy. Our Father …
Oratio finalis	Final prayer

As said above, the nature of this sacramental is different from the St. Benedict Medal; so also is the prayer of blessing different. In a way, this blessing could have been considered a bridge between the old and the new form, because, on the one hand, the object is blessed (the Miraculous Medal), and, on the other hand, the person who wears this medal devoutly is placed under the protection of the Immaculate Conception.

However, this bridging over did not happen. To simply omit both of these important blessings, from which many and great graces have emanated, is what Fr. Gabriele Amorth referred to as a grave sin of omission. In this manner, the faithful are deprived of precious spiritual support. Priests can and must have recourse to the old form in order to make accessible the richness of the sacramentals to the faithful.

✠ ✠ ✠

Conclusion

Now we have reached the conclusion, although there is much more that might be said regarding the nature and use of sacramentals and other important subjects related to this topic — such as, for example, the significance of relics,[632] sacred places, liturgical vestments, processions, funerals, and so on, which either are sacramentals themselves, or are closely linked to them. But in this book, we have tried to focus on the essentials, since they need to be addressed first.

The approach used was based on a "sacramental perspective," as indirectly proposed by the International Theological Commission in 2020.[633] In suggesting this approach, they, in turn, draw on the Post-Synodal Apostolic Exhortation *Sacramentum Caritatis*, issued by Pope Benedict XVI.[634] In that document, the pope from Germany addressed the mystery of the Eucharist and how it might be explained to the world. He developed a so-called "eucharistic spirituality," affirming that the Eucharist "itself powerfully illuminates human

---

[632] Cf. Giovanni Battista Proja, *Immagini, reliquie e benedizioni*, (Rome: Città Nuova Editrice, 2005). See also the remarks by Sergius Bulgakov, *Relics and Miracles. Two Theological Essays*, trans. Boris Jakim, (Grand Rapids: William B. Erdmans Publishing Company, 2011).
[633] Cf. International Theological Commission, "The Reciprocity."
[634] Ibid., 11, footnote 10.

history and the whole cosmos. In this sacramental perspective we learn, day by day, that every ecclesial event is a kind of sign by which God makes himself known and challenges us. The eucharistic form of life can thus help foster a real change in the way we approach history and the world. The liturgy itself teaches us."[635] With this, the pope proposes a viable way for correct understanding. Thus, the unity of faith in the duality of the natural and supernatural is assured; any type of dualism between the supernatural and the natural is avoided. Sacramentals, by their nature, are related to the sacraments; they are, then, closely associated with them. Like the sacraments, the spiritual effect of supernatural grace comes to bear through them. Therefore, it has been necessary to approach them in a manner that not only excludes dualism (i.e., an understanding in this context that the natural and the supernatural are two completely separate things) but also pushes back against any tendency to minimize the importance and nature of sacramentals, either through an overemphasis on rationalism or a simplistic version of faith that does not grant them the complexity and full dimensions of their nature.

A theological examination of the sacramentals has, up until now, been regarded and treated as the stepchild of theology.[636] Usually, the subject is approached either through a lens of historical interpretation, which cannot do justice to the living mystery of sacramentals, or the topic is simply ignored. Thus, the faithful are deprived of these powerful means of spiritual assistance; this leads them to search wherever they can to find something else. This is why there is such a proliferation of esotericism and esoteric practices in the world today. Where faith dwindles, superstition grows.

Recognizing the importance of sacramentals and restoring their proper understanding, use, and application should be an emergency

---

[635] Benedict XVI, *Sacramentum Caritatis*, 92.
[636] Cf. Ralph Weimann, "Die Sakramentalien."

priority for the Church. But their benefits are not derived by a simple flick of the proverbial lightswitch. They are a challenge for modern man, because they presuppose a living faith, and without faith, they become incomprehensible and meaningless; the actual crisis of faith will not be easily reversed. They are a challenge because understanding them requires a theological approach that is based and rooted in faith. This is clearly affirmed in the Encyclical Letter *Lumen fidei*:

> Since faith is a light, it draws us into itself, inviting us to explore ever more fully the horizon which it illumines, all the better to know the object of our love. Christian theology is born of this desire. Clearly, theology is impossible without faith; it is part of the very process of faith, which seeks an ever deeper understanding of God's self-disclosure culminating in Christ. It follows that theology is more than simply an effort of human reason to analyze and understand, along the lines of the experimental sciences. God cannot be reduced to an object. He is a subject who makes himself known and perceived in an interpersonal relationship. Right faith orients reason to open itself to the light which comes from God, so that reason, guided by love of the truth, can come to a deeper knowledge of God.[637]

Thus, the only viable way to "decode" and understand the sacramentals requires a sacramental perspective, one that makes the invisible become visible. It is based on this theological approach that sacramentals were explained in this book, with the intention of shining the light of faith on their value, their spiritual fruits, and their richness — for priests as well as for the faithful. God willing, this will inspire other theologians to pay renewed attention to this important topic and spur the faithful to avail themselves of these rich sources of grace. And now, through a brief review, some concluding thoughts can be formulated.

---

[637] Francis, LF, 36.

The introduction not only gave an overview of the historical development of sacramentals, but also pointed out a problem that has accompanied the genesis of this text all along: The question of hermeneutics, of the right interpretation and development of faith, is of crucial importance, especially concerning the sacramentals. Any rupture and discontinuity with the Tradition of the Church would be the opposite of true development, causing damage to the living organism: the Church.[638] Meanwhile, the principle of organic development has time and again proved to be the only viable way forward, explicitly outlined by the Second Vatican Council.[639]

Important distinctions have been made concerning the theological notion of "sacramentals," helping to frame these broad issues. As a part of this, distinctions were drawn among consecrations, blessings, exorcisms, and sacred objects. This was followed by explanations of their theological nature. The doctrine of Original Sin has also proved to be a jumping-off point in theological debates, especially as regards the *Book of Blessings*. If this doctrine is believed and accepted, then evil and its influence in the world is also acknowledged. Thus, all sacramentals must necessarily respond to this reality, which means that they must include apotropaic elements. In addition to their biblical foundation and their anti-demonic purpose, the "incarnational principle" is the guiding element for understanding their nature — together with their ecclesiological and liturgical dimensions. Finally, it was shown that sacramentals have a threefold dimension regarding their place in time, i.e., that they are related to the past, present, and future. All of these elements come together to shape the theological understanding of sacramentals.

---

[638] I have demonstrated this in great detail in my doctoral dissertation. Cf. Ralph Weimann, *Dogma und Fortschritt*.
[639] Cf. SC, 23.

With this theological understanding, it was possible to provide some important indications for the use and the effects of sacramentals. Although they are related to the sacraments, they are fundamentally different because they work according to the principle of *ex opere operantis Ecclesiae*, meaning that deriving positive spiritual effects from them requires devout participation, a concept which must be understood correctly. At the same time, the formula and the sacred signs of sacramentals have a special significance and have an impact on their efficacy. In this context, those principles were highlighted that characterize the renewed form of sacramentals — and this has demonstrated the serious deficiencies of that form, rooted in the problem that it is a form based in large part on a hermeneutic of rupture.

This leads to consequences when considering the minister and recipient of the sacramentals; they were discussed in the fourth chapter. Without falling into the heresy of Donatism, it was concluded that personal holiness is of particular importance with regard to the ability to obtain the spiritual fruits of sacramentals. The distinction between common and ministerial priesthood has also proved to be of special relevance.

The second part of the book focused on the practical application of sacramentals. Pastoral ministry must be based on the solid foundation of theology, which, in turn, is a reflection of faith. On this basis, the importance of the invocation of the name of Jesus Christ for the sacramentals was described. Imperative and deprecative invocations in particular can produce spiritual fruits of great significance.

From there, the following chapter focused on explanations about the sign of the cross. Through this sacred sign, fruits of purification, liberation, and sanctification can be obtained. The importance of the sign of the cross was obscured during the liturgical reform, sometimes so much so that its use was even abolished; nevertheless, in the administration of sacramentals, it should always be used. Essentially and unavoidably, a truly Christian blessing must include the sign of salvation as *the* distinguishing mark.

Given the importance of the anti-demonic character of sacramentals, more extensive considerations were presented in the seventh chapter going over relevant material. Some basics of angelology and demonology were recalled, basics which are a precondition to understanding what the Church calls exorcism. Only with these foundational principles clarified and defined can misunderstandings and narrow views be overcome and proper orientation on the subject be offered. The devil, as a fallen angel, operates according to ordinary and extraordinary actions. Within the category of extraordinary action, four varieties were presented, namely infestation, vexation, obsession, and possession. In the final part of that chapter, it was indicated what priests who are not exorcists can do to help affected persons and what measures of assistance are strictly reserved for exorcists. Finally, the distinction between major and minor exorcisms was covered, which is as fundamental as the distinction between healing and deliverance.

In the last chapter, the focus was on the blessings of the Church, the most common office of the priest. Those elements were highlighted that are helpful to obtaining spiritual fruits. Within this framework, a proper understanding of symbolism is of great importance. And, in this context, distinctions were made between what can and what cannot be blessed, giving basic criteria and fundamental structures for how to bless persons and/or objects. Among many significant distinctions, concrete examples were provided for some of the most common sacramentals.

Ultimately, the explanations provided in this book should make it undeniably clear that the sacramentals are of great importance. They must be rediscovered and made accessible to the faithful because, through them, significant spiritual fruits may be obtained. At the same time, it would be appropriate to further develop a theology that embraces the sacramental perspective in order to express anew the beauty and greatness of faith.

For this reason, the faithful ought to request and the priests ought to learn and know the treasuries of the old form of the Roman Rite, which remains the principle by which all other principles are measured (*princeps analogatum*). Thus, a reform of the reform should be undertaken, which does not invent itself as a novelty, but rather places itself in that great flow of Tradition that leads to the origin of all faith, grace, and salvation: Jesus Christ. This is the true goal of administering the sacramentals, for they are powerful means of purification, liberation, protection, and sanctification.

Glossary

Ad fontes: meaning "to the sources", refers to the whole of Tradition that reaches out to its foundation: Revelation itself.

Anamnesis, Epiclesis, and *Doxology*: *Anamnesis* refers to God's healing deeds, looking to the past; *epiclesis* is the invocation of the Holy Spirit making present and effective the merits of salvation for today; *doxology* is a prayer of praise and glory to the Trinity, directed to the future.

Anathema sit: from the Greek word *anathema*, which means being accursed, and, therefore, excommunicated.

Apotropaic: anti-demonic elements.

Blessing: visible sign through which the faithful receive spiritual benefits (grace).

Christology: doctrine concerning Jesus Christ.

Clericalism: interprets the ministry received as a power to be exercised rather than as a free and generous service to the revealed truth.

Common Blessing: the minister implores divine grace to grant some spiritual good.

Common Priesthood: participation in the priesthood of Christ based on Baptismal grace; it differs in essence from the ministerial priesthood.

Consecration (constitutive Blessing): a constitutive blessing that separates the sacred from the profane; it signifies the permanent sanctification of a person, object, or place.

Dedication: synonymous for consecration.

Deliverance: liberation from an extraordinary action of the devil.

Deprecative Invocations: something or someone is addressed indirectly in the name of Jesus Christ.

Diagnostic Exorcism: minor exorcism that helps to discern the presence of an extraordinary diabolic action.

Dogma: revealed teachings of Christ, proclaimed with the highest authority of the Church's Magisterium; the faithful are obliged to believe the truth contained in them and adhere to it.

Donatism: heretical position that assumed among other things that the clergy must be faultless to be effective dispensers of the sacraments.

Dualism: division of something into two opposing aspects.

Dubia: a standard procedure within the Church, consisting in the submission of one doubt (*dubium*) or several doubts (*dubia*) concerning faith and morals to the Magisterium for final clarification.

Ecclesiology: doctrine concerning the Church.

Economy of Salvation: God's plan for the salvation of the world.

Ex Opere Operantis: from the work of the doer; the effectiveness depends mainly on the moral condition of the persons who intervene.

Ex Opere Operantis Ecclesiae: from the work of the doer that is the Church; it refers to the minister acting in the person of the Church.

Ex Opere Operato: from the work which has been worked; sacraments confer grace when they are validly administered.

Excommunication *latae sententiae*: a canonical penalty that is inflicted automatically, at the very moment a law is contravened.

Exorcism: invocation of the name of God, made with the aim of removing the devil from a person, animal, place, or thing.

Extraordinary Actions (of the Devil): specific demonic activity of preternatural force.

Fides quae: objective revealed content of faith (dogmas of faith).

Fides qua: the personal acceptance of faith and the assimilation of the revealed objective truth.

Fides Quaerens Intellectum: faith seeking understanding, thus faith precedes theology.

Healing: restoration of the original harmony with God and man.

Hermeneutic of Reform: interpretation of the doctrine as a renewal within the continuity of the Church, which increases in time and develops, yet always remains the same.

Hermeneutic of Rupture: interpretation of the doctrine as a discontinuity with the living tradition of the Church and splitting it in a pre-conciliar and post-conciliar Church.

Immanentism: reality is reduced to self-consciousness.

Imperative Invocations: direct form of invoking the name of Jesus Christ, it usually implies an appeal to His authority.

Incarnational Principle: "The Word became flesh" is the concrete way of realizing the divine plan of salvation. This is reflected in the sacraments and in the sacramentals, where material things are granted spiritual significance.

Indwelling Efficiency: spiritual effects (graces), produced due to the intercessory power of the Church.

Infestation: demonic powers that possess inanimate objects, like houses and places, but also animals.

Invocative Blessing: intended to grant some temporal good, however, they do not affect any change of condition.

Lex Celebrandi: the law of celebration; official articulation of faith that corresponds to the law of faith.

Lex Credendi: the law of faith is the *regula fidei* that corresponds to the dogma.

Lex Orandi: the law of prayer; articulation of faith that corresponds to the law of faith.

Lex vivendi: it refers to the life of the Church, the manner of living.

Liberation: generally called exorcism, aiming toward the liberation from one or more demoniac presence(s).

Major (solemn) Exorcism: directed at the liberation from demonic possession through the spiritual authority which Jesus entrusted to His Church; it can be performed only by a priest with the permission of the bishop.

Minor Exorcism: called "Exorcism against Satan and his Apostate Angels" aims at the liberation from extraordinary demonic activity, possessions excluded.

Natural vs. Preternatural vs. Supernatural: natural corresponds to the order of creation; preternatural indicates a category that goes beyond the natural possibilities of any human being; supernatural refers to the power of God.

Nunc Stans: in God, there is no past nor future but only present, also called eternity.

Obsession: extraordinary action of the devil, an interior torment on the psychic level that affects the inner senses of the person.

Ontological: nature of being.

Ordinary Actions (of the Devil): temptation; it is not a sin in itself, but it becomes a sin when consented to.

Participatio Actuoso – Devout Participation; its goal is to achieve full and conscious participation in the mystery of salvation and to obtain the greatest amount of spiritual benefits leading to sanctification.

Peritus: an expert, who assists and advises the hierarchy.

Petitio Principii: circular reasoning.

Pneumatology: doctrine concerning the Holy Spirit.

Possession: extraordinary action of the devil, when one or many demonic spirits exercise despotic control over a human body.

Princeps Analogatum: valid point of reference, e.g. Jesus Christ is the point of reference for all Christians.

Private use of the exorcism: the minor exorcism used outside of any pastoral context and/or requested by the faithful, and as a *pia oratio*, can be used by priests without further permission.

Public use of the exorcism: done in the name and by the authority of the Church; exclusively by ministers appointed by the Church; in the form determined by the Church.

Purification: basic dimension concerning the practical application of all sacramentals; it is the precondition for sanctification and refers to sin and evil.

Rationalism: reality is reduced to reason alone.

Regula Fidei: rule of faith refers to the norm and measure extrinsic (external) to our faith; it is given from God and therefore Divine and infallible; faith is the supernatural assent to the divine truth.

Sacrament: efficacious sign of grace, instituted by Christ and entrusted to the Church, by which divine life is dispensed.

Sacred Signs: Associated with *the* sacred, for the most part, instituted by the Church and they cause invisible effects (grace).

Sacramental idea: principle based on creation but at the same time transcending the biological sphere reaching out to the supernatural reality of God.

Sacramental Reality: surpasses the visible and includes the supernatural existence.

Sanctification: is obtained in Jesus Christ, and linked to justification, it is the goal of Christian life.

Vetus form: it is the principle in the liturgy by which all other forms must be measured, to be part of the living tradition.

Vexation: extraordinary action of the devil in form of physical aggression against a person that can affect health, affections, and feelings.

Bibliography

Magisterial Documents
(Chronologically Ordered)

Council of Nicaea II 787, in Henry Denzinger (ed.), *Enchiridion Symbolorum, The Sources of Catholic Dogma*, trans. by Roy J. Deferrari, 13th ed. (London: Herder, 1957), 302.

Pius V, Papal Bull *Quo Primum*, 14.7.1570, in *Missale Romanum*, Ex Decreto SS. Concilii Tridentini restitutum Summorum Ponfificum cura recognitum, Editio iuxta typicam (Thalwil: C. H. Beck, 2012), (7)-(8).

The Roman Ritual: Christian Burial, Exorcisms, Reserved Blessings, Etc., vol. II, trans. and ed. by Philip T. Weller, 2nd ed. (Hawthorne, CA: Caritas Publishing 2017).

The Roman Ritual: The Blessings, vol. III, trans. and ed. by Philip T. Weller, 2nd ed. (Hawthorne, CA: Caritas Publishing, 2008).

Rituale Romanum, Pauli V Pontificis Maximi issu editum aliorumque Pontificum cura regognitum atque ad normam codicis iuris canonici accommodatum SSMI D.N. PII Papae XII auctoritate ordinatum et actum (Bonn: nova et vetera, 2010).

Canons and Decrees of the Council of Trent, trans. by H. J. Schroeder (Rockford: TAN Books and Publishers, 1978).

Pius IX, Bull *Ineffabilis Deus*, 8.12.1854, in DH, 2800–2804.

S. Congregatione Rituum, Benedictionis et impositionis S. Numismatis I. M. V., vulgo Medaglia miracolosa (S. R. C. 19. April. 1895), in ASS 28 (1895–96): 442–443.

Pius X, Motu Proprio Tra le sollecitudini, in ASS 36 (1903–1904): 329–339.

———. Motu Proprio *De musica sacra*, in ASS 36 (1903–1904): 387–395.

Pius X, Motu Proprio *De Musica Sacra*, in Congregationis Sacrorum Rituum (ed.), *Decreta authentica*, Collecta, vol. VI (Rome, Typis Polyglottis Vaticanis, 1912), 29–38.

Pius XII, Encyclical Letter *Mediator Dei*, November 20, 1947, in http://www.vatican.va/content/pius-xii/en/encyclicals/documents/hf_p-xii_enc_20111947_mediator-dei.html [3.5.2023].

———. Apostolic Letter *Carissimis Russiae Populis*, July 7, 1952, in https://w2.vatican.va/content/pius-xii/la/apost_letters/documents/hf_p-xii_apl_19520707_sacro-vergente-anno.html [10.5.2023].

Pius XII, Encyclical Letter *Haurietis Aquas*, May 15, 1956, in http://w2.vatican.va/content/pius-xii/en/encyclicals/documents/hf_p-xii_enc_15051956_haurietis-aquas.html [10.5.2023].

John XXIII, Apostolic Letter *Inde a Primis*, June 30, 1960, in https://www.vatican.va/content/john-xxiii/la/apost_letters/1960/documents/hf_j-xxiii_apl_19600630_indeaprimis.html [9.5.2023].

———. Encyclical Letter *Mater et Magistra*, May 15, 1961, in http://www.vatican.va/content/john-xxiii/en/encyclicals/documents/hf_j-xxiii_enc_15051961_mater.html [10.5.2023].

Constitution on the Sacred Liturgy, *Sacrosanctum Concilium*, December 4, 1963, in https://www.vatican.va/archive/hist_councils/ii_vatican_council/documents/vat-ii_const_19631204_sacrosanctum-concilium_en.html [12.6.2022].

Congregation for Divine Worship, Instruction *Liturgicae Instaurationes*, n. 9, in AAS 62 (1970): 701.

Sacred Congregation for Divine Worship, Decree, Prot. No. 600/70, May 31, 1970, in ibid. (ed.) *The Roman Pontifical*, Renewed by Decree of the most Holy Second Ecumenical Council of the Vatican, promulgated by authority of Pope Paul VI and revised at the direction of Pope John Paul II (Vatican City: Libreria Editrice Vaticana, 2012), 291.

Paul VI, Omelia Solemnità dei Santi Apostoli Pietro e Paolo, June 29, 1972, in http://w2.vatican.va/content/paul-vi/it/homilies/1972/documents/hf_p-vi_hom_19720629.html [10.5.2023].

———. General Audience, November 15, 1972, in https://www.ewtn.com/library/papaldoc/p6devil.htm [26.3.2019].

———. *Ordo Dedicationis Ecclesiae et Altaris* (Vatican City: Libreria Editrice Vaticana, 1977).

John Paul II, Discours dans la Chapelle de la Médaille Miraculeuse, May 31, 1980, in https://www.vatican.va/content/john-paul-ii/fr/speeches/1980/may/documents/hf_jp-ii_spe_19800531_medaglia-miracolosa.html [10.5.2023].

———. Preghiera di affidamento e di consacrazione alla Vergine, May 31, 1982, in http://w2.vatican.va/content/john-paul-ii/it/speeches/1982/may/documents/hf_jp-ii_spe_19820513_vergine-fatima.html [10.5.2023].

———. Apostolic Letter *Salvifici Doloris*, February 11, 1984, in http://www.vatican.va/content/john-paul-ii/en/apost_letters/1984/documents/hf_jp-ii_apl_11021984_salvifici-doloris.html [9.5.2023].

———. L'Atto di Affidamento, March 25, 1984, in https://www.vatican.va/content/john-paul-ii/it/letters/1983/documents/hf_jp-ii_let_19831208_vescovi-immacolata-concezione.html [10.5.2023].

CDF, *Inde ab aliquot annis*, English translation, Letter to Ordinaries regarding norms on Exorcism, September 29, 1985, in http://www.vatican.va/roman_curia/congregations/cfaith/documents/rc_con_cfaith_doc_19850924_exorcism_en.html [10.5.2023].

Congregation for Divine Worship and the Discipline of the Sacraments, Letter from April 13, 1985, Prot. N. 481/85, in Leges Ecclesiae VI, n. 5122, 9135.

John Paul II, Encyclical Letter *Dominum et vivificantem*, May 18, 1986, in http://www.vatican.va/content/john-paul-ii/en/encyclicals/documents/hf_jp-ii_enc_18051986_dominum-et-vivificantem.html [12.5.2023].

———. General Audience August 13, 1986, trans. by Lawrence J. Gesy, in https://www.ewtn.com/library/NEWAGE/JP2DEVIL.htm [26.3.2022].

———. Address to the participants of the Study Week of the Pontifical Academy of Sciences, September 26, 1986, in https://w2.vatican.va/content/john-paul-ii/en/speeches/1986/september/documents/hf_jp-ii_spe_19860922_simposio-maria-gesu.html [12.5.2023].

———. Discorso alla Popolazione di Monte Sant'Angelo, May 25, 1987, in http://w2.vatican.va/content/john-paul-ii/it/speeches/1987/may/documents/hf_jp-ii_spe_19870524_monte-sant-angelo.html [9.5.2023].

———. Apostolic Letter *Vicesimus Quintus Annus*, December 4, 1988, in http://www.vatican.va/content/john-paul-ii/en/apost_letters/1988/documents/hf_jp-ii_apl_19881204_vicesimus-quintus-annus.html [4.5.2023].

Decree, in National Conference of Catholic Bishops (ed.), *The Roman Ritual Revised by Decree of the Second Vatican Ecumenical Council and Published by Authority of Pope John Paul II* (New York: Catholic Book Publishing Corp., 1989).

International Commission on English in the Liturgy (eds.), *Ceremonial of Bishops*. Revised by Decree of the Second Vatican Ecumenical Council and Published by the Authority of Pope John Paul II (Collegeville: The Liturgical Press, 1989).

John Paul II, Apostolic Exhortation *Vita Consecrata*, March 25, 1996, in http://w2.vatican.va/content/john-paul-ii/en/apost_exhortations/documents/hf_jp-ii_exh_25031996_vita-consecrata.html [12.5.2023].

CDF et al., *Ecclesiae de Mysterio*, August 15, 1997, in http://www.vatican.va/roman_curia/pontifical_councils/laity/documents/rc_con_interdic_doc_15081997_en.html [3.5.2023].

John Paul II, Encyclical Letter *Fides et Ratio*, September 14, 1998, in http://www.vatican.va/content/john-paul-ii/en/encyclicals/documents/hf_jp-ii_enc_14091998_fides-et-ratio.html [12.5.2023].

Congregatio De Cultu Divino Et Disciplina Sacramentorum, *Notificatio de ritu Exorcismi*, Prot. 1280/98/L, in *Notitiae* 35.3–4 (1999): 156.

Apostolic Penitentiary, *Manuel of Indulgences. Norms and Grants*, trans. United States Conference of Catholic Bishops, 4th ed. (Washington, D.C.: USCCB, 1999).

CDF, Declaration *Dominus Jesus*, August 6, 2000, in https://www.vatican.va/roman_curia/congregations/cfaith/documents/rc_con_cfaith_doc_20000806_dominus-iesus_en.html [12.5.2023].

———. Instruction on Prayers for Healing, September 14, 2000, in https://www.vatican.va/roman_curia/congregations/cfaith/documents/rc_con_cfaith_doc_20001123_istruzione_en.html [6.5.2023].

———. The Message of Fatima, April 19, 2000, in https://www.vatican.va/roman_curia/congregations/cfaith/documents/rc_con_cfaith_doc_20000626_message-fatima_en.html [10.5.2023].

Code of Canon Law, English translation taken from: John P. Beal et al. (eds.), *New Commentary on the Code of Canon Law* (New York: Paulist Press, 2000).

Congregation for Divine Worship and the Discipline of the Sacraments, *Decretum*, in AAS 94 (2002): 684.

———. *Decree*, Unofficial English Translation, in http://notitiae.ipsissima-verba.org/show/135 [14.5.2023].

John Paul II, Apostolic Letter *Rosarium Virginis Mariae*, October 16, 2002, in https://w2.vatican.va/content/john-paul-ii/en/apost_letters/2002/documents/hf_jp-ii_apl_20021016_rosarium-virginis-mariae.html [10.5.2023].

———. Encyclical Letter *Ecclesia de Eucharistia*, April 17, 2003, in http://www.vatican.va/holy_father/special_features/encyclicals/documents/hf_jp-ii_enc_20030417_ecclesia_eucharistia_en.html [10.5.2023].

Rituale Romanum, *De exorcismis et supplicationibus quibusdam*, Editio typica (Vatican City: Librariae Editricis Vaticanae, 2004).

Congregation for Divine Worship and the Discipline of the Sacraments, *Instruction Redemptionis Sacramentum*, March 25, 2004, in https://www.vatican.va/roman_curia/congregations/ccdds/documents/

rc_con_ccdds_doc_20040423_redemptionis-sacramentum_en.html [3.5.2023].

Benedict XVI, Address to the Roman Curia offering them his Christmas greetings, December 22, 2005, in http://w2.vatican.va/content/benedict-xvi/en/speeches/2005/december/documents/hf_ben_xvi_spe_20051222_roman-curia.html [12.5.2023].

———. Post-Synodal Apostolic Exhortation *Sacramentum Caritatis*, February 22, 2007, in http://www.vatican.va/content/benedict-xvi/en/apost_exhortations/documents/hf_ben-xvi_exh_20070222_sacramentum-caritatis.html [10.5.2023].

———. Motu Proprio *Summorum Pontificum*, July 7, 2007, in http://www.vatican.va/content/benedict-xvi/en/motu_proprio/documents/hf_ben-xvi_motu-proprio_20070707_summorum-pontificum.html [5.5.2022].

———. Letter to the Bishops on the Occasion of the Publication of the Apostolic Letter "Motu Proprio Data" *Summorum Pontificum*, July 7, 2007, in http://www.vatican.va/content/benedict-xvi/en/letters/2007/documents/hf_ben-xvi_let_20070707_lettera-vescovi.html [11.5.2023].

Pontificale Romanum, Editio Typica 1961–1962, Edizione anastatica e Introduzione (eds.) Manlio Sodi and Alessandro Toniolo (Vatican City: Libreria Editrice Vaticana, 2008).

Benedict XVI, Letter to the Bishops of the Catholic Church concerning the remission of the excommunication of the four bishops consecrated by Archbishop Lefebvre, March 10, 2009, in http://www.vatican.va/content/benedict-xvi/en/letters/2009/documents/hf_ben-xvi_let_20090310_remissione-scomunica.html [12.5.2023].

———. Homily in Conclusion of the Year for Priests, June 11, 2010, in http://www.vatican.va/content/benedict-xvi/en/homilies/2010/documents/hf_ben-xvi_hom_20100611_concl-anno-sac.html [12.5.2023].

———. Apostolic Letter *Porta fidei*, October 11, 2011, in http://www.vatican.va/content/benedict-xvi/en/motu_proprio/documents/hf_ben-xvi_motu-proprio_20111011_porta-fidei.html [10.5.2023].

The Roman Missal, 3rd Chapel Edition (New Jersey: Catholic Book Publishing, 2011).

Congregation for Divine Worship and the Discipline of the Sacraments, *The Roman Pontifical*, Renewed by Decree of the Most Holy Second Ecumenical Council of the Vatican, promulgated by authority of Pope Paul VI and revised at the direction of Pope John Paul II (Vatican City: Libreria Editrice Vaticana, 2012).

———. *The Rites of Ordination in the Roman Ritual and Pontifical*, renewed by Decree of the Most Holy Second Ecumenical Council of the Vatican (Vatican City: Libreria Editrice Vaticana, 2012).

Missale Romanum, Ex Decreto SS. Concilii Tridentini restitutum Summorum Ponfificum cura recognitum, Editio iuxta typicam (Thalwil: C. H. Beck, 2012).

Francis, Homily in *Missa pro Ecclesia*, March 14, 2013, in http://www.vatican.va/content/francesco/en/homilies/2013/documents/papa-francesco_20130314_omelia-cardinali.html [12.5.2023].

———. Encyclical Letter *Lumen Fidei*, June 29, 2013, in http://www.vatican.va/content/francesco/en/encyclicals/documents/papa-francesco_20130629_enciclica-lumen-fidei.html [10.5.2022].

———. Blessing of the New Statue of St. Michael the Archangel, July 5, 2013, in https://www.vatican.va/content/francesco/en/speeches/2013/july/documents/papa-francesco_20130705_statua-san-michele.html [9.5.2023].

CDF, Pontificia Commissio "Ecclesia Dei," Prot. N. 153/2009, June 26, 2015.

Francis, Post-Synodal Apostolic Exhortation *Amoris Laetitia*, March 19, 2016, in http://www.vatican.va/content/dam/francesco/pdf/apost_exhortations/documents/papa-francesco_esortazione-ap_20160319_amoris-laetitia_en.pdf [12.5.2023].

CDF, Letter *Placuit Deo*, March 1, 2018, in https://press.vatican.va/content/salastampa/en/bollettino/pubblico/2018/03/01/180301a.html [12.5.2023].

Congregation for Institutes of Consecrated Life and Societies of Apostolic Life, Instruction *Ecclesiae Sponsae Imago*, June 8, 2018, Vatican City, in http://www.vatican.va/roman_curia/congregations/ccscrlife/documents/rc_con_ccscrlife_doc_20180608_istruzione-ecclesiaesponsaeimago_en.html [8.5.2023].

The Roman Ritual, The Order of Baptism of Children, English trans. according to the Second Typical Edition, For the Use in the Dioceses of the United States of America (Collegeville: Liturgical Press, 2020).

Francis, Apostolic Letter Motu Proprio *Traditiones Custodes*, July 16, 2021, in https://www.vatican.va/content/francesco/en/motu_proprio/documents/20210716-motu-proprio-traditionis-custodes.html [10.5.2023].

Francis, Act of Consecration to the Immaculate Heart of Mary, March 25, 2022, in https://www.vatican.va/content/francesco/en/prayers/documents/20220325-atto-consacrazione-cuoredimaria.html [10.5.2023].

Literature (Alphabetically Ordered)

Amorth, Gabriele, *An Exorcist Tells His Story*, trans. by Nicoletta V. MacKenzie (San Francisco: Ignatius Press, 1999).

———. with Paolo Rodari, *L'ultimo Esorcista. La mia battaglia contro Satana* (Milan: Piemme, 2011).

Andreopoulos, Andreas, *The Sign of the Cross: The Gesture, the Mystery, the History* (Brewster, Massachusetts: Paraclete Press, 2010).

Anselm, *Proslogion, Proemium,* in F. S. Schmitt (ed.), *S. Anselmi Cantuariensis Archiepiscopi Opera omnia* (Dehli: Isha Books, 2013).

Aquinas, Thomas, De Pot.

———. *Summa Theologiae*, English Translation in https://www.newadvent.org/summa/1.htm [12.5.2023].

———. *Summa Contra Gentiles*, Book IV, trans. by Charles J. O'Neil, St. Isidore e-book library, in https://isidore.co/aquinas/ContraGentiles4.htm [12.5.2023].

Association of International Exorcists (eds.), *Proceedings of the National Congress of Italian Exorcists, 9th–13th September 2013*, trans. by IAE English Secretariat (Rome, Association of International Exorcists, 2013).

———. (eds.), *Linee guida per il ministero dell'esorcismo. Alla luce del rituale vigente* (Padua: Edizioni Messaggero Padova, 2020).

Augustinus, *Tractatus in Joannis Evangelium*, 84, 1–2, PL 35.

Auer, Johann, "*Militia Christi*. Zur Geschichte eines christlichen Gottesbildes," in *Geist und Leben*, 32 (1959): 340–351.

Ball, Ann, *The How-To Book of Sacramentals* (Huntington: Our Sunday Visitor Publishing Division, 2005).

Bamonte, Francesco, *Diabolical Possession and Exorcism. How to Recognize the Shrewd Deceiver*, trans. by Benedict Ejeh (Somolu Lagos: Bertie-John Nig. Printers, 2008).

———. *Gli Angeli Ribelli. Il mistero del male nell'esperienza di un esorcista* (Milan: Paoline Editoriale, 2008).

———. "The Evangelical Fundaments of the Signs of Diabolical Possession Mentioned in the Ritual of Exorcism," in Association of International Exorcists (eds.) *Proceedings of the National Congress of Italian Exorcists, 9th–13th September 2013*, trans. by IAE English Secretariat (Rome, Association of International Exorcists, 2013), 59–93.

Barry, William J., *The Sacramentals of the Holy Catholic Church, or Flowers from the Garden of the Liturgy* (London: FB &c Ltd., 2017).

Biliniewicz, Mariusz, *The Liturgical Vision of Pope Benedict XVI. A Theological Inquiry* (Bern: Peter Lang, 2013).

Blai, Adam C., *Hauntings, Possessions, and Exorcisms* (Steubenville, Ohio: Emmaus Road Publishing, 2017).

Bonet Alcón, José, *Los Sacramentos menores. Estudio histórico sobre la naturaleza de los sacramentales* (Buenos Aires: ACS Publications, 1993).

Bonino, Serge-Thomas, *Angels and Demons. A Catholic Introduction*, trans. by Michael J. Miller, vol. 6 (Washingthon, D.C.: The Catholic University of America Press, 2016).

Bradshaw, Paul F., *Ordination Rites of the Ancient Churches of East and West* (New York: Liturgical Press, 1990).

Brett, Laurence F. X., *Redeemed Creation. Sacramentals Today* (Delaware: Pilgrim Reader Books, 1984).

Bugnini, Annibale, *The Reform of the Liturgy 1948–1975*, trans. by Matthew J. O'Connell (Collegeville: Liturgical Press, 1983).

Buonaiuto, Aldo, *Le mani occulte viaggio nel mondo del satanismo* (Rome: Città Nuova, 2005).

Burke, Raymond Leo (ed.), *An Introduction to the Vocation of Consecrated Virginity Lived in the World*, vol. 1 (Lansing, Michigan: United States Association of Consecrated Virgins, 2012).

Bulgakov, Sergius, *Relics and Miracles. Two Theological Essays*, trans. by Boris Jakim (Grand Rapids, Michigan: William B. Erdmans Publishing Company, 2011).

Bux, Nicola, *Benedict XVI's Reform. The Liturgy between Innovation and Tradition*, trans. by Joseph Trabbic (San Francisco: Ignatius Press, 2012).

Cardó, Daniel, *The Cross and the Eucharist in Early Christianity. A Theological and Liturgical Investigation* (Cambridge: Cambridge University Press, 2019).

Daniélou, Jean, *The Angels & Their Mission*, trans. by David Heimann (Manchester, New Hampshire: Sophia Institute Press, 2009).

De Montfort, Louis, *True Devotion to Mary with Preparation for Total Consecration*, trans. by Frederick W. Faber (Gastonia: Tan Books, 2010).

Denzinger, Henry (ed.), *Enchiridion Symbolorum*, The Sources of Catholic Dogma, trans. by Roy J. Deferrari, 13th ed. (London: Herder, 1957).

Dermine, François-Marie, *Carismatici, sensitivi e medium. I confini della mentalità magica* (Bologna: Edizioni Studio Domenicano, 2010).

Depré, Louis, *Symbols of the Sacred* (Grand Rapids: William B. Eerdmans Publishing Company, 2000).

De Sales, Francis, *Philothea or An Introduction to the Devout Life* (Charlotte, North Carolina: TAN Books, 2010).

Dodaro, Robert, "The Argument in Brief," in ibid. (ed.), *Remaining in the Truth of Christ. Marriage and Communion in the Catholic Church* (San Francisco: Ignatius Press 2014), 11–35.

Donghi, Antonio, "Sacramentali," in Domenico Sartore and Achille M. Trajacca (eds), *Nuovo dizionario di liturgia* (Rome: Edizioni Paoline, 1988), 1253.

Dougherty, Jude Patrick, "Naturalism," in *New Catholic Encyclopedia*, vol. X (Washington, D.C.: The Catholic University of America, 1967), 271–274.

Dulles, Avery, "The Theology of Worship: Saint Thomas," in Matthew Levering and Michael Dauphinais (eds.), *Rediscovering Aquinas and the Sacraments: Studies in Sacramental Theology* (Chicago: Hillenbrand Books, 2009), 1–13.

Eijk, Willem Jacobus con Galli, Andrea, *Dio vive in Olanda. "Ma il Figlio dell'uomo, quando verrà, troverà la fede sulla terra?" Lc 18,8* (Milan: Ediziones Ares, 2020).

Faul, Denis, Art. "Donatism," in New Catholic Encyclopedia, vol. IV (Washington, D.C.: The Catholic University of America, 1967), 1001–1003.

Flores, Juan Javier, "La partecipazione liturgica punto di partenza del movimento liturgico," in Agostino Montan – Manlio Sodi (eds.), *Actuosa Participatio. Conoscere, comprendere e vivere la Liturgia* (Vatican City: Libreria Editrice Vaticana, 2002), 229–245.

Forstner, Dorothea, *Die Welt der Symbole* (Innsbruck: Tyrolia Verlag, 1961).

Frank, Adolph, *Die Kirchlichen Benediktionen im Mittelalter*, vol. 1+2 (Bonn: nova et vetera, 2006).

Fiedrowicz, Michael, "Saint Michael, Defender of the Church Militant," Gregorius Magnus vol. 10 (2020): 20–24.

———. *Theologie der Kirchenväter. Grundlagen frühchristlicher Glaubensreflexion*, 2nd ed. (Freiburg im Breisgau: Herder, 2010).

Gamber, Klaus, *The Reform of the Roman Liturgy: Its Problems and Background*, trans. by Klaus D. Grimm (Harrison, N.Y.: Una Voce Press, 1993).

Garrigou-Lagrange, Reginald, *The Theological Virtues. Volume One: On Faith*, trans. by Thomas a Kempis Reilly, vol. 1 (Binghamton: Herder, 1965).

Ghezzi, Bert, *Recovering the Power of the Ancient Prayer. The Sign of the Cross* (Chicago: Loyola Press, 2006).

Gil Hellín, Francisco, *Constitutio de sacra liturgia, Sacrosanctum Concilium. Concilii Vaticani II synopsis in ordinem redigens schemata cum relationibus necnon patrum orationes atque animadversiones*, vol. 5 (Vatican City: Libreria Editrice Vaticana, 2003).

Gnocchi, Alessandro and Palmaro, Mario, *L'ultima Messa di Padre Pio. L'anima segreta del santo delle stigmate* (Milan: Piemme, 2010).

Graf, Friedrich Wilhelm, "Liberale Theologie," in LThK, vol. 6, 3rd ed. (Freiburg im Breisgau: Herder, 1995), 884–885.

Gregory the Great, *Dialogue*, trans. by Odo John Zimmerman (Washington D.C.: The Catholic University of America Press, 2002).

Grou, Jean-Nicolas, *Handbüchlein für innerliche Seelen*, trans. by Wilhelm Schamoni (Arensberg: Verlagsdruckerei Josef Kral, 1983).

Guardini, Romano, *Sacred Signs*, trans. by Grace Branham (St. Louis: Pio Decimo Press, 1956).

———. *The Spirit of the Liturgy*, trans. by Joanne M. Pierce (New York: The Crossroad Publishing Company, 1998).

Guéranger, Prosper, *The Medal or Cross of St. Benedict. Its Origin, Meaning and Privileges*, trans. by Laurence Shepherd (London: Burns and Oates, 1880).

Gunter, Paul, "Active Participation in the Renewal and Promotion of the Liturgy of Vatican Council II," in ibid. (ed.) *Sacrosanctum Concilium. Sacred Liturgy and the Second Vatican Council* (London: Carrigboy, 2015), 126–141.

Gy, Pierre-Marie, "Labores coetuum a studiis: De benedictionibus," in *Notitiae* 7 (1971): 123–132.

Hauke, Manfred, "The Theological Battle over the Rite of Exorcism, 'Cinderella' of the New *Rituale Romanum*," in Antiphon 10.1 (2006): 32–69.

Hitchcock, Helen Hull, "Pope Benedict XVI and the 'reform of the reform,'" in Neil J. Roy and Janet E. Rutherford (eds.), *Benedict XVI and the Sacred Liturgy* (Dublin: Four Courts Press, 2011), 70–87.

Hitchcock, James, "Continuity and disruption in the liturgy: a cultural approach," in Neil J. Roy and Janet E. Rutherford (eds), *Benedict XVI and the Sacred Liturgy* (Dublin: Four Courts Press, 2011), 88–97.

Hitchcock, James, *Recovery of the Sacred* (San Francesco: Ignatius Press, 1995).

Huels, John M., "A Juridical Notion of Sacramentals," in *Studia canonica*, 38 (2004): 345–368.

———. "Part II Other Acts of Divine Worship [cann. 1166–1204]," in John P. Beal et al. (eds.), *New Commentary on the Code of Canon Law* (New York: Paulist Press, 2000), 1400–1423.

———. "The Most Holy Eucharist," in John P. Beal, et al. (eds.), *New Commentary on the Code of Canon Law* (New York: Paulist Press, 2000), 1095–1137.

International Association of Exorcists (ed.), *Guidelines for the Ministry of Exorcism. In the Light of the Current Ritual* (Dover: Two Hearts Media Organization, 2022).

Istituto Sacerdos (ed.), *Esorcismo e preghiera di liberazione. Atti del corso*, 2nd ed. (Monterotondo: Edizioni Art, 2012).

Ivers, Therese, *A Practical Guide to Consecration Planning for Virgins Being Consecrated to a Life of Virginity in the World under the Provisions of Canon 604* (CreateSpace Independent Publishing Platform, 2013).

Johnson, Cuthbert, *Prosper Gueranger (1805–1875) A Liturgical Theologian. An Introduction to his liturgical writings and works*, Analecta Liturgica 9 (Rome: Edizioni Abbazia S. Paolo, 1984).

Jone, Heribert, *Gesetzbuch der lateinischen Kirche. Erklärung der Kanones*, vol. II, 2nd ed. (Paderborn: Ferdinand Schöningh, 1952).

Journet, Charles, *The Mass. The Presence of the Sacrifice of the Cross*, trans. by Victor Szczurek (South Bend, St. Augustine Press, 2008).

Jungmann, Josef, "Constitution on the Sacred Liturgy," in Herbert Vorgrimler (ed.), *Commentary on the Documents of Vatican II*, vol. 1, 2nd ed. (New York: Herder, 1967), 1–87.

Kaczynski, Reiner, "Blessings in Rome and the Non-Roman West," in Anscar J. Chupungco (ed.), *Handbook for Liturgical Studies*, vol. 4, *Sacraments and Sacramentals* (Collegeville: Liturgical Press, 1997), 393–410.

Kaczynski, Reiner, "5 Die Benediktionen," in Hans Bernhard Meyer et al. (ed.), *Sakramentliche Feiern II*, vol. 8 (Regensburg: Friedrich Pustet Verlag, 1984), 233–274.

Kähler, Martin, *Der sogenannte historische Jesus und der geschichtliche, biblische Christus: Mit einem Nachwort von Sebastian Moll* (Berlin: Berlin University Press, 2013).

Kluger, Florian, *Benediktionen. Studien zu kirchlichen Segensfeiern* (Regensburg: Verlag Friedrich Pustet, 2011).

Lampe, Geoffrey W. H., *The Seal of the Spirit: A Study in the Doctrine of Baptism and Confirmation in the New Testament and the Fathers*, 2nd ed. (London: SPCK, 1967).

Lang, Uwe Michael, "Sacred Architecture at the Service of the Mission of the Church," in Alcuin Reid (ed.), *Sacred Liturgy. The Source and Summit of the Life and Mission of the Church* (San Francisco: Ignatius Press, 2014), 198–211.

———. *Signs of the Holy One. Liturgy, Ritual, and the Expression of the Sacred* (San Francisco: Ignatius Press, 2015).

———. "Theologies of Blessing: Origins and Characteristics of *De benedictionibus* (1984)," in Antiphon 15.1 (2011): 27–46.

———. *The Voice of the Church at Prayer. Reflections on Liturgy and Language* (San Francisco: Ignatius Press, 2012).

———. *Turning Towards the Lord. Orientation in Liturgical Prayer* (San Francisco: Ignatius Press, 2009).

Leclerq, Henri, "Sacramentals," in Charles G. Herbermann et al. (eds.), *The Catholic Encyclopedia*, vol. 13 (New York: Robert Appleteon, 1912), 293.

Lefebvre, Gaspare, "XXI. I Sacramentali," in R. Aigrain (ed.), *Enciclopedia Liturgica*, trans. by M. Mignone and A. Stella, 2nd ed. (Alba: Edizioni Paoline, 1957), 724–766.

Leo the Great, *Sermo 8 de passione Domini*, 6–8; PL 54.

Lessi-Ariosto, Mario, Linee interpretative dell'iter redazionale del *De benedictionibus*, in Rivista liturgica 73 (1986): 214–230.

Lozano, Neal, *Resisting the Devil. A Catholic Perspective on Deliverance* (Huntington, Indiana: Our Sunday Visitor Publishing Division, 2010).

Henry E. Manning, *The Eternal Priesthood*, a reprint of the 8th ed. (New York: Catholic Publications Society Co., 2014).

Marchetto, Agostino, *Il Concilio Ecumenico Vaticano II. Contrappunto per una storia* (Vatican City: Libreria Editrice Vaticana, 2005).

Marmion, Columba, *Christ – The Ideal of the Priest. Spiritual Conferences*, trans. by Matthew Dillon (St. Louis: Herder, 1952).

McManus, Frederick R. (ed.), *Parish Ritual* (New York: Benzinger Brothers, 1962).

Mongelli, Giovanni, *Gli Angeli Buoni. Ministri di Dio per la salvezza degli uomini*, vol. 1 (Caposele: Edizioni Michael, 2009).

———. *Gli Angeli cattivi. Nostri avversari nell'opera della salvezza*, vol. 2 (Caposele: Edizioni Michael, 2009).

Mosca, Vincenzo, "I luoghi e i tempi sacri (cann. 1205–1253)," in Gruppo Italiano Docenti di Diritto Canonico (eds), *La funzione di santificare della Chiesa* (Milan: Edizioni Glossa, 1995), 193–219.

Mosebach, Martin, *The Heresy of Formlessness. The Roman Liturgy and Its Enemy*, trans. by Graham Harrison (San Francisco: Ignatius Press, 2006).

Müller, Michael, *God the Teacher of Mankind, or Popular Catholic Theology, Apologetical, Dogmatical, Moral, Liturgical, Pastoral, and Ascetical: Sacramentals, Prayer, Vices and Virtues, Christian Perfection, etc.* (St. Louis: Fr. Pustet & Co., 1888).

Nebel, Johannes, "Die *participatio plena et actuosa* im Lichte der *sacra potestas*. Klärungsversuche zur Sinnerhellung christlicher Liturgie," in Forum katholische Theologie 32 (2016): 1–22.

Öfele, Maria Luisa (ed.), *Jungfrauenweihe: Altes und neues Charisma* (Heiligenkreuz: Medien-GmbH Heiligenkreuz, 2017).

Oswald, Johannes Heinrich, *Angelogie. Das ist die Lehre von den guten und den bösen Engeln im Sinne der Katholischen Kirche*, 2nd ed. (Kulmbach: Verlagsbuchhandlung Sabat, 2019).

Palacios Blanco, Fernando, *El Romano Pontífice y la liturgia. Estudio histórico-jurídico del ejercito y desarollo de la potestad del Papa en materia litúrgica* (Toledo: Instituto Teológico San Ildefonso, 2018).

Palilla, Benigno, *Il diavolo esiste io lo'ho incontrato* (Milan: Paoline Editoriale Libri, 2008).

———. "Solemn Exorcism in the Context of Spiritual Warfare," in Association of International Exorcists (eds.) *Proceedings of the National Congress of Italian Exorcists,* 9th – 13th September 2013, trans. by IAE English Secretariat (Rome, Association of International Exorcists, 2013), 137–164.

Pennesi, Alessandro, "Some Criteria for the Discernment of Some of the Reasons Why People Wish to Meet an Exorcist," in Association of International Exorcists (eds.) *Proceedings of the National Congress of Italian Exorcists, 9th–13th September 2013*, trans. by IAE English Secretariat (Rome, Association of International Exorcists, 2013), 51–58.

Peters, Edward N. (ed.), *The 1917 or Pio-Benedictine Code of Canon Law* (San Francisco: Ignatius Press, 2001).

Pieper, Josef, *In Search of the Sacred. Contributions to an Answer*, trans. by Lothar Krauth (San Francisco: Ignatius Press, 1991).

———. *Über den Begriff der Sünde* (Kevelaer: Topos, 2019).

Proja, Giovanni Battista, *Immagini, reliquie e benedizioni* (Rome: Città Nuova Editrice, 2005).

Quellet, Mark, *Amici dello sposo. Per una visione rinnovata del celibato sacerdotale* (Siena: Cantagalli, 2019).

Ratzinger, Joseph, Collected Works, *Theology of the Liturgy*, trans. by John Saward et al., vol. 11 (San Francisco: Ignatius Press, 2014).

———. "Die neuen Heiden und die Kirche," in ibid., *Kirche - Zeichen unter den Völkern. Schriften zur Ekklesiologie und Ökumene*, in JRGS, vol. 8/2 (Freiburg im Breisgau, et al.: Herder, 2010), 1143–1158.

———. *Introduction to Christianity. With a New Preface*, trans. by J. R. Foster (San Francisco: Ignatius Press, 2004).

———. *Jesus of Nazareth. Part Two: Holy Week. From the Entrance into Jerusalem to the Resurrection*, trans. Vatican Secretariat of State (San Francisco: Ignatius Press, 2011).

———. *On the Way to Jesus Christ*, trans. by Michael J. Miller (San Francisco: Ignatius Press, 2005).

———. *Pilgrim Fellowship of Faith. The Church as Communion*, trans. by Henry Taylor (San Francisco: Ignatius Press, 2005).

———. Preface, in Alcuin Reid, *The Organic Development of the Liturgy*, 2nd ed. (San Francisco: Ignatius Press, 2005), 9–13.

———. *The Nature and Mission of Theology, Essays to Orient Theology in Today's Debates*, trans. by Adrian Walker (San Francisco: Ignatius Press, 1995).

———. *The Transforming Power of Faith. General Audiences* (San Francisco: Ignatius Press, 2013).

Ratzinger, Joseph with Messori, Vittorio, *The Ratzinger Report. An Exclusive Interview of the State of the Church*, trans. by Salvator Attanasio and Graham Harrison (San Francisco: Ignatius Press, 1985).

Reifenberg, Hermann, "Art. Blut Christi III. Liturgisch u. frömmigkeitsgeschichtlich," in LThK, vol. 2, 3rd ed. (Freiburg im Breisgau: Herder, 1994) 537.

Righetti, Mario, *Manuale di storia liturgica. I Sacramenti – I Sacramentali*, vol. IV, 2nd ed. (Milan: Ancora, 1998).

Roccasalvo, Joan L., *The Eastern Catholic Churches: An Introduction to their Worship and Spirituality* (Collegeville: Liturgical Press, 1992).

Rossetti, Stephen J., *The Priestly Blessing. Rediscovering the Gift* (Indiana: Ave Maria Press, 2018).

Scerri, Hector, *Koinonia, Diakonia and Martyria. Interrelated Themes in Patristic Sacramental Theology as expounded by Adalbert-G. Hamman* (Malta: University of Malta, 1999).

Scheeben, Matthias, *Handbook of Catholic Dogmatics. Book One Theological Epistemology*, trans. by Michael J. Miller (Steubenville, Ohio: Emmaus Academic, 2019).

Schmaus, Michael, *Dogma. The Church as Sacrament*, vol. 5 (Maryland: Roman & Littlefield Publishers, 1975).

Schmid, Franz, *Die Sacramentalien der Katholischen Kirche: in ihrer Eigenart beleuchtet* (Brixen: Verlag der Buchhandlung der Kath.-polit. Pressvereins, 1896).

Striet, Markus, *Ernstfall Freiheit: Arbeiten an der Schleifung der Bastionen* (Freiburg im Breisgau: Herder, 2018).

Suárez, Federico, *About Being a Priest* (Dublin: Scepter Publishers, 1997).

Sullivan, John F., *The Externals of The Catholic Church, Her Government, Ceremonies Festivals Sacramentals, and Devotions*, 5th ed. (New York: Kenedy & Sons, 1942).

Vagaggini, Cyprian, *Theological Dimensions of the Liturgy. A General Treatise on the Theology of the Liturgy*, trans. by Leonard J. Doyle and W. A. Jurgens (Collegeville: Liturgical Press, 1976).

Van Slyke, Daniel G., "The Order for Blessing Water: Past and Present," in Antiphon 8:2 (2003): 12–23.

Verheul, Ambrosius, *Introduction to the Liturgy. Towards a Theology of Worship* (Hertfordshire: Anthony Clarke Books, 1972).

Vošicky, Bernhard, *Sakraltheologie III. Die Sakramentalien der Kirche* (Punitz: Hochschule Heiligenkreuz, 1999).

———. *Schau auf den Herrn! Begegnungen mit Gott und seinen Heiligen* (Heiligenkreuz: Be&Be Verlag, 2010).

Weimann, Ralph, *Bioethical Challenges at the End of Life. An Ethical Guide in Catholic Perspective* (Brooklyn, NY: Angelico Press, 2022).

———. "Die Sakramentalien – Stiefkind der Theologie," in Markus Graulich and Karl-Heinz Menke (eds.), *Fides incarnata* (Freiburg im Breisgau: Herder, 2021), 391–406.

———. "Die Krise der Kirche als Krise des Klerus," in NOrd 73 (2019): 244–256.

———. *Dogma und Fortschritt bei Joseph Ratzinger. Prinzipien der Kontinuität* (Paderborn: Ferdinand Schöningh, 2012).

———. "Hermeneutik der Reform als Erneuerung in Kontinuität," in Mitteilungen Institut Papst Benedikt XVI (4/2011): 59–82.

———. "Verschiedenheit der Formen und die Einheit in der Liturgie. *Lex celebrandi* als Spiegelbild der *lex credendi*," in M. Graulich (ed.) *Zehn Jahre Summorum Pontificum. Versöhnung mit der Vergangenheit – Weg in die Zukunft* (Regensburg: Friedrich Pustet, 2017), 86–116.

———. "The Crisis of Faith and the Crisis of the Church, in Nova et Vetera," vol. 19, No. 2 (2021): 199–216.

Ziegenaus, Anton, *Die Heilsgegenwart in der Kirche. Sakramentenlehre*, vol. VII (Aachen: MM Verlag, 2003).

Online Sources (alphabetically ordered)

Augustine, Tractate 84 (John 15:13), English Translations, in http://www.newadvent.org/fathers/1701084.htm [22.3.2023].

Amorth, Gabriele, An Exorcist Explains Demonic Possession and Vexation, October 12, 2018, in https://catholicexchange.com/an-exorcist-explains-demonic-possession-and-vexation [8.2.2023].

———. Interview with Father Amorth, Exorcist, on the Reform of the Rite of Exorcism after Vatican II, in https://www.fisheaters.com/praeternaturalworldamorth.html [4.5.2023].

Armstrong, Patti, An Exorcist Comments on Walmart's Satanic Products, March 25, 2019, in http://www.ncregister.com/blog/armstrong/an-exorcist-comments-on-walmarts-satanic-products [8.5.2023].

Barrett, Michael T. (ed.), Art. "Holy Water," Catholic Encyclopedia, in http://www.newadvent.org/cathen/07432a.htm [12.5.2023].

Blessing and Investiture With the Medal of the Immaculate Conception, in http://www.rosarychurch.net/rituale/miraculous_medal.html [12.5.2023].

Blessing of an Expectant Mother at the approach of confinement, in https://latinmassbaptism.com/blessing-of-expectant-mothers/ [12.5.2023].

Cassian Folsom, Sacred Signs and Active Participation at Mass, Adoremus Conference held in Los Angeles on November 22, 1997, in http://www.ewtn.com/library/liturgy/SIGNS.HTM [29.6.2021].

Comunicato della Sala Stampa della Santa Sede, September 29, 2018, in https://press.vatican.va/content/salastampa/it/bollettino/pubblico/2018/09/29/0707/01504.html [12.5.2023].

Gregory the Great, Book Two of the Dialogues: The Life of Saint Benedict, in https://www.osb.org/gen/greg/dia-05.html [25.2.2023].

International Theological Commission, The Reciprocity Between Faith and Sacraments in the Sacramental Economy, March 3, 2020, in http://www.vatican.va/roman_curia/congregations/cfaith/cti_documents/rc_cti_20200303_reciprocita-fede-sacramenti_en.html [10.5.2023].

Leo the Great, *Sermo 8 de passione Domini*, 6–8; PL 54, 340–342, trans. by: https://www.crossroadsinitiative.com/media/articles/power-of-the-cross-st-leo-the-great/ [9.5.2023].

Lovasik, Lawrence, St. Michael, Strength of God, in http://www.catholictradition.org/saint-michael4.htm [9.5.2023].

Office for the Liturgical Celebrations of the Supreme Pontiff, Liturgical Vestments and the Vesting Prayers, in http://www.vatican.va/news_services/liturgy/details/ns_lit_doc_20100216_vestizione_en.html [6.5.2023].

Rauch, Raphael, Ausländerstimmrecht, Krankensalbung durch Frauen, Dreikönig: Was diese Woche wichtig wird, January 4, 2021, in https://www.kath.ch/newsd/auslaenderstimmrecht-krankensalbung-durch-frauen-dreikoenig-was-diese-woche-wichtig-wird/ [12.5.2023].

Sherwood, Harriet, Robot priest unveiled in Germany to mark 500 years since Reformation, May 30, 2017, in https://www.theguardian.com/technology/2017/may/30/robot-priest-blessu-2-germany-reformation-exhibition [12.5.2023].

Smith, Gregory A., Just one-third of U.S. Catholics agree with their church that Eucharist is body, blood of Christ, August 5, 2019, in https://www.pewresearch.org/fact-tank/2019/08/05/transubstantiation-eucharist-u-s-catholics/ [10.5.2023].

The Franciscan Archive, in https://franciscan-archive.org/misc/michael.html [10.5.2023].

The Order of Saint Benedict, The Medal of Saint Benedict, in https://www.osb.org//gen/medal.html [22.3.2023].

USCCB, Art. "Exorcism," in https://www.usccb.org/prayer-and-worship/sacraments-and-sacramentals/sacramentals-blessings/exorcism [10.5.2023].

Appendix 1

EXORCISMUS IN SATANAM ET ANGELOS APOSTATICOS[640]	EXORCISM AGAINST SATAN AND HIS APOSTATE ANGELS
In nómine Patris, et Fílii, et Spiritus Sancti. Amen.	In the Name of the Father, and of the Son, and of the Holy Spirit. Amen.
Ad S. Michaelem Archangelum Precatio	Prayer to St. Michael the Archangel
Princeps gloriosíssime, cæléstis milítiæ, sancte Michael Archángele, défénde nos in prælio adversus príncipes et potestátes, advérsus mundi rectóres tenebrárum harum, contra spirituália nequítiæ, in celéstibus. Veni in auxilium hóminum; quos Deus ad imáginem similitúdinis suæ fecit, et a tyránnide diáboli emit prétio magno. Te custódem et patrónum sancta veneratur Ecclésia; tibi trádidit Dóminus ánimas redemptórum in supérna felicitáte locándas. Deprecáre Deum pacis, ut cónterat sátanam sub pédibus nostris, ne ultra váleat captivos tenére hómines, et Ecclésia nocére. Offer nostras preces in conspéctu Altíssimi, ut cito antícipent nos misericórdiæ Dómini, et apprehéndas dracónem, serpéntem antíquum qui est diábolus et sátanas, et ligátum mittas in abyssum, ut non sedúcat ámplius gentes.	O most glorious Prince of the heavenly militia, St. Michael the Archangel, defend us in the battle against the principalities and powers, against the rulers of the world of this darkness, against the spirits of wickedness, in the heavens. Come to the assistance of men; whom God has made to the image of His likeness, and has purchased from the tyranny of the Devil at a great price. Holy Church venerates thee as Her guardian and patron; to thee has the Lord handed over the souls of the redeemed to be placed in supernal felicity. Beseech the God of peace, to crush Satan beneath our feet, so that he may no longer prevail to hold men bound, and do injury to the Church. Offer our prayers in the sight of the Most High, so that the mercies of the Lord may swiftly go before us, and apprehend the dragon, the ancient serpent, who is the Devil and Satan, and cast him bound into the abyss, so that he may no more seduce the nations.

---

[640] RR, 602–605. English translation The Franciscan Archive, in https://franciscan-archive.org/misc/michael.html [10.5.2023].

Exorcismus
In nómine Iesu Christi Dei et Dómini nostri, intercedénte immaculáta Vírgine Dei Genetrice María, beáto Michaéle Archángelo, beátis Apóstolis Petro et Paulo et ómnibus Sanctis,

si es in ordine exorcistae, dicas; alioquin omittas:
et sacra ministérii nostri auctoritáte confisi,

deinde omnes simul, dicendo:
ad infestatiónes diabólicæ fraudis repelléndas secúri aggrédimur.

Psalmus 67
Exsúrgat Deus, et dissipéntur inimici eius, et fúgiant qui odérunt eum, a fácie eius.
Sicut déficit fumus, deficiant: sicut fluit cera a fácie ignis, sic péreant peccatóres a fácie Dei.

V. Ecce Crucem Dómini: fúgite, partes advérsæ.
R. Vicit Leo de tribu Iuda, radix David.
V. Fiat misericórdia tua, Dómine, super nos.
R. Quemádmodum sperávimus in te.

Exorcizámus te, omnis immúnde spíritus, omnis satánica potéstas, omnis incúrsio infernális adversárii, omnis légio, omnis congregátio et secta diabólica, in nómine et virtúte Dómini nostri Iesu ✠ Christi, eradicáre et effugáre a Dei Ecclésia, ab animábus ad imáginem Dei cónditis ac pretióso divíni Agni sánguini redémptis ✠.

Exorcism
In the Name of Jesus Christ, Our God and Lord, with the intercession of the Immaculate Virgin Mary, Theotokos, of blessed Michael the Archangel, of the blessed Apostles Peter and Paul, and of All the Saints,

if one is an exorcist, let him say the following, here:
and having confided in the sacred authority of our ministry,

all continue, together, by saying:
we step forward safely to repel the infestations of diabolic deceit.

Psalm 67
Let God arise, and let His enemies be scattered, and let those who hate Him flee before His Face. As smoke is driven away, let them be driven away: as wax melts before the face of fire, so may sinners perish before the Face of God.

V. Behold the Cross of the Lord: flee, bands of enemies.
R. He has conquered, the Lion of the tribe of Judah, the Root of David.
V. May Thy mercy, Lord, be upon us.
R. As much as we have hoped in Thee.

We exorcize thee, every unclean spirit, every satanic power, every assault of the infernal adversary, every legion, every diabolic congregation and sect, in the Name and by the Virtue of our Lord Jesus ✠ Christ, be uprooted and flee from the Church of God, from the souls established according to the image of God and redeemed by the Precious Blood of the Divine Lamb ✠.

Non ultra áudeas, serpens callidíssime, decípere humánum genus, Dei Ecclésiam pérsequi, ac Dei electos excútere et cribráre sicut tríticum ✠. Imperat tibi Deus altíssimus ✠, cui in magna tua supérbia te símililem habéri adhuc præsúmis; qui omnes hómines vult salvos fíeri, et ad agnitiónem veritátis veníre. Imperat tibi Deus Pater ✠; ímperat tibi Deus Fílius ✠; ímperat tibi Deus Spíritus Sanctus ✠. Imperat tibi Christus, ætérnum Dei Verbum caro factum ✠, qui pro salúte géneris nostri tua invídia pérditi, humiliávit semetípsum factus obédiens usque ad mortem; qui Ecclésiam suam ædificávit supra firmam petram et portas ínferi advérsus eam numquam esse prævalitúras edixit, cum ea ipse permansúrus ómnibus diébus usque ad consumatiónem sǽculi. Imperat tibi sacraméntum Crucis ✠, omniúmque christiánæ fídei Mysteriórum virtus ✠. Imperat tibi excélsa Dei Génetrix Virgo Maria ✠, quæ superbíssimum caput tuum a primo instánti immaculátæ suæ Conceptiónis in sua humilitáte contrivit. Imperat tibi fides sanctórum Apostolórum Petri et Pauli ceterorúmque Apostolórum ✠. Imperat tibi Mártyrum sanguis, ac pia Sanctórum et Sanctárum ómnium intercéssio ✠.

Dare no more, cunning serpent, to deceive the human race, persecute the Church of God, drive out God's elect and sift them as wheat ✠. The Most High God commands thee ✠, He to whom thou in thy great pride still presume to consider thyself similar; He who wants all men to be saved, and to come to the acknowledgement of the truth. God the Father commands thee ✠; God the Son commands thee ✠; God the Holy Spirit commands thee ✠; Christ, the Eternal Word of God made flesh, commands thee ✠, He who on behalf of the salvation of our race, destroyed by thy envy, humbled His very self, being made obedient even unto death; He who has built His Church upon the firm Rock and has declared that the gates of Hell shall never prevail against Her, being Himself with Her all days even unto the consummation of the age. The Sacrament of the Cross commands thee ✠, as does also the virtue of all the Mysteries of the Christian Faith ✠. The exalted Virgin Mary, the Theotokos, commands thee ✠, She who in Her humility didst crush thy most proud head from the first instant of Her Immaculate Conception. The faith of the holy Apostles Peter and Paul and of all the other Apostles commands thee ✠. The blood of the Martyrs, and the pious intercession of all the Saints commands thee ✠.

E̲rgo, draco maledicte et omnis légio diabólica adiurámus te per Deum ✠ vivum, per Deum ✠ verum, per Deum ✠ sanctum, per Deum, qui sic diléxit mundum, ut Filium suum unigénitum daret, ut omnis, qui credit in eum, non péreat, sed hábeat vitam ætérnam: cessa decípere humánas creatúras, eisque ætérnæ perditiónis venénum propináre: désine Ecclesiæ nocére et eius libertáti láqueos inícere. Vade, sátana, invéntor et magister omnis fallaciæ, hostis humánæ salútis. Da locum Christo, in quo nihil invenísti de opéribus tuis; da locum Ecclesiæ uni, sanctæ, cathólicæ, et Apostólicae, quam Christus ipse acquisívit sánguine suo. Humiliáre sub potenti manu Dei; contremísce et éffuge, invocato a nobis sancto et terríbili Nómini Iesu, quem ínferi tremunt, cui Virtútes cælórum et Potestátes et Dominatiónes subiéctæ sunt; quem Chérubim et Séraphim indeféssis vócibus laudant, dicéntes: Sanctus, Sanctus, Sanctus Dóminus Deus Sábaoth.

℣. Dómine, exaúdi oratiónem meam.
℟. Et clamor meus ad te véniat.
℣. Dóminus vobíscum.
℟. Et cum spíritu tuo.
Oratio
Oremus:

T̲herefore, cursed dragon and you, every diabolic legion, we adjure thee by the Living ✠ God, by the True ✠ God, by the Holy ✠ God, by the God, who so loved the world, that He gave His only begotten Son, that everyone, who believes in Him, might not perish, but have eternal life: cease deceiving human creatures and giving them the venom of eternal perdition to drink: desist in doing injury to the Church and in laying snares for Her liberty. Be gone, Satan, inventor and master of every fallacy, enemy of human salvation. Give place to Christ, in whom thou hast found nothing of thy works; give place to the One, Holy, Catholic, and Apostolic Church, which Christ Himself has acquired with His own Blood. Humble thyself beneath the powerful Hand of God; tremble throughout and flee, as we invoke the Holy and Terrible Name of Jesus, at which Hell does tremble, to which the Virtues and Powers and Dominations of Heaven have been subjected; which the Cherubim and Seraphim praise with unfailing voices, saying: Holy, Holy, Holy, the Lord God Sabbaoth.

V. O Lord, hear my prayer.
R. And let my cry come unto Thee.
V. The Lord be with you.
R. And with thy spirit.
Final Prayer
Let us pray:

Deus cæli, Deus terræ, Deus Angelórum, Deus Archangelórum, Deus Patriarchárum, Deus Prophetárum, Deus Apostolórum, Deus Mártyrum, Deus Confessórum, Deus Virginum, Deus qui potestátem habes donáre vitam post mortem, réquiem post labórem: quia non est Deus præter te, nec esse potest nisi tu, creátor ómnium visibílium et invisibílium, cuius regni non erit finis: humíliter maiestáti glóriæ tuæ suplicámus, ut ab omni infernálium spirítuum potestáte, láqueo deceptióne et nequítia nos poténter liberáre, et incólumes custodíre dignéris. Per Christum Dóminum nostrum.
℟. Amen.

℣. Ab insídiis diáboli,
℟. Libera nos, Dómine.
℣. Ut Ecclésiam tuam secúra tibi fácias libertáte servire,
℟. Te rogámus, audi nos.
℣. Ut inimícos sanctæ Ecclésiae humiliáre dignéris,
℟. Te rogámus, audi nos.
Et aspergatur locus aqua benedicta ✠.

God of Heaven, God of Earth, God of the Angels, God of the Archangels, God of the Patriarchs, God of the Prophets, God of the Apostles, God of the Martyrs, God of Confessors, God of Virgins, God who has power to grant life after death, rest after labor: because there is no God besides Thee, nor can there be any but Thee, the Creator of all things visible and invisible, of whose reign there shall be no end: we do humbly supplicate the Majesty of Thy Glory, that Thou may deign to liberate us powerfully from every power of the infernal spirits, from their snare, their deception and their wickedness, and to keep us safe and sound. Through Christ our Lord.
R. Amen.

V. From the snares of the Devil,
R. Liberate us, O Lord.
V. That Thou may cause Thy Church to serve Thee in secure liberty,
R. We beg Thee, hear us.
V. That Thou may deign to humble the enemies of the Church,
R. We beg Thee, hear us.
Now sprinkle the surroundings with holy water ✠.

Appendix 2

Ordo Ad Faciendam Aquam Benedictam	The Blessing of Holy Water
V. Adjutórium in nómine Dómini. R. Qui fecit caelum et terram.	V: Our help is in the name of the Lord. R: Who made heaven and earth.
Deinde absolute incipit exorcismum salis:	*The exorcism of salt follows:*
Exorcízo te, creatúra salis, per Deum ✠ vivum, per Deum ✠ verum, per Deum ✠ sanctum, per Deum, qui te per Eliséum Prophétam in aquam mitti jussit, ut sanarétur sterílitas aquæ: ut efficiáris sal exorcizátum in salútem credéntium; et sis ómnibus suméntibus te sánitas ánimæ et córporis; et effúgiat, atque discédat a loco, in quo aspérsum fúeris, omnis phantásia, et nequítia, vel versútia diabólicæ fraudis, omnísque spíritus immúndus, adjurátus per eum, qui ventúrus est judicáre vivos et mórtuos, et sáeculum per ignem. R. Amen.	Thou creature of salt, I purge thee of evil by the living ✠ God, by the true ✠ God, by the holy ✠ God, by the God Who ordered thee through Eliseus, the prophet to be cast into the water to cure its unfruitfulness. Be thou a purified salt for the health of believers, giving soundness of body and soul to all who use thee. In whatever place thou are sprinkled, may phantoms and wickedness, and Satan's cunning be banished. And let every unclean spirit be repulsed by Him Who shall come to judge the living and dead, and the world by fire. R. Amen.
Orémus. Imménsam cleméntiam tuam, omnípotens aetérne Deus, humíliter implorámus, ut hanc creatúram salis, quam in usum géneris humáni tribuísti, bene ✠ dícere et sancti ✠ ficáre tua pietáte dignéris: ut sit ómnibus suméntibus salus mentis et córporis; et quidquid ex eo tactum vel respérsum fúerit, cáreat omni immundítia, omníque impugnatióne spiritális nequítiæ. Per Christum Dóminum nostrum. R. Amen.	Let us pray. O almighty, everlasting God! Humbly we implore thy boundless mercy that thou wouldst deign of thy goodness to bless ✠ and sanctify ✠ this creature of salt which thou hast given for the use of mankind. May all that use it find in it a remedy for soul and body. And let everything which it touches or sprinkles be freed from uncleanness and assault from evil spirits. Through our Lord. R. Amen.
Exorcismus aquæ: et dicitur absolute:	*Exorcism of water:*

Exorcízo te, creatúra aquae, in nómine Dei ✠ Patris omnipoténtis, et in nómine Jesu ✠ Christi, Fílii ejus Dómini nostri, et in virtúte Spíritus ✠ Sancti: ut fias aqua exorcizáta ad effugándam omnem potestátem inimíci, et ipsum inimícum eradicáre et explantáre váleas cum ángelis suis apostáticis, per virtútem eiúsdem Dómini nostri Jesu Christi: qui ventúrus est judicáre vivos et mórtuos, et saéculum per ignem. R. Amen.

Orémus.
Deus, qui ad salútem humáni géneris, máxima quaeque sacraménta in aquárum substántia condidísti: adésto propítius invocatiónibus nostris, et eleménto huic multímodis purificatiónibus praeparáto, virtútem tuæ bene ✠ dictiónis infúnde; ut creatúra tua, mystériis tuis sérviens, ad abigéndos daémones, morbósque pelléndos, divínæ grátiæ sumat efféctum; ut quidquid in dómibus, vel in locis fidélium, haec unda respérserit, cáreat omni immundítia, liberétur a noxa: non illic resídeat spíritus péstilens, non aura corrúmpens: discédant omnes insídiæ laténtis inimíci; et si quid est, quod aut incolumitáti habitántium ínvidet, aut quiéti, aspersióne hujus aquæ effúgiat: ut salúbritas, per invocatiónem sancti tui nóminis expetíta, ab ómnibus sit impugnatiónibus defénsa. Per Christum Dóminum nostrum. R. Amen.

Hic mittat sal in aquam in modum crucis, dicendo:

Thou creature of water, I purge thee of evil in the name of God ✠ the Father almighty, in the name of Jesus ✠ Christ, His Son, our Lord, and in the power of the Holy ✠ Spirit, that thou mayest be water fit to brace us against the envious foe. Mayest thou be empowered to drive him forth and exile him together with his fallen angels by the power of the selfsame Jesus Christ, our Lord Who shall come to judge the living and the dead, and the world by fire. R. Amen.

Let us pray.
O God, for man's salvation dost dispense wondrous mysteries with the efficacious sign of water, hearken to our prayer — pouring forth thy benediction ✠ upon this element which we consecrate with manifold purifications. Let this creature serve Thee in expelling demons and curing diseases. Whatsoever it sprinkles in the homes of the faithful, be it cleansed and delivered from harm. Let such homes enjoy a spirit of goodness and an air of tranquility, freed from baneful and hidden snares. By the sprinkling of this water may everything opposed to the safety and repose of them that dwell therein be banished, so that they may possess the well-being they seek in calling upon Thy holy name, and be protected from all peril. Through our Lord. R. Amen.

Now salt is thrice put into the water in the form of a cross, saying only once:

Commíxtio salis et aquae páriter fiat, in nómine Pa ✠ tris, et Fí ✠ lii, et Spíritus ✠ Sancti. R. Amen.	May this salt and water be mixed together, in the name of the Father ✠, and of the Son ✠ and of the Holy ✠ Spirit. R. Amen.
V. Dóminus vobíscum. R. Et cum spíritu tuo.	V. The Lord be with you. R. And with thy spirit.
Orémus. Deus, invíctae virtútis auctor, et insuperábilis impérii Rex, ac semper magníficus triumphátor: qui advérsæ dominatiónis vires réprimis: qui inimíci rugiéntis saevítiam súperas: qui hostíles nequítias poténter expúgnas: te, Dómine, treméntes et súpplices deprecámur, ac pétimus: ut hanc creatúram salis et aquae dignánter aspícias, benígnus illústres, pietátis tuae rore sanctífices; ut, ubicúmque fúerit aspérsa, per invocatiónem sancti nóminis tui, omnis infestátio immúndi spíritus abigátur: terrórque venenósi serpéntis procul pellátur: et praeséntia Santi Spíritus nobis, misericórdiam tuam poscéntibus, úbique adésse dignétur. Per Dóminum nostrum Jesum Christum Fílium tuum: Qui tecum vivit et regnat in unitáte ejúsdem Spíritus Sancti Deus, per ómnia saécula saeculorum. R. Amen.	Let us pray. Author of invincible strength and king of an unconquerable empire, ever the gloriously Triumphant One! Who restrainest the force of the adversary, Who overcomest the fierceness of the devouring enemy, Who valiantly putteth down hostile influences! Prostrate and fearsome we beseech Thee, Lord, consider kindly this creature of salt and water, make it honored, and sanctify it with the dew of Thy sweetness. Wherever it is sprinkled in Thy name, may devilish infection cease, venomous terror be driven afar. But let the presence of the Holy Spirit be ever with us as we implore Thy mercy. Through our Lord, Jesus Christ, Thy Son, Who liveth and reigneth with Thee in unity of the same Holy Spirit, God, eternally, and ever. R. Amen.

About the Author

Fr. Ralph Weimann studied in the United States, Italy, and Germany and obtained a diploma in humanities, a bachelor's degree in philosophy, and a licentiate degree in theology. He earned a doctorate in theology in 2010 on the thesis "Dogma and Progress in the Theology of Joseph Ratzinger." He earned a second doctorate in 2013 on the thesis "Bioethics in a Secularized Society." He has worked as a military chaplain since 2015. Fr. Weimann lectures at various colleges and universities in Rome, particularly the Pontifical University of St. Thomas Aquinas (Angelicum) and the International Online University Domuni.

Sophia Institute

Sophia Institute is a nonprofit institution that seeks to nurture the spiritual, moral, and cultural life of souls and to spread the Gospel of Christ in conformity with the authentic teachings of the Roman Catholic Church.

Sophia Institute Press fulfills this mission by offering translations, reprints, and new publications that afford readers a rich source of the enduring wisdom of mankind.

Sophia Institute also operates the popular online Catholic resource CatholicExchange.com. *Catholic Exchange* provides world news from a Catholic perspective as well as daily devotionals and articles that will help readers to grow in holiness and live a life consistent with the teachings of the Church.

In 2013, Sophia Institute launched Sophia Institute for Teachers to renew and rebuild Catholic culture through service to Catholic education. With the goal of nurturing the spiritual, moral, and cultural life of souls, and an abiding respect for the role and work of teachers, we strive to provide materials and programs that are at once enlightening to the mind and ennobling to the heart; faithful and complete, as well as useful and practical.

Sophia Institute gratefully recognizes the Solidarity Association for preserving and encouraging the growth of our apostolate over the course of many years. Without their generous and timely support, this book would not be in your hands.

www.SophiaInstitute.com
www.CatholicExchange.com
www.SophiaInstituteforTeachers.org

Sophia Institute Press° is a registered trademark of Sophia Institute.
Sophia Institute is a tax-exempt institution as defined by the
Internal Revenue Code, Section 501(c)(3). Tax I.D. 22-2548708.